Joe,

Enjoy the

Antarctic Tears

adventure & make
your own. You'll
never regret pursuing
your dreams!

Aaron Linsdau

Aug 19, 2015

ANTARCTIC TEARS

Determination, adversity, and the pursuit
of a dream at the bottom of the world

AARON LINSDAU

SASTRUGI PRESS

Sastrugi Press / Published by arrangement with the author

Sastrugi Press: 2907 Iris Avenue, San Diego, CA 92173, United States
www.sastrugipress.com

Antarctic Tears: Determination, adversity, and the pursuit of a dream at the bottom of the world

The author has made every effort to accurately recreate conversations, events, and locales from his memories of them. To maintain anonymity, some names and details such as places of residence, physical characteristics, and occupations have been changed. The publisher does not have any control over and does not assume any responsibility for author or third-party websites or their content.

Library of Congress Control Number: 2014905337
Linsdau, Aaron
Antarctic Tears - 1st U.S. ed.
Summary: Aaron Linsdau attempts to become the first American to ever ski from the coast of Antarctica to the South Pole and back, without aid or support.
ISBN-13: 978 0 9960206 0 2
ISBN-10: 0 9960206 0 8

910.4
Printed in the United States of America

Editor: Brian Scrivener

10 9 8 7 6 5 4 3 2

To Mom who taught me perseverance
To Dad who taught me to dream
To Kelly, my biggest supporter

Contents

Foreword i

Acknowledgements vii

Welcome to the Big Leagues 1

Antarctica's Short History 9

The Course Was Charted Long Ago 19

How to Camp in the Snow 31

Goodbye, Bits and Bytes 45

Crushed by History 59

So the Expedition Begins 67

A Cold Antarctica, Days 1-3 83

Days 4-8 99

Days 9-12 113

Days 13-17 123

Days 18-24 139

Days 25-34 157

Days 35-41 181

Days 41-51 197

Days 52-57 219

Days 58-62 235

Days 63-68 253

Days 69-73 269

Days 74-79 279

Days 80-82 293

Something More Difficult 311

Other major Antarctic expeditions 318

FOREWORD

I am a fan of the underdog, the rags to riches tale. I'm the one who cries when the little league team with the geek and the fat kid and the introvert beats the arrogant hot shot team; I am the most entranced of all when Ugly Betty takes off her glasses to reveal her unexpected beauty; when Forest Gump meets the President and is decorated for his Vietnam heroism and brings home the shrimp haul and gets the girl, I believe, I am there every step of the way, my faith in the long-shot unwavering. And why? Maybe because I am one or, at least, I used to be.

Back in 2001 a couple of life changing things happened to me. The first was that my beloved godfather died, leaving me a pretty signif-icant legacy. It wasn't enough to make me rich for life so I'd never have to work again or anything, but it was enough to give me some freedom. The second thing that happened was that I discovered really big places. A break up with my long term boyfriend combined with a love affair with Michael Ondaatje's Booker Prize winning novel The English Patient, lead me on a mission to find some way of visiting the remotest heart of the Sahara to see for myself the mysterious Cave of Swimmers, made famous in that book. I soon discovered that pretty much the only person accessing that most inhospitable part of the world at the time was a Hungarian rock art researcher called Andras Zboray. For the next three months I bombarded this poor man with pleading emails, begging him to take me on one of his expeditions to the Libyan Desert and, at last, after a meeting in London, where I either confirmed or allayed his doubts about my sanity, to this day I'm not sure which, he finally agreed. The area Andras was focused on was the eastern Sahara, known as the Western Desert (west of the Nile) or the Libyan Desert, a completely uninhabited area the size of the Indian subcontinent in southern Egypt, eastern Libya and Northern Sudan, the second biggest wilderness on the planet. For the next three years, twice a year for three or four weeks at a time, I traveled far out into the depths of nothing, into the heart of emptiness and discovered that after a lifetime of being big, I was in fact, very, very small.

There is nothing like visiting the second biggest wilderness on the planet for making you start wondering about the biggest wilderness on the planet, Antarctica, and by 2003 that is where my imagination was wandering. When you look at the map of Antarctica and start thinking about visiting it, you pretty quickly come to the naïve conclusion that there is only one thing on the map, the South Pole, and that is probably the place to go. Just after that conclusion you quickly think, "Well, if I'm going to go to the South Pole, I really aught to do some epic overland ski trip to get there. It's only right and proper." The problem for me was, I had never been on so much as a school ski trip, I had never spent time in snow, I had never climbed a mountain, I had done pretty much nothing of any relevance to such an expedition in my life. I was the ultimate rookie.

In October 2004 I joined an ANI expedition from Hercules Inlet to the South Pole, the same route that Aaron came and attempted to tackle as a return journey eight years later. I knew nothing, I had no skills, all I had was a sunny demeanor, a stubborn streak that would have made any mule proud and two secret weapons: four amazing team mates who shared their strength and resilience with me every day and a professional guide, Denise Martin, who it turns out ended up being the single most influential person in my life.

Over the next 56 days, we struggled and suffered and laughed and cried and fought and reveled our way across Antarctica. Every day, Denise delivered her winter wisdom, her polar knowledge, her respect and reverence for this environment into me, her eager pupil. Antarctica was ferocious and exuberant and wild and untamed and I got it, I just got it: this was my place, my environment, I belonged here, it was like coming home, and I soaked up everything about it like a sponge.

Two years later, with a wealth more knowledge and experience under my belt I returned to the white continent and undertook a solo, unsupported expedition on the Hercules Inlet to Pole route, this time completing it in 39 days 9 hours and 33 minutes, at the time, a new speed record for the journey. After this, the polar community seemed to nod its approval and for the past 7 years to the present time of writing I have been working as a guide every season for ANI, the company that first took me on as a novice client, and have now clocked up more full South Pole expeditions than anyone ever. This polar underdog has come good.

On the 24th November, 2012, I had just arrived on the ice at ANI's base camp at Union Glacier. I was about to undertake my 6th long expedition to the South Pole as a guide for ANI with two clients. At dinner that night our Operations Manager Steve Jones asked if I could come and have a chat to one of the solo expeditioners already in the field at the evening scheduled calls, a guy called Aaron Linsdau, who was having a bit of a tough time. "Sure! No problem!" I readily agreed. It was not uncommon for me to get called in to chat to ski expeditions in the field. Our Comms Operators are the best in the world and a more caring and attentive group you could not wish to speak to, but there is sometimes no substitute for talking to someone who has been through exactly what you are going through and who can offer some tips and advice.

I didn't know anything about this Aaron Linsdau, I didn't know his background or experience, I'd only heard his name a few days earlier when I'd arrived in southern Chile to start work. All I knew was that he was attempting to complete the return journey from Hercules Inlet to the South Pole and back again, solo and unsupported, arguably one of the toughest undertakings in the world of polar travel.

As I strolled into the comms box that evening and sat down to wait for Aaron's call I reached for his expedition comms sheet that would show me all his daily position data and updates and started to read. Within a few minutes my eyes were wide with astonishment and I was sitting to attention intently taking in the terrible information before me. This was the slowest moving expedition I had ever witnessed on Antarctica. If this person had simply prostrated himself one body length at a time for 9 hours a day like some Tibetan pilgrim he would surely be moving faster than he was currently? Something was very, very wrong here. I read through the notes and saw that Aaron had been suffering with illness, which partly explained his progress, but I could see it wasn't the full story.

When the phone eventually rang, my heart immediately went out to the voice at the end of the faint, crackling line. Within minutes, I could identify with what I was hearing. Aaron was trying to be cheerful, each sentence containing a little, self deprecating laugh. I could sense his determination, but also his mounting desperation. I liked him.

For the next 40 minutes I questioned Aaron and listened carefully to what he told me, trying to piece together a remote image of everything he was doing and the shape of his expedition. It became clear that here was a person who had plunged head first into the deep end of polar expeditions with little experience and little prior knowledge and who was puzzling it out day by day and running on his wits alone. It was both alarming and brilliant all at once. I brain dumped as much as I could think of that would help him over the phone and, by the time we finished talking, Aaron seemed more cheerful and fired up for the next day.

"Well, what do you think?" asked Steve Jones, as I hung up the phone and looked thoughtfully out the window into the snow. "Is he going to make it?"

"I have no idea! Probably not. But you know what? I really, really want him to!" This underdog had completely won me over.

For the next couple of months, we watched Aaron's painstaking progress across the continent. I spoke to him a couple of times and was always impressed by his indomitable good humor. I went out into the field myself and undertook my own expedition from the coast to the pole with my clients on the slightly shorter 500 nautical mile Messner route, and when I got back Aaron was still plugging away.

My own experience of these long expeditions on Antarctica has always been less about suffering and more about meditation. Even when the place is raging I try to stoically slip through it unnoticed, I move regardless of weather and hardship, my journeys much more internal than external. Reading in these pages about Aaron's very different journey, his trials and his suffering, has been like reading about something I could never imagine on Antarctica, but to have persevered for so long through such physical and emotional and environmental torment is tremendous and this honest account makes for a jolly good story. Aaron may not quite have achieved what he originally envisioned at the start of his trip, but what he did achieve took terrific spirit, and this will forevermore remain one of my favorite and, for all the wrong reasons and for all the right reasons, most admired polar expeditions.

Hannah McKeand
World record fastest solo female to the South Pole

Acknowledgments

Thanks go out to my family, friends and supporters who made the expedition and this book possible. Without the vast number of people who worked on this project with me, I would have never made it to Antarctica, let alone stepped into the ski bindings and took the first step toward finally realizing my dream.

A special thank you goes out to Kelly Gaffney, my expedition manager and girlfriend. Although you had never managed an expedition before, you stepped up and produced some novel ideas of how to bring people together, making sure I had everything I needed while training in Jackson Hole in the summer of 2012. You were my motivator and kept me going even when I did not feel like dragging my tire. Your thoughtfulness and caring made me feel confident in my chances of success. Without you, I doubt I would have ever reached Antarctica. You printed shirts with the expedition website and told everyone you could about it. Without your love and encouragement, I never would have been able to do what I did. When I felt down, your quick laugh brightened my day and made me excited for the challenge. I eagerly await spending many more days with you.

Without dad and mom, I would have never made it into the outdoors. Dad, your encouraging me to join the Boy Scouts and do something you enjoyed as a child made a huge difference in my life. Without you, earning the rank of Eagle Scout would never have happened because I never would have shown up to the first meeting. Earning that honor was something I completely owe to both of you. Mom, your patient encouragement and helping me work through problems when I wanted to give up was invaluable.

My brother Jason and his wife Nicole, along with their two sons Justin and Jake, provided me with a place to sleep. That and Nicole's superior cooking (to my lame culinary skills) kept me going so many times when I was away from my Temecula home.

Wendy Davis, where would I be without you? Had you not said that cross country skiing was the most difficult and annoying sport you ever did on skis, I would never have taken up the sport in the first place. You were a huge impetus for me taking my first trip across Yellowstone and discovering what a joy trekking through the snowy cold was. Your resourcefulness in setting up flights to and from Chile from all the way in Japan was unmatched. Your friendship and thoughtfulness has and always will be cherished.

During the expedition, Hannah McKeand and Vilborg Arna Gissurardóttir played pivotal roles in helping me reach the Pole. Without your advise and wisdom, I would still be out on that Antarctic plateau, slogging away and making poor mileage. It was an honor to be schooled by Hannah, the most experienced skier in Antarctica, holding a Guinness World Record for Antarctic skiing. And Vilborg, I had no idea I was in the presence of a woman who has the prime minister and president of Iceland practically on speed dial.

Thank you to my aunt Nancy Takeda for providing me a home base in Jackson for all those years I drove there to camp, backpack, and trek into the northwest Wyoming wilderness. For without your help, I never would have had the resources to ski across Yellowstone and test my different ideas prior to the expedition.

Thank you to the Wort Hotel staff for cheering me on all the way.

Thank you to my grandfather Roy (Akira) Takeda. Without your support, sage wisdom and insight, I might have never undertaken this venture in the first place. When I'm falling asleep on the recliner watching NASCAR, I will be able to look back and remember skiing across Antarctica.

Thank you very much to the Prostate Cancer Foundation. Being listed as an athlete with your organization was a great honor. Without your research, efforts, and support, my dad might not be alive today. It is through the tireless work of your organization that so many more men are alive today. Prostate cancer is such a preventable disease, so I'm glad you are leading the charge to get the word out.

Thank you to the Boy Scouts of America. Your organization has instilled leadership, skills, and responsibility into boys for over 100 years. As an Eagle Scout, I am honored to be listed among your ranks. Being able to speak at different Scouting functions has been enjoyable and I look forward to many more such events.

It would have not been possible without the support of all of my sponsors, without who's help, I would not have been able to fund this venture. I look forward to building long-term relationships with all of you: Micro-USA, Gonediggin.com, It's Jackson Time, ExplorersWeb.com, Jackson Hole Boot and Shoe Repair, Hilleberg Tents, TVL Video, Hybridge Group, Snowsled.com, and Massage Professionals of Jackson Hole.

Thank you to the North County Times, San Diego Union Tribune, Jackson Hole News and Guide, The Daily, Jackson Hole Planet, and the Carlsbad Patch newspapers for providing coverage both before and after the expedition. A special thank you goes out to Brandon Stone and the staff at KUSI-TV in San Diego for featuring my expedition on your television station. All of you were instrumental in broadcasting my message about the Prostate Cancer Foundation.

Thank you to the congregation of St. James Church in Imperial Beach, CA, for your love, support, and prayers during my expedition. I have been amazed and honored when so many people at the church have come up to me and told me they followed my efforts in Antarctica.

Thank you to all the private donors to the expedition. Your help made it possible for me to stand at 90ºS. I am indebted to all of you: Steve Corman, Peter & Emily Ligotti, Patricia Thompson, Stephanie Cronin, Cheryl Hlatkey, Allen Ripingill, Joann Luu, Holyann Buderus, Dr. James Little, Joanne VanMeter, James Clayton, Ben Meyers, Gerald and Linda Linsdau, Esther and Raymond Seid, Steve Escoto, and Georgia Andrews.

Thank you to Jim Linsdau and Ron Moody for additional edits.

And a final thank you to all the people who stopped and chatted while I was towing my tires through Carlsbad and Jackson. I hope my message of never giving up, accepting change, and pursuing your dreams touched your lives as you touched mine.

I

Welcome to the Big Leagues

KNEELING DOWN ON THE SNOW, I gasped for breath. Coughing, I ripped off the protective mask. The racking spasm overpowered my body and shook me as though a gorilla pummeled me with its fists. Even though I had a silicone rubber mask over my mouth, the airborne powdery snow bypassed the shield and penetrated my already weakened lungs. Attempting to suck in air though what felt like a straw, I coughed hard enough to hear my back crack. There, before me in the snow, was a bright crimson splotch of blood.

Staring at this glaring stain in the otherwise perfect Antarctic whiteness drained the color out of my face. Part of that had to do with my tuberculosis-like cough and an inability to breathe. The other part was a palpable fear. In no way was coughing up blood normal. Had I been in San Diego there would have been plenty of options should the problem worsen. But I was not. I was thousands of miles away from any significant hospital anywhere on the globe. The constant dry cough and the absolute roaring of the tent buffeted by persistent 40 knot winds made sleep impossible. I felt glum. Crawling back inside the tent, I flopped down on my sleeping bag and lay there, my energy spent.

My immediate reaction was to inform Antarctic Logistics and Expeditions (ALE) about what had happened. And after that, I would have to tell my expedition manager and girlfriend, Kelly Gaffney, too. But a crushing sense of fear overtook me. Should I reveal this new and alarming detail? I lay motionless, simultaneously holding back a sob and a scream for an hour. Flipping from one side to the other, I tested for the telltale sloshing of fluid in my lungs. Should I feel anything, I knew my expedition was over.

I was attempting to trek from the geographic coast of Antarctica to the South Pole and back, thousands of miles from help. Crude methods of self diagnosis were all I had. I feared that if I let the ALE doctors know what had occurred, they would insist that I abandon the expedition. After coming this far and investing everything I had, the quarter-sized blot of red snow represented the weight of ten years on my shoulders.

A dry, irritating cough is common for people first arriving in Antarctica. It clears up in a week or two after the person acclimatizes to the desiccated conditions on the continent. The air has less humidity than found on commercial airliners due to the complete lack of moisture. In fact, the whole continent of Antarctica is considered a desert, due to its average precipitation being less than ten inches per year. For having an ice cap three miles thick and persistent bad weather, there was little actual snowfall. However, my cough was not only from the arid environment. Rather, it was from a lung infection that had developed from a cold I caught on the way to Punta Arenas, Chile, the jumping off point for most expeditions heading to Antarctica.

Thus far the expedition had not gone as planned. Although my spirits were high despite having been afflicted with a serious illness far away from medical help, I had fallen badly behind my schedule. It was common for expeditions to take between 40 and 60 days to reach the pole. I had only 90 days not only to ski to the pole, a distance of over 700 miles, but to perform the return journey of the same distance. Normally one way expeditions were one quarter of the way to the pole by this point, roughly 180 miles. I had only covered a measly 24 miles.

Conditions had been nasty, making matters worse. Starting at Hercules Inlet on the Ronne Ice Shelf in the Weddell Sea, I had to climb two thousand vertical feet in a few miles to gain the Antarctic plateau where, hopefully, the surface would level out. But a few surprises lurked around and beyond the steep slope. Right at the beginning of the trek two prominent crevasse fields stood between me and the South Pole. This meant that following a dogleg path toward the Ellesworth Mountains was necessary before finally connecting with the route to the South Pole. It added a frustrating 20 miles to the expedition. Though the circuitous start was annoying, the acute real danger of dying in a crevasse fall overwhelmed any impatience I had. Training by flipping a tire end-over-end for miles to teach myself patience now paid off.

Traveling in Antarctica also means traveling blind one out of five days. There are two reasons for this: goggles fogging and whiteout conditions. Goggles fog from overheating cause by exertion. Becoming too hot in cold conditions causes skin to steam. This moisture coats the inside of the goggles and flash freezes, making the lenses completely opaque. Managing my body's heat was a constant battle. With the variability of each day's conditions, anticipating what the best clothing was to prevent overheating or freezing was impossible.

The more insidious problem for travel in Antarctica is whiteout. Once away from the coastal mountains, there is only ice, snow and sky. When the clouds obscure the sun, the surface contrast is reduced to the point of being shadowless. It is like being inside a massive ping pong ball. The only objects to see are skis, self and a sled. Each looked as though they are suspended inside a pool filled with milk.

For the difficulty of traveling with ice on the goggles and in a whiteout, there was another serious problem with attempting to ski a round-trip in Antarctica. The expedition has to begin in November when the weather is dreadful. The winds are even more fierce than in December, routinely exceeding 40 knots (46 miles per hour), and often much higher. And although the continent is a desert, deep snow builds up north of the coastal mountains. The buildup is not necessarily due to falling snow but rather to blowing snow coming over and being deposited on the leeward side of the mountains. Strong winds made for deep snow conditions early in the trekking season.

This is exactly what I found myself in.

The snow was deep enough that my skis repeatedly sank eight inches and my two sleds, loaded with 330 pounds of supplies, turned into a pair of snowplows. Many times, I was unable to budge the sleds. Turning back, I saw that they had plowed themselves under disrupting forward progress. Other times, one ski runner would ride up on a hardened patch of snow, dumping the other side into soft snow and tilting the whole mess over. This required me to stop, right the sleds and yank them into a position where they would not fall over the moment I started towing them again. On the day I coughed up blood, my speed dropped to 0.4 miles per hour on skis. The snow was so waterless that my skis floated on the top surface, but as I pulled, the snow broke apart below the surface causing me to slip backward and sink. So, I stowed the skis and tried walking. Although having the skis not pulling well was annoying, postholing in shin-deep snow reduced my speed to an aggravating 0.3 mph. Crawling on my hands and knees backwards would have been faster. As troublesome as the slipping skis were, walking was that much worse.

For all the troubles I had up to the second week of the expedition I was still energized. Yes, I was slogging through deep snow and making impossibly slow progress. Yes, I had hacked up blood and in it saw the end of my expedition. Despite these challenges I was having the best outdoor experience I'd had. Ever. Looking back on the past couple of years of struggles, this was absolutely the finest undertaking I had ever embarked upon. There was the pure thrill of being in Antarctica, far away from anything and anyone all by myself. Antarctica had no arbitrary deadlines, no hidden agendas, no bosses telling me one story and then stabbing me in the back later. It was simply me versus an entire continent. Being there provided greater clarity of purpose, was easier to understand, and was far more enjoyable than working at any job ever had been.

As I dragged my expedition forward, I wondered what Roald Amundsen and Robert Scott felt as they led their expeditions across this frozen wasteland a century earlier. Thus far, my expedition was turning out more similar to Scott's than Amundsen's. I hoped I would not perish starving and frozen, trapped by a ten day blizzard. Reading Alfred Landsing's Endurance and Apsley Cherry-Garrard's The Worst Journey in the World cover to cover, I researched, in depth, what they experienced, day by day. Although Cherry-Garrard's account had a detailed daily account of their journeys, the emotional detail was thin in true British fashion. So many psychological details were left out of the text. For as much as I desired to know what the men struggled with internally, to have a better idea of what to expect, I also wanted to have my own experience uncolored by their tales. I desired to succeed and was having an enjoyable time being there, but based on the previous year's expeditions, my expedition deteriorated into a fight for survival.

In the 2011 to 2012 season, two teams had been able to pull off a round-trip journey. I wanted to make that journey as the first American soloist. That season was the centennial celebration of Amundsen and Scott achieving the South Pole, and as such, there was a plethora of teams from around the globe competing for their place in the spotlight. As I read about the expeditions last year, I suffered both a pang of guilt and a twinge of jealousy for not being there. This was something I had planned to do for an entire decade. Yet with the preparations and time required to execute the trip, it was impossible to have made it without making major changes in my life.

As much as I had infiltrated terra incognita on the Earth, I had entered the same place inside of myself. Antarctica was still a barely visited place. Humans had not crawled all over it. In fact, no humans had even sighted the continent until 1820. In 2009, ten previously unknown penguin colonies numbering up to 9,000 birds were discovered along the periphery of ice barrier. For all the technology swarming the world, it seemed impossible that acres of birds remained undiscovered until three years prior to my expedition. This is what made Antarctica particularly appealing to me: the purity of the experience and that so many skills had yet to be learned. But to make it there, I had to pour in every effort, dollar and time to prepare for the experience.

For as much training as I put in over the previous summer and winters in Jackson Hole, I discovered that it was inadequate. Over the hundreds of miles I had dragged tires, arguably the best simulation of sled towing, I still had not experienced the frustration of stumbling on the flattest of ice, skiing blind or constantly having my sleds go awry. A better simulation would have been to drag a love seat through a swamp while wearing hazy white plastic over my face, although the swamp would not have provided the piercing cold. As much as pulling 50 pounds of tires up mountain trails was difficult, doing so did not present enough psychological challenge. Though the training had toughened my tendons and ligaments, there was no way I could have prepared for bronchitis and the incessant equipment failures.

Being a solo expedition was vastly different experience from traveling as a team in Antarctica. There was no one to lean on, to commiserate with or to figure out problems. Trekking alone was not new to me, as I had skied and snowshoed solo across Yellowstone Park, in the winter, for three consecutive years. I had backpacked solo on Greenland's Arctic Circle Trail over frozen tundra and through ice-choked rivers. Being self contained was satisfying, though lonely. Having grown up partly in Wyoming, stories of 19th century trappers appealed to me. It seemed unimaginable that they left civilization and ventured into the wilderness, for a year or more at a time, surviving alone. And conceivably they had a pleasant time doing it while bringing back goods and stories to their world. That was something I hoped to do, too.

And yet I was a polar nobody. In the world of Antarctic exploration, I was not even on the map, as this was my first foray into it. Although I made a risky dash across the Greenlandic tundra a full month after the travel season ended in 2008, postholing for days in thigh-deep snow, the trip did not register on anyone's radar. Other than the paperwork I provided to ALE, they knew nothing about me. I had no proven track record. However, I had ski-towed before in Yellowstone, been in tough situations, and struggled through them. My experience was better than what other expeditions possessed to ski to the South Pole. A few have arrived in Union Glacier to do a ski-all-the-way trip and had never cross country skied. At least I wasn't one of those.

I knew that the expedition was difficult and doing it solo was even more so. Many experienced polar travelers have not attempted a solo expedition and for good reason. Lacking human companionship for so long is difficult to cope with. The loneliness, risk and having no one to cover my back in a crisis was not to be taken lightly. Some have even given up only because they wanted to quit, not because they were injured, suffered a catastrophic gear failure or exhausted their supplies. These dangers were familiar, and I looked forward to handling them on a larger scale. I dreamt about Antarctica, tested myself and prepared everything to handle the worst and do my best. Training at high elevation and physically pushing myself to the limit was only a small part of skiing across Antarctica.

Little did I anticipate all the events that were to unfold.

(Right) *The wind creates sastrugi, dramatic and beautiful ice sculptures that are the bane of Antarctic explorers.*

(Below) *Sundogs appear around the sun when there is ice in the upper atmosphere. Bad weather soon follows these displays.*

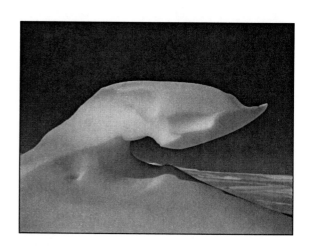

2

ANTARCTICA'S SHORT HISTORY

O N FABIAN GOTTLIEB VON BELLINGSHAUSEN'S ship, the crew had to be miserable and cold. They were assaulted by heavy snow fall and had sailed along what they hoped was a continental landmass, only to discover it was a mere island. On January 27, 1820, Bellingshausen reported seeing a "solid stretch of ice running from east through south to west." The Russian ship *Vostok* had been only 19 miles from it, the dangerous ice floes choking the waters made closer inspection impossible. The next day, he and his compatriot crew wrote and believed that they were looking at a continental mass of indeterminate size. They had seen Antarctica. This was the first record of anyone having seen the last continent to be discovered. It was unbelievable that expeditions had circled the globe centuries before and yet had been unable to penetrate the southern ocean.

During the age of exploration from the 15th to the 17th century, explorers prowled the globe but never discovered the fifth largest continent. Sir Francis Drake was blown far south off course while passing through the Straits of Magellan in 1578 during a massive storm, yet had not glimpsed land. Not until Captain James Cook attempted to find the fabled southern continent did anyone cross the Antarctic Circle in 1773, while America broiled for independence. After three failed attempts, Cook declared that due to the nature of the ice and what he had observed, there was no large landmass to be found. It was not until Bellingshausen's expedition 47 years later that anyone again penetrated the Antarctic Circle. The seas were so difficult and dangerous from weather and ice that navigating these waters was precarious at best, lethal at worst.

And yet the waters surrounding Antarctica were far from unspoiled. British sealing ships had decimated the elephant and sea lion populations of South Georgia island by the time Bellingshausen visited in January 1820. The only known surviving logbook of the time notes that sealing captain John Davis was likely the first person to set foot on Antarctica. For all their efforts, the British and American sealers never saw Antarctica proper. The Russians happened to beat both by only a few weeks to the first sighting. Americans, British, and Russians were all vying to claim various lands in the southern hemisphere for whales, seals and elephant seal oil to meet the increasing demand in their respective nations. However, the unmanaged killing of these animals permanently destroyed the populations on many islands without regard to sustainability. Soon, sealing ships pushed farther and farther south to find viable hunting grounds. They failed to realize that their bountiful harvest would never again be realized.

For the better part of the next century, France, Britain, the United States and Russia made various efforts at establishing colonies and making territorial claims all throughout Antarctica. Due to the ice barrier sealing off the continent, landing and performing the 19th century ceremonies for claiming lands was suicidal in the best of times. Ironically, the seas surrounding Antarctica were named for captains who ventured into them but found little. Sealing captain James Weddell of the British brig *Jane* was able to sail south to latitude 74ºS 34ºW, much farther south than any navigator had reached before. His crew was displeased at having found only open sea, as they were searching for seals and, without land or beaches, there were none to be had and no money to be made. To console his crew, Weddell passed out grog, raised the colors and fired off guns to celebrate the navigational event. Though the wayward captain named the sea after King George IV, the sea would eventually bear his name. The ice conditions on that February 20, 1823 were unique, as the feat of sailing that far south would not be repeated for another century.

In December 1840, the famous British explorer James Clark Ross sailed his way through ice-choked waters by following the 170° meridian southward. This was an attempt to find the magnetic pole located off the coast of Antarctica. Making various claims on islands with hasty ceremonies, he continued south on the *Erebus* and *Terror*. These two mortaring ships were designed to withstand heavy gunfire from their decks and thus handled the icy waters without issue. With care, he picked his way through the ice until he realized that sailing to the magnetic pole by ship was impossible. On gaining his farthest south approach, he happened upon two massive volcanoes, "one of which was emitting flame and smoke in great profusion." The explorer did not know that these two volcanoes were attached to Antarctica's main landmass by an isthmus of ice. He was stopped from venturing farther south by what is now known as the Ross Ice Shelf.

By 1902, the Swedish geologist Otto Nordenskjöld made the first significant sledging journey into Antarctica. His ship, the *Antarctica*, was destroyed by pack ice, forcing him and his now separated ship's and sledging crews to make their way independently to Snow Hill Island where they were miraculously saved by an Argentine relief ship in 1903. In the same year, Edward Wilson, Robert Falcon Scott and Ernest Shackleton made the first attempt at reaching the South Pole. By the time they reached 82°15'S, they had contracted scurvy and were suffering snow blindness. They made an unprecedented trip of 270 miles toward the pole. But, they had hundreds of miles more to go. The failure of the expedition was partly due to Scott's refusing to bolster the rations with seal meat, an effective scurvy deterrent. Shackleton had been coughing up blood and was so weak he was unable to help pull the sledge. Scott took Wilson with him and traveled another mile south so that Shackleton would not be able to share in the honor of the feat. This forever ruined the relationship between Scott and Shackleton. Though Scott's actions were celebrated back in Britain, failing to mind the health and honor of his men reflected badly on his leadership and forever left a mark on his name.

Through various intrigues and maneuverings, Shackleton mounted an attempt on the South Pole in 1908. Starting out in October, he, Eric Marshall, Jameson Adams and Frank Wild trekked across the continent. In a mere 30 days they had surpassed Scott's old record and were able to keep skiing. They were within a hair's grasp of penetrating to the Pole, only 97 nautical miles out. But both illness and severe malnourishment plagued them, forcing the team to abandon their efforts. Again, Antarctica rebuffed anyone from reaching the South Pole.

Norwegian Roald Amundsen used sledges, dogs and skis during his expedition. He only had a fast journey in mind. His team took only 57 days to reach the Pole, using previously placed caches to keep them stocked on their departing and returning journeys. Amundsen knew from previous failed expeditions that traveling fast and light was the best way to achieve the Pole with hopes of making it back alive. He left on September 8, far too early in the season. His team was repelled from the continent's interior by temperatures down to -68°F. He bided his time and left again on October 15.

It was not until Amundsen and his team of four members skied within a mile of the Pole on December 15, 1911, that anyone was able to claim reaching the southernmost point on the Earth. With the inaccuracy of navigation instruments, compounded by the difficulty of making sightings at the Earth's apex, Amundsen arguably came as close as Scott did on January 16, 1912. Without modern surveying and satellites, determining the exact spot of the Pole did not happen for some time. To avoid the Peary and Cook North Pole controversies of not attaining exactly 90°S, Amundsen had his men leave tracks and markers all over the area, signifying his team had made the best possible effort to touch the Pole, claiming it for Norway.

Once Scott's team neared to within two miles of the Pole, they saw a black tent on the horizon and knew they had been beaten. Unexplainably, Scott eschewed the use of skis and had his team walk the distance. His initial plan to use ponies and heavy machinery failed, leaving his team to man haul impossibly heavy sleds. Again, Scott failed to provision properly for the journey. By the time they reached the Pole, the team was malnourished and suffered from scurvy and exhausted from the effort of dragging the sledges. To compensate for not being the first, they collected over 30 pounds of rocks as scientific specimens, further slowing their return. Being dangerously late in the season, adding weight certainly contributed to the expedition's fate.

Edgar Evans, the strongest of their group, collapsed on February 17 and died that night. A month later, Lawrence Oates, his feet frostbitten and gangrenous, famously walked away from their tent, never to return. Several days later, Scott convinced his team to stay in the tent, starving and freezing until they perished. Due to the failure of Scott's navigation equipment, they did not know they were a mere ten miles from their cache. It seemed Scott would rather not perish walking but rather die in the tent while leaving messages for posterity. Their bodies were not discovered until months later. No one again reached the pole overland until Edmund Hillary and his team in 1958.

Stewing over the snubbing by Scott, Shackleton mounted a journey of his own for both science and glory. He planned to cross the whole of Antarctica. On arriving at South Georgia island in late 1914, he was informed of the bad ice in the Weddell Sea that year. Nevertheless, he pressed on toward his destination. By the end of January 1915, he, his crew and the ship *Endurance* were trapped in the ice pack while within sight of his destination, Vahsel Bay. From there, they and the ship drifted northward through the austral winter and into early spring. By October, the ship disintegrated from the unceasing ice pressure. On October 27, the *Endurance* was crushed by the pack ice, forcing the crew onto the ice. She then sank on November 21, leaving the crew with little shelter and scant supplies.

For another five months, they drifted north until the pack ice started breaking up in April. The desperate crew took three open boats recovered from the *Endurance* on April 9 and headed toward the desolate Elephant Island. With no one knowing their whereabouts, they had no hope of rescue. The chance of a ship passing by was scant to none. With limited shelter and only a few hapless animals to eat, they were marooned in the worst conditions imaginable. At the dawn of the 20th century, the radio was only a curiosity and not reliable. As such, the *Endurance* had no radio. Once trapped, Shackleton knew that they would never be rescued.

On April 24, 1916, Shackleton and five of his crewmen set off on the *James Caird*, named after the chief sponsor of the expedition, toward South Georgia, 650 nautical miles away. With only four navigational sightings over their journey, Frank Worsley, captain of the *Endurance*, guided the tiny boat to within sight of the island. During their attempt to reach the shore, nightmarish seas made landing impossible. The crew was forced to spend one more night on the ocean through, of all things, a hurricane. But once they landed, they were still not saved. Their single hope, a whaling station, was on the opposite side of the island. Instead of taking to sea and risking destruction, Shackleton took Tom Crean and Worsley on a trek across the uncharted portion of South Georgia, a forbidding and mountainous island with no shelter.

On reaching the whaling station, Shackleton coordinated rescues for his three stranded boat mates on the other side of the island and then the rest of his crew on Elephant Island. Three times the rescue attempts were repulsed until on August 30, 1916, Shackleton sailed onshore and found that all 22 of his men had survived the additional five months. Not until 2013 was anyone able to recreate the ocean-crossing feat Shackleton's crew achieved, and then only escorted by a ship for safety.

After Shackleton's crossing of South Georgia, there was not another successful crossing until 1955. Sir Earnest Shackleton and his men had but a 50 foot section of rope and a carpenter's adze for climbing equipment. Modern expeditions, with the world's best climbers, have used modern technical gear with significant support from safety teams. No one has ever matched Shackleton's minimalist feat without backup or rescue support.

Relatively little in American literature lauds the feat of Amundsen. Perhaps that's because he was not English and thus too foreign for

American audiences. That, or his expedition was too efficient and got right to the point, whereas Scott not-so-nobly perished in his pursuit. And both stories are always overshadowed by Shackleton's inadvertently commanding one of the greatest survival stories of the modern era. Other than William Bligh's escape from the *Bounty*, no one had made such a voyage in a diminutive craft through the 19th century. At least no one who lived to tell about it.

The motivations of early polar explorers during the Edwardian age of exploration were not as noble as would be assumed. Instead, Scott, Amundsen and Shackleton used these explorations as vehicles for fame and fortune back home. Only with modern technology and transport is it possible to make treks across Antarctica for the pure satisfaction of the activity. Aircraft, satellite phones and other modern amenities have forever altered travel in Antarctica.

For the first half of the 20th century, various claims and disputes embroiled Antarctica. Government stations were established, colonies planted, and many countries worked to gain a toe-hold. Australia established a post office on Heard Island in part to declare its intention of being an active player on the continent. However, without a base and outside supplied transported in for support, continuous living in Antarctica is impossible. There is no growing land, no place for livestock to be tended, or anything else that would support life. The *Belgica antarctica*, a species of flightless midge, is the largest terrestrial animal on the continent. It is at most a quarter-inch-long insect. Humans would be hard pressed to harvest these tiny arthropods for all but a mouthful of food.

Yet, for all the lifelessness of the interior of the continent, the surrounding waters team with life. Krill, whales, seals, fishes, penguins and their ilk all make Antarctic waters some of the most abundant on the planet. But the separation between life and lifelessness is all but a few miles from the coast. Penguins travel inland and overwinter while bearing their young. As they are water dwelling birds, they are not considered land animals. Neither are the seals, sea lions, elephant seals, skuas and others that make the beaches their temporary refuge from the sea.

In an attempt to allay any significant and possibly destructive exploration on the continent, the Antarctic Treaty was established in 1961. Even so, there have been many disputes. Some nations continue modern-day whaling operations while others look to the continent as a source of mineral and oil wealth. Each country staking a claim has established a system of permits and allowances for humans to visit the continent for science, exploration and adventure. Even with the treaty, there have been near fights and a minor war in and around Antarctica. The Falkland Islands, claimed by Britain, is a vital way station on the sea voyage to Antarctica. Argentina historically disputed the British claim. On April 1, 1982, Argentine forces invaded the island. At the same time, British forces were keeping a close eye on the Argentine military at South Georgia. Once fighting broke out on the Falklands, Argentine forces attacked the British on South Georgia, too. Fighting continued until, on June 14, Argentine forces surrendered to the British.

Greenpeace even held a minute base in Antarctica from 1987 until 1992. They attempted to force various treaty governments to declare Antarctica a world park, eliminating commercial exploitation and allowing only limited science research. The organization's only major action was the successful blockade of the construction of an airstrip at the French Dumont D'Urville base in 1989. All treaty organizations refused to acknowledge Greenpeace's base, named World Park, and refused any request for assistance other than for life-threatening events.

For now, Antarctica is a semi-permanent home to scientific bases and seasonal explorers. The largest base is McMurdo, the American station on the south tip of Ross Island, on the edge of the Ross Ice Shelf. Supply ships dock during the austral summer, keeping McMurdo and the South Pole station supplied for the year. During the winter, McMurdo is cut off by sea from the rest of the world. After the end of February, the South Pole station cannot receive or send transportation until October due to the extreme cold and darkness.

Cruise ships depart from Ushuaia, Argentina, for the peninsula and the main islands in the Atlantic and Weddell seas from October to March. These cruises afford those who want to see Antarctica the chance without suffering through the continent's interior conditions. ALE and Adventure Network International (ANI) provide expedition support services at Union Glacier in the Ellsworth Mountains, near the Ronne Ice Shelf. From the end of October until the end of January, the company shuttles supplies, expeditions and their own maintenance staff needs between Punta Arenas, Chile, and their Union Glacier base. They are currently the only private company on the western side of Antarctica to do so.

(Upper Left) *Receiving the Eagle Scout award, the highest rank the Boy Scouts of America bestows.*

(Upper Right) *Backpacking in Sequoia National Park, north of Timber Gap.*

(Right) *Spinal compression by a backpack and sleeping bag larger than myself.*

(Below) *What I looked like after a night in my "survival" shelter. I was thankful it was a warm summer evening, otherwise it would have been a real survival experience.*

3

The Course Was Charted Long Ago

SOME 75 YEARS after both Amundsen and Scott reached the South Pole, my father introduced me to the Boy Scouts, an organization founded on teaching boys both outdoor and personal skills, helping them to mature and succeed in life. They are famous for introducing boys from around the world to camping and high adventure. Once I learned what they enabled me to do, I was hooked and spent my teen years with them. Although I did not rapidly advance in rank, I enjoyed learning about the outdoors, knots, canoeing, backpacking and everything else the program offered. Being academically oriented from a young age, reading and recalling key portions of the *Boy Scout Handbook* came easily to me. After I had practiced a skill a few times, I retained it for life. Even years later, as an adult in the organization, I was able to recall most of what I learned. This ability was handy at both work and in the outdoors.

My first backpacking experience was with the Boy Scouts in 1988. We hiked up Harvey Moore trail in the Cuyamaca National Forest, an hour east of San Diego, California. There I learned what it was like to overpack. Weighing in at a whopping 50 pounds, my pack was a spine crusher. Though I did not wear any of the denim jeans I brought with me, I dutifully carried them anyway. We were lucky the weather was warm with no chance of rain. Otherwise, my cotton clothes would have made me miserable. Reflecting on the trip, I learned that though adults were well meaning, sometimes they did not know what they were doing, either. Why they let me carry such a pack and with improper clothing still evades me to this day. Understanding the importance of packing light had not permeated my troop's thinking at the time. The trip worked out and everyone enjoyed it, but it took a decade before I learned, on my own, what not to bring.

Too, I found that learning leadership and responsibility required effort and patience, far more than I had as a teenager. On one particular desert camp trip, my patrol leader delegated me the task of bringing condiments for the not-so-gourmet hot dogs we planned to eat for dinner. Being all of 14 years old, I was distracted and soon forgot my assignment. When it was time to prepare the hot dogs and I was asked to produce ketchup, mustard and relish, I developed that wretched sinking feeling that comes right at the dawning of something unpleasant happening. Although no one died from eating dry buns and hot dogs, I was not popular with my patrol that night. As other patrols and the adults planned different dishes, there was no one to bail me out with their condiments. From then on, I never forgot any all-important ingredient. I learned to write lists and to check them off prior to departure.

In 1980, my dad was laid off from his produce clerk job in Jackson, Wyoming. The economy in the town was floundering, prior to the billionaire boom hitting the area. Living in a cramped trailer, my dad had a small savings so we were not cast out on the street. Still, joblessness and having a wife and two sons made the slow fall season stressful. Dad's brother also was laid off right at the same time. Being seven years old, the concept of work and being laid off was alien to me. All I knew was that I had to walk to school and not fight with my brother, both a challenge at times. Since we lived in the Rocky Mountains, the winters were always difficult for adults. But for me, snow was a wonderland.

My main goal that winter was to build a full size snow man. With a significant amount of powder blanketing the lawn, I decided that conditions were ripe and it was time to embark on realizing my goal. Mom obliged my eagerness to go outside, so she carefully bundled me up so that I would not catch a cold. Since I was always a sickly child and suffered from asthma, she must have stressed out every time I ventured outside to do anything. In contrast, my brother Jason was more resilient and rarely fell ill. In the world of immunity, I had not inherited fitting genes for living in Jackson. Knowing none of this at the time, I only cared about building my snow man, so outside I went. I instantly discovered the amount of work it took. Though my brother had better genetics, being four years old made him of little help, as he could barely waddle in the snow.

Unsure of how to build something taller than I was, I piled up snow to see what I could make of it. After only a few minutes, the pile looked nothing like the snowmen I had seen in town. Unsatisfied, I determined that the only way to do this was to roll the snow. Making the largest snow ball I could, I put it on the ground and gingerly pushed it forward. If I was not careful, the snow ball crumbled instead of building up, so I minded the growing mass cautiously. After rolling it three-quarters of the way around the trailer, I was impressed by how big the ball had grown. But now it was so large I was unable to push it with my arms. I put my back against it and used my stick-thin legs to continue the work. I did not want to leave the snowman in the side yard, but rather have it be proudly displayed out front. For the next fifteen minutes, I gasped and shoved with all the force my scrawny body could muster. Finally, after a seeming eternity, I lay panting against one snowball centered in the front yard.

Though I was proud of the accomplishment, I had not thought this project through. One problem was I had consumed the loose snow in the yard. There was not enough to build two additional balls. Then there was the bigger problem of construction. I was barely able to roll the base. How was I to set two smaller balls on top of this one staring back at me? Being sapped from what I had done already, I had to accept this as the end product. I finished the ball off with a face and arms. Though it bothered me to leave the snowman in this state, it was time for lunch. A boy has his priorities. My parents were impressed with the squat snowman but asked where the other two snowballs were. After explaining my dilemma, dad helped me polish up the project, making it into a proper snow man.

Some weeks later, my parents announced that we were moving to California and would live nearby the ocean. As I had no idea what an ocean was, I was scared but excited.

"Mom, is an ocean just a giant lake?" I asked.

"No, it's much bigger than that," she replied.

Though my mom was unhappy to be leaving her parents, mine knew they needed to make a change. My dad and uncle had made a reconnaissance mission to San Diego a few weeks before and, mutually, thought it was a smart idea to live in a sizable city for better job opportunities. Also, they were tired of the hard Wyoming winters, as the previous two years (1978 and 1979) had recorded temperatures below -40°F and, in town, near -60°F without wind chill. During those years, the pipes in the trailer froze. Dad crawled under the house and thawed them with a torch. My parents had no interest in seeing how cold that winter would be. So with neither jobs nor even a place to stay waiting for them, they packed my brother and me up and headed off for San Diego. I remember looking at the remains of my snow man, sitting alone in the yard as we left.

It was the biggest risk I've seen my parents take, relying on faith that all would work out. I have always been inspired to think that our little family showed up in San Diego with nothing but a U-haul full of 1970's furniture and a Datsun pickup. They left the Ford Pinto behind. We even were able to visit the beach on our first day there and I learned what an ocean looked like.

One day when I was at my parents' house in 2002, I took a moment to dig through the piles of magazines that always adorned the end table. Although the cover image of the December 2001 issue of *National Geographic* featured Rembrandt's "Sacrifice of Isaac", the painting barely grabbed my attention. What did was the bold yellow text of the first article.

"Antarctica: Life at the Bottom of the World"

I could actually see photographs of a place I barely learned about in both high school and college. The *Geographic* was always exemplary for learning about new places, so, I contented myself with sitting down, consuming Roff Smith's text and Maria Stenzel's photographs, and studied a place that seemed impossible to travel to. I might as well have been looking at photographs of the moon. Yet I longed for more information. My dial-up internet was next to worthless for serious research, so I borrowed the magazine and brought it home with me. For as much as I wanted to stomp off to the library and shuffle through the few books available on Antarctica, I was distracted by a new job and buying a home. Neither afforded much time to spend dreaming of far off lands. And then, I asked myself, what would I do with that information? Although I felt as though I could do anything, I had a problem figuring out how to make it happen. How would I ever travel down there? It looked to be as inaccessible a place as it had been for the explorers in the early 20th century. I had no ship, aircraft, and most importantly, finances to fly there. The magazine sat on a bookcase I had built, shuffling into the background as I acquired more books. Soon, I forgot it.

Plus, I was advancing in my engineering career. Having earned a degree in electrical engineering from California State University, San Diego, I learned I had an ability to write embedded software that would run on the circuits I designed. For a techno-geek, this was a dream. Now, instead of being beholden to whatever products I could purchase, I had the ability to design any electronics I needed. And then, I could write the software to drive those circuits to do anything I wanted. I found myself fairly absorbed in enjoying the art of creation. As an engineer, devising electronics and watching customers use them was a heady thrill.

One of my buddies, Alfonso Limon, with whom I had kept in perpetual contact since junior high school, was working on a degree in Computational Science. He invited me to register for a class at the university and see what I thought.

"Why don't you sign up for the computer graphics visualization class?" he asked.

At first I thought up a bunch of meaningless excuses not to, then realized I was missing an opportunity.

"Well, why not. I don't have anything else to do with my time," I replied.

"Great. Classes start next week."

If nothing else, it gave me a chance to return to the university and learn something new and exciting. As my employer paid for continuing education in a related field, it made sense to take the classes. Granted, it was not a field of study that allowed me to go outside, like geology or environmental science, but it was related so it would be paid for. The only requirement I had was to turn in excellent grades, something easy for me to do. I figured three years were going to pass no matter what. I wanted to pass the time constructively.

As I was now tied up working on a master's degree, there was no way I could take off to do any real exploring or even consider embarking on an expedition. The thought did not cross my mind. Between driving to work 40 miles, then driving to the university another 20 miles three times a week, I had little spare time. At most, I kept myself somewhat in shape by jogging. Returning to the student life did not cause me to gain weight. Though my immunity genes were poor, my weight management ones were excellent. So even though computational science was a degree earned in a windowless basement, I was in no particular danger of falling apart physically. This allowed me to take an occasional hike but nothing more adventurous. That was, until summer 2002.

While sitting at my desk at work, I sensed the call of the outdoors rise in my subconscious. For an unknown reason, probably from web surfing at my desk during lunch, the random thought of backpacking through the California Sierras flashed into my mind. After reading around, I found Mineral King in Sequoia National Park. The few online photos available showed it to look like the Alps, all without the international plane flight. As it had been over a decade since I had backpacked, I had little in the way of equipment. After drifting away from Boy Scouts, I saw little reason to keep equipment that crushed my spinal column. The thought of suffering up steep mountain trails depressed me, making the dreamy look of Mineral King appear imposing and miserable. I had no desire to lug a 50 pound pack up a mountain. While reading the park's trail description, I stumbled upon the phrase "lightweight backpacking".

This piqued my interest.

In a mere 15 minutes, I was introduced to a whole new psychology of traveling through the outdoors. Rather than striving to carry as much as possible, there were people now who did everything they could to shave ounces off their gear. They even chopped their toothbrushes in half. One website even described how to assemble a denatured alcohol stove out of soda cans. It seemed fanciful, but I kept reading. Another website featured the Spanish proverb, "En largo camino una paja pesa," which translates to "On a long journey even a straw weighs heavy." Farther down on the page, the author listed his equipment and compared the weight to that of a traditional backpacker. The difference was stunning. The author carried 11 pounds, whereas I had thought carrying 30 pounds was packing "light". The light bulb winked on. Setting out to learn about the best and lightest gear, I spent a few days calling and researching. I shopped around at different outdoor sports stores in San Diego and purchased newer, far lighter equipment. Weighing my new cadre of gear, I was elated. The scale showed it all added up to a scant 12 pounds.

I was ready to go on my first backpack into the Sierras. After leaving a route description with my parents in case of an untimely bear encounter, I drove the six hours into the Sierras. Unsure what to expect, I hiked off toward Franklin Pass over to Ranger Lake. Even with the light pack, the trail kicked my butt. For all the research and pack lightening technology I had invested in, I failed to consider one critical element. I had not performed a shakedown hike. Though my Boy Scout troop did not know about lightweight packing nor make it to the Sierras, they were wise enough to have shakedown hikes. At the time, those seemed like a waste of time. Now, not being active constantly, I saw their value. After my 16 mile tour in the Sierras, I was destroyed. My joints ached all six hours during the drive back. I stumbled out of my car when I arrived home and I hobbled for four days afterward. Yet, I was satisfied. I had researched my equipment, used much of my Boy Scout training but ditched the crippling over-weight pack, and had slept overnight in the Sierras. Alone. My mosquito bitten face glowed with pride.

Now I understood that I needed constant physical training so that, at a moment's notice, I could pack my gear and be ready to hit the Sierras. This brought me into the next phase of my active life. I learned about running and strung together a few races until I finished a marathon. At the same time, I purchased a road bike and discovered the joys of that sport, too. Pushing myself with running and riding, I developed strength and stamina. As a result, I found hauling a backpack to a far-off mountain peak much easier. Even though the trips were strenuous, I did not return crippled. Extending the length and complexity of each trip, I pushed how far I hiked on these weekend trips. Finding a new joy in the challenge of being in the outdoors, my perspective of what I was doing with my life began to shift. Instead of being completely geek obsessed, putting countless hours into learning about the latest microprocessor, I now collected a select library of outdoor and adventure non-fiction books. National Geographic had released their Adventure Classics reprint series, one of which was titled *The Worst Journey in the World*. Written by Apsley Cherry-Garrard, one of Robert Falcon Scott's men, it recounted the ill-fated Antarctic expedition. It sat on my bookshelf, unread, due to other distractions.

In 2003, I met a girl and began dating her. After mustering my scant powers of observation, I noticed that she had adorned her house with Parisian art. After only dating for a month, I suggested we take a trip to Paris.

"Are you serious? I mean, like the real Paris?"

"Yes, of course. I certainly do not mean Paris, Texas."

"Oh, very funny."

She gaped at me in astonishment. It was rather obvious she would love to visit France and tour the country. As we already possessed passports, we only needed to take time off work, purchase tickets, and find our way there. We were both excited, as this would be our first off-continent trip. Several people asked if we would be okay traveling there, as my high school French was rusty by this point. I always replied that we would have no problem. Paris was a vast city, so there should be plenty of options. I assured everyone that I knew what I was doing and that we did not require any reservations. We would arrive in the city and figure it out.

I had no clue.

We eventually did find some places to stay and ended up learning about the cultural gulf between America and France. It was all utterly thrilling to me. I was somewhere that I had never been, my language skills were marginally passable at best, and I was duty-bound to ensure someone else had an enjoyable time, all while barely able to read and translate menus and museum descriptions. One day, while we were walking along the banks of the Seine, she asked me where I always had wanted to go in the world. Without thinking, I blurted out "Antarctica". She looked at me puzzled but laughed. She must have thought I was being a fool for wanting to go somewhere so cold. It was not exactly the most romantic place to mention. A smarter man would have said, "Rome, with you of course!"

I was still working on dialing in the romantic part at 30 years old.

Several months later, I was visiting at her house when she randomly dropped a magazine in front of me.

"What is this for?" I asked, not even glancing at it.

"Look at the cover."

"Yes, it's a very nice painting, probably of Abraham sacrificing..."

Then realization dawned on me. It was the same issue of *National Geographic* sitting lost in my house, the one I'd borrowed from my parents. Except this copy had a pen mark circling the feature story about Antarctica.

"I think you are completely crazy for wanting to go there, but you should read the article anyway."

"Alright, so I'm crazy. I've actually seen this article before."

"No kidding. I saw it at your place and thought I'd emphasize the point. You are nuts."

Again, my mind rushed as I thumbed through the images and text. I brought the magazine home and placed it on the coffee table. That way I could refer to it time and again. Over a year after seeing the magazine for the first time, I was again enticed by the topic, location and challenge of traveling to such a forbidding place. I found myself searching for my copy of *The Worst Journey in the World*. This time I devoured it in a few evenings.

(Main) While backpacking in the Sierras in the winter, I wanted to cut as much weight as possible. Switching from a heavy tent to a lightweight tarp made difficult travel more enjoyable.

(Below Left) Looking at me sleeping in my snow tunnel from the outside. It took 2 hours to chisel out the ice so I would fit.

(Below Right) Sleeping in a snow cave is not for the claustrophobic. This was one of the warmest and quietest nights I ever had camping in the winter.

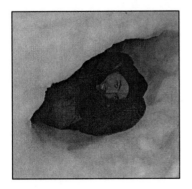

(**Upper Left**) *Arrival at the Kangerlussuaq airport in Greenland. It was -10°F when I walked off the jet and onto the tarmac.*

(**Upper Right**) *The first church constructed in Sisimiut has a whale bone arch entrance to the courtyard.*

(**Right**) *Testing what it would be like to wear caribou antlers on the way to Lake Taserssuaq.*

(**Below**) *While hiking toward Oles Lakseelv along the Arctic Circle Trail, I encountered snow and -25°F temperatures with only a 5°F rated sleeping bag.*

4

How to Camp in the Snow

WHILE I RELATED THE STORIES of my backpacking trips into the Sierras, coworkers routinely asked if I had ever climbed Mt. Whitney. I had given little thought to it. All I knew was that a permit was required to climb it in the summer. Besides, I was fully absorbed in completing my master's thesis. Being a typical student, I worked on it for a while, then I did not touch it again for a month. After repeating this cycle for the better part of a year, I realized the only way to finish writing it was if I sat down and cranked it out. After several months' worth of concerted effort, I defended the work and was awarded my masters of science in computational science.

Now I was ready for an outdoor challenge.

One issue that bugged me about planning a Mt. Whitney climb was the lottery system. Hikers had to bid on time slots during the summer. Although I understood why the Forest Service did this, it still irked me. Coming from the 1970's Wyoming, where people wandered as much as they pleased, anything that restricted me in the mountains was a real bother. Without the permit system, though, the place would have turned into a disgusting garbage heap. During the hiking season, the trail is crammed with people; I did not want to climb up the mountain in a mule train of bodies. I sought a purer experience. I opted to wait beyond the permit period and into November, when there was considerable snow coverage in 2003. With snowshoes, crampons and ice axe in hand, I drove to Lone Pine to climb the snow-covered mountain.

In no time, I figured out that I was in trouble. It took a full hour to drive the last mile to the Whitney Portal store where I had planned to start. The snow was deep on the road, making even rear-locked 4x4 travel close to impossible. Undaunted, I shoveled over a hundred pounds of snow and piled a bunch of rocks into the pickup bed. This still barely gave me traction, even with chains on. Heedless of these obstacles, I ground my way up to the end of the road. When I exited my truck, I only saw one set of footprints, so I knew that I had the place to myself. It was a real joy from the otherwise Disneyland experience I had been warned about.

Even though I had camped in the snow, I had never scaled a high mountain before. There was a trail all the way up, so I was not concerned about becoming lost. With my trusty GPS and a stream of waypoints to guide me, I awoke at 3 a.m. and began my slow march up the mountain.

At first I made decent time, as I managed to follow the trail in the dark with my headlamp, even with the snow. But as I gained altitude, the trail became more indistinct until I used my GPS full time to tramp from point to point in the darkness. This all did not bother me, as I knew that at dawn, I would have a much easier time. That was, until I started walking in even deeper fresh snow. Once I put on my snowshoes, I continued the climb undiscouraged. Well into the morning, I forged on with dogged determination. Even though my snowshoes were doing a decent job and the trail was visible, I still sank ten inches per step. The fresh snow made travel laborious. Near noon, I checked the GPS. I was not even half way up the mountain. For several moments, I stared at the device in disbelief, irritation and disappointment welling up inside of me. I had been denied my first summit bid. Disgusted, I turned back and slogged back to my truck.

Two years later, my climbing partner Dan King and I attempted an even later season bid on Mount Whitney. This time we did not even reach as far as I had the first time. The fluffy snow was now chest deep, rendering the snowshoes useless. A blizzard roared down the mountain face.

"It's only a longer walk back," Dan yelled above the winds.

"Yes, I know. This really stinks to have failed at this twice, now," I hollered back.

"Don't worry. At least we didn't get stuck higher and have to bivvy [sleep overnight unplanned]."

"You're right. I'm still fond of my toes and fingers."

This winter travel business started to gall me. Attempting to hike to the top of Whitney in one day in deep snow was not working out. After hearing a few avalanches roar out of sight, we decided to beat a hasty retreat. The mountain would be there another day. It was not until 2006 that I finally stood on the peak of Whitney. I had driven there on a whim and scored a walk-up permit near the end of the season. With only a tiny patch of snow that year, I easily reached the summit. Conditions made all the difference. Even though walking up a clear trail made achieving the goal easy, I did not find it completely satisfying. Failing previous times was still worse, though. On the peak, I recalled the words of Ernest Shackleton: "Superhuman effort isn't worth a damn unless it achieves results."

By the time I had summited Mt. Whitney, I had a number of solo backpacking and travel trips under my belt, so I felt confident. Knowing that I was self contained and reliant only on myself brought me a great deal of satisfaction. On each trip, I stretched myself farther. Eventually, I was strong enough to drive seven hours to Kings Canyon National Park, backpack 40 miles with 10,000 feet of elevation gain over one night, and then drive another seven hours back home. I took pride in now being able to cover difficult miles in a short time. Yet I realized what I did paled in comparison to polar explorers or high-altitude mountain climbers. It felt as though I played at a respectable level with the junior varsity but still nowhere near the big leagues.

By 2008, I was ready for something different.

Near the end of spring, I grew restless with my job. In fact, I began to feel out of place in my career. Engineering had been a challenge up to this point but had recently begun to become a grind. Each project became less of a creative activity and more like mindless work. What I once enjoyed as art was now only a day job. The 12 years I had dedicated to being a nerd's nerd had paid off in my ability to conquer most any problem, yet I felt as though I had reached a plateau. At the time, my employer had no management positions available. It would be the only way to advance in my career. There was no technical ladder for me to climb up, either. That meant I would have to change jobs to a larger company and settle into advancing myself. However, my plateau happened right in the early depths of the Great American Recession. The job offer emails had dried up. What had once been a lucrative industry had suddenly left me in a meager lifeboat of a company.

So, I resigned myself to stay where I was. At the time it was okay. I had a reasonable amount of responsibility and there was no lack of work for me to do. That certainly beat out some of my friends who had been out of work for several months. Yet I wanted to run and bail off the ship. By the end of summer, I needed to escape work for a while. Another trip to the Sierras would not to satisfy me. The next place needed to be remote, somewhere that I was not familiar with and which presented a whole new experience. I expanded my search to international destinations. I wanted to travel to somewhere far away. But what was far away, anyway? Opening up my dusty world atlas, I poured over the world overview page to see what would catch my attention. Immediately something did.

Greenland.

I had no idea what was in Greenland other than rocks or snow. I had flown over it several times while traveling back and forth to Europe but had never set foot on the massive island, one-third the size of Australia. It was a minor continent unto itself. I knew no one who had been to Greenland, let alone trekked across the Arctic tundra. After surfing the web, I happened upon the mention of a ski competition held in Greenland during spring, where skiers traverse over 100 miles from the icecap of Greenland to the coast. I wasn't ready for that. But people also hiked the Arctic Circle Trail during the summer months. With only a barely adequate Danish-to-English translation of the trail description, I researched how to travel to Greenland. It took a few days to purchase the air ticket, as my credit card kept rejecting the transaction as fraud. Random airfare purchases out of Copenhagen must have set off some alarms.

Now that I had my first international mini-expedition planned, work seemed more enjoyable. Although working on repeated late projects was discouraging, I now had something to look forward to. It was not too long before I dug out my passport, packed my bags and made my way to Greenland via Denmark. I watched Greenland streak under me on my way to Europe. Flying over the place I was going to did not make much sense, but the only direct flight from the United States to Greenland, from Baltimore to Kangerlussuaq, had been canceled the year before. In total it took three days to reach Greenland. Now I knew I had gone somewhere.

During the landing approach, the plane banked steeply and circled into the landing strip in Søndre Strømfjord, the Danish name for the settlement. While pressed against my seat, I saw that there was little snow on the ground. During the flight from Copenhagen to Greenland, I imagined that the trail was buried by impassable snow. As I had opted not to bring snow shoes to save weight, I was taking a risk. As we turned, I saw rocks poking out of the snow cover in the fjord, allaying my fears and instilling hope that the journey was possible. I wanted to do this trek without a guide, all on my own.

Permits to hike the trail were available at the police station. As I sidled into the constricted trailer, the desk officer gazed at me quizzically.

"Can I help you?" he asked in lightly accented English.

"May I have a permit to hike the Arctic Circle Trail?"

"Certainly. But when exactly are you planning to go?"

Checking my watch, I replied, "As soon as we can finish the permit and I can find a ride to the trail."

"Oh. That is not good. You realize that you are very late in the season and the passes are filled with snow?"

"Yes, I understand, but I've come a long way to hike through your country."

"Do you have a radio or satellite phone?"

I was worried he would deny me a permit at this point.

"No, I do not."

"That is risky. We had three German hikers in August calling us on the radio constantly. They asked for directions and help. Eventually, one broke his leg and we had to evacuate them. Do you have insurance?"

I produced my international medical and repatriation insurance form. After reviewing over the paperwork, he stared at me.

"You seem to have everything in order. Have you hiked in winter mountain conditions before?"

"Yes, without too much trouble."

Shaking his head, he pulled out the permit, scratched lines through the radio and satellite phone sections, and filled out the rest of it.

"Please, check in with the police station when you reach Sisimiut. We will try to watch out for you. This is risky and you understand we may not be able to rescue you immediately.

"I understand."

"Let us finish this up and get you on your way. You have a difficult trek ahead of you."

Thanking him, I headed over to the airport gift shop, purchased the last three Greenland hiking maps on the shelf and found a driver to take me to Kellyville, a science station at the start of the Arctic Circle Trail. I opted for the expensive taxi rather than walking ten dusty miles with nothing but salt water for drinking. As the driver spoke only a few words of English and I no useful Greenlandic, we rode in silence. He smiled and was cheerful though, so he was not disagreeable company. Once we stopped at the trailhead, he morphed his face into one of concern.

"Okay?" he said with a grave voice.

"Ja!" I replied in my laughable Danish.

Grinning, I took his hand, shook it and was off.

Eleven days later, I emerged from the Arctic wilderness and entered Sisimiut, smelling like a garbage dump in a heat wave. The ice-choked river crossings did nothing to abate my elegant aroma. I had made it. Even though my legs and feet were incredibly sore, I had trekked across Greenland's tundra, seen the aurora borealis and had more experiences packed into a week and a half than in years of working as an engineer. Elated, I walked through the village, smiling at the cordial people. Thoughts of my having crossed multiple icy rivers, postholing through knee deep snow, and crossing the treeless and swampy tundra buoyed my otherwise weary feet.

I was hooked on international trekking.

In spring of 2009, I watched a show on public television about winter in Yellowstone. One of the people featured in the documentary Christmas in Yellowstone was photographer Tom Murphy of Bozeman, Montana. He was shown traversing the Yellowstone backcountry, pitching a tarp tent (which I used in the winter, too), and sleeping in his -20°F sleeping bag. He woke up smiling. I was blown away. I had no idea one could trek across the backcountry in winter. After some research, I found Murphy's information and contacted him about an idea. Although he had only skied from Flagg Ranch to Yellowstone Lake, I wanted to travel all the way across the park. I didn't have a clue how to arrange it. He was accommodating and let me in on a few of his travel secrets. He also said that given the toughness of the winters in the park, there was no shame in traveling the roads all the way from Gardiner, Montana to Flagg Ranch, Wyoming. He was not sure how long it would take but advised me to be prepared for viciously cold temperatures.

Nancy Takeda, one of my aunts, lived in Jackson, Wyoming. Her home was the perfect place to use as a base camp to make a foray into Yellowstone. Once I told her and my parents about my idea to cross the park, they thought I damaged my brain while in Greenland. I told them who I had spoken with, what I planned to do and how I had already begun preparations. Nancy had been through some harsh northwest Wyoming winters, so she knew what I was up against.

"Are you sure you want to do that? I know you have camped in the snow but Yellowstone is different," Nancy said.

"Don't worry," I told her. "If I can backpack across the Greenland tundra by myself, I'm sure I'll be able to ski across Yellowstone, too."

Her concern was mirrored by my parents. They told me how cold Yellowstone could be. Sure, I knew it can drop down below -20°F. I had camped in that in Greenland. Although they acknowledged that I knew the temperatures and altitude there, I still heard reservation and concern in their voices. They reminded me that I had grown up in San Diego, a perpetual summer resort city, and had not lived through a bitter winter, let alone camped in it. I took their warnings to heart and made rushed preparations. I needed to leave town for a while; I wanted to travel and survive.

By late fall, I was having trouble managing my two fissuring personalities. One, the dedicated engineer and scientist, loved the technical challenges but was frustrated by being unable to express my best artistry of the craft. The other, an ardent outdoorsman and adventurer, was not content sitting at a desk, working to make someone else rich. One said to stay the course to keep my brain challenged, while the other said to ditch it all and live life larger. Somewhere there must be an agreeable compromise that would keep both halves of me satisfied. I hoped Yellowstone would provide inspiration on how to do that.

After purchasing tickets and finalizing logistics, I was on my way across Yellowstone in snow truck mat-tracks, passenger vans outfitted with miniature tank treads. Immediately, I ran into my first problem. The tails of my skis were damaged on the trip across the park to Mammoth Hot Springs. Placed in the rack on the van, the constant bouncing cracked the tails to pieces. The Xanterra folks were most accommodating in effecting a repair, as their carrier rack had caused the damage. In an hour, they fixed the skis and I was on my way.

My hope was to go from the north to the south entrances to the park. However, the northern half of Yellowstone tends to be drier than the southern, so there was no snow on the road from Gardiner to the Indian Creek campsite. As my entire rig was based on snow travel, I walked the first couple of miles from Roosevelt Arch to Mammoth, then rode in a shuttle to Indian Creek. This eliminated my status of walking across the entire park under my own power. I put the asterisk there on my own, as it was essential to be honest about what was and, more importantly, was not done.

The first day of travel was enjoyable until a storm blew in, with winds directly out of the south. The same direction I was headed. As I had to reach Norris Basin for my first night, I discovered two realities. The first was the sled I brought had too much drag. It was designed with side-hilling in mind, not traveling in flat, soft snow. On flat ground it dragged like a boat anchor. The second discovery was that my ski setup was all wrong. I had no ski skins. Ski skins are made from fuzzy fabric that, when rubbed one direction, is smooth, while rubbing in the other direction grabs snow and makes towing and uphill travel possible. The patterned base on the skis should have provided excellent traction, but I had no way to test them in San Diego. By the time I was in Yellowstone, I learned these skis were not the right size. All they did was slip.

"These skis are junk," I yelled into the building storm. I flopped on my sled and abjectly stared at the skis as snow built up on my jacket. As a backup, I had brought snow shoes. Sighing, I strapped the skis to the sled, mounted the snow shoes and started trudging my way across the park. Snow shoeing was 50 percent slower than skiing, so I ended up being out in the field much longer than I expected.

By the time I had traveled 60 miles to Yellowstone Lake, I was not only discouraged but destroyed. My muscles were cramping up. The first few days of stormy weather provided constant headwind, slowing me down even more. Gritting my teeth, I shoved the skis out of the way, sat on my sled, and sighed. I knew I would be able to slog this out but at the expense of enjoying myself. Tired and beaten, I stared out over Yellowstone Lake. I knew the deep runners made the sled difficult to drag. But how could I render it easier? Suddenly, my engineering brain kicked in.

"Hello, you doof," it said. "Why hadn't you thought of this before? You are carrying what you need to make the sled easier to pull."

Of course! I had been carrying skis for a week. If there was only a way to mount the sled to them…

Sure enough. I manhandled the sled onto the skis, then shoved the whole rig. It slid away from me downhill fifteen feet until the sled slipped off the bindings. Now all I had to do was figure out how to keep the sled attached to the skis. Not wanting to waste daylight, I strapped the skis back on and continued yanking the sled with all my strength. It took half an hour to scheme something up. Using the rope I had brought, I jury rigged a harness with knots, lashings and cross-bracing. It took a while to tie it all together, as the weather was bitterly cold, -25ºF. The setup was reliant on gravity, but with the crossed traces to the tips of the skis, it held together. I figured that, even if the rigging crumbled every hour, I moved so much faster that it was worth the annoyance.

All of a sudden, I snowshoed without straining my legs each step. This was an absolute dream. Then, in 100 yards, the whole rig collapsed. I didn't care. I walked without pain. The complex arrangement of ropes needed tuning, and soon I was on my way. What had equated to a nine hour leg press session was reduced to walking with a little weight tugging at me. I was so excited I whooped and hollered every few minutes until I grew hoarse. That was okay because I had merged problem solving with adventuring. I was elated. Having my voice fade to a whisper for celebration was worth it. I even spoke with the lodgepole pines surrounding me to have something to tell how happy I was. What had degenerated into drudgery was turned into an absolute thrill. My failure to figure it out was obvious. I was using my adventure spirit to the exclusion of my engineering brain. Now that I had both working in concert, I felt whole again. It was as though I had woken up.

The last night of the trip, the temperature dropped precipitously. My cereal partially froze while I ate it. My boots shrank two sizes. Each time I stood on the snow, my feet burned from the cold. They felt as though I had stepped on broiling asphalt. Fearing frostbite, I yelled, stomped and flapped my arms while simultaneously packing the tent. In deep snow, this was no minor effort. One mat-track stopped and the driver rolled his window down.

"Hey buddy, are you okay? The thermometer shows -45ºF," said the driver with alarm.

"Yes, I'm fine. It's a bit cold so, if you don't mind, I need to keep working on getting moving."

"Okay, buddy. That's crazy. That is just crazy."

Most of the way down from the plateau, I flailed my arms and jumped up and down to keep the blood circulating. Every time I did, sensation returned to my feet. Later that afternoon, I arrived at Flagg Ranch, the end of the trek. Fearing that I had frozen my toes off as I no longer felt them, I tottered over to the fireplace and gingerly removed the boots and socks. Inspecting each toe, I found nothing amiss. I had survived and kept everything attached. Jumping up barefooted, I thrust my arms into the air in victory and hissed out an audible, "Yes!" People looked at me perplexed for a moment, then resumed their conversations. I had walked across Yellowstone unscathed, conquering my fear, weather, design and technical issues. And the best part: I enjoyed the whole trip.

Over the next two years, I refined my gear and approaches to cold weather camping while trekking across Yellowstone two more times. One of the major changes I made was to bolt skis to the sleds. This produced a huge difference in the sled performance and my overall enjoyment of the trip. Now, I could go farther in less time.

After the 2010 trip through Yellowstone, I began to surmise that skiing across Antarctica was possible. I had started talking more about it with my family and friends. They all still thought I was nuts but were somewhat used to my outlandish trips. I still compared myself against the titans of exploration, feeling like an amateurish child while reading about their exploits. But I knew that all polar explorers had, at one time, not been anyone either. This was difficult to reconcile. How did they transform themselves from a nobody to having a place in history books? It was not a matter of following a defined path. I needed confidence that I was moving along the right path. There was no instruction manual. Had I desired to undertake activities defined by manuals, I should have taken up a different career. At work, I now saw myself as that: someone defined by manuals.

I wanted to do an excellent job and deliver a quality product, so I knew that once my attitude toward my job deteriorated, I was in trouble. The artistry had dissolved and what was left in its place felt rather dull and leaden. Every project seemed to be done in a rush, requiring incessant and repeated late nights. Much as I relished the challenge, I knew that I was missing time with my family and friends. If I was going to be under constant pressure and putting in long hours all the time, I knew it should be for me and those I cared about.

It was time to plan for Antarctica or forget it and do something else.

(Main) *Along the Yellowstone Park Road, over the pass between Norris Junction and Canyon Village. This was the most difficult hill climb of this expedition.*

(Below Left) *When things become difficult on an expedition, this sign says it all.*

(Below Right) *The snow during the 2009-2010 season in Yellowstone was deep and soft. Even with snowshoes, I sank up to my shins repeatedly.*

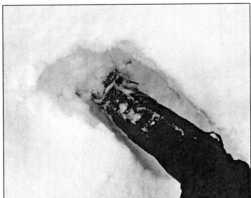

(Main) *Showing off my ration bag, I enjoyed camping while listening to sizzling geothermal features.*

(Below Left) *Smiling while packing my gear, I enjoyed every minute of my first long-distance ski expedition. The rope rigging from the sled to the skis can be seen in this photo.*

(Below Right) *At the end of the expedition across Yellowstone, I made sure to take the picture in front of the South Entrance park sign. It was -45°F the morning this was taken, the perfect Antarctic simulation.*

Goodbye, Bits and Bytes

BUT WHAT TO DO? I combed the internet searching for what other people had done and the feats accomplished. I thirsted to do something original, something outlandish that no one had done before. Part of the reason had to do with originality and the other with securing possible sponsors for the expedition. It seemed that originality was key, though not always. There was no end to people attempting to summit Everest, which has been done thousands of times, and yet these people secured sponsorships. So originality was not an absolute criterion for securing sponsorships, but experience was. The one fact I learned was there had been several round trip attempts to the pole. According to ALE, many expeditions which planned to ski to the pole and return via ski or kites quit for any number of reasons. Now I had originality.

What impeded me was being a complete unknown, someone who had achieved nothing more than long backpack and cross-country ski trips in the winter. Though fairly impressive to the non-outdoor audience, these were but a pittance compared to what major expeditions had done and were, no doubt, planning on doing. Even Will Steger, an Antarctic legend, had terrible trouble securing sponsorships in his early days. He wanted to dogsled to the North Pole but needed a trial run to prove he could do it. So he put together a successful expedition from Minnesota to Point Barrow, Alaska. With that success in hand, sponsors were more willing to fund his expedition. However, I knew I did not have the time or money to cross country ski to Alaska. Instead, I opted to begin saving my dollars and cut back on spending. My commute wasted $400 in gas each month in addition to two hours daily. More if there was traffic. To escape this wasteful cycle, I rented out my house in Temecula and moved to Carlsbad, only 10 minutes from work. After one week, I realized I should have done this long before. This change was the first of many to come.

None of the attempts to ski to the South Pole and ski back without aid or support had succeeded, yet several worthy challengers had attempted it. It was exciting to read these people's credentials, yet to learn that they had given up on the idea was disheartening. Who was I? I had no Special Forces background, nor had I backing from a Royal Family, nor any vast source of financial support. It seemed that everyone who tried this had a substantial resume and an excellent network of people. But contacting these people proved fruitless. That was, until I found Todd Carmichael.

Carmichael was one of only a few Americans to ski solo from Hercules Inlet to the South Pole, a trip of 720 miles. Solo meant alone in the world's biggest wilderness. I was stunned. After learning about the endless list of people who had climbed Everest, I expected this would have been a well-trodden path, too. Now I began to grow excited. He was kind enough to email me his perspective on what he had done in Antarctica and all the troubles he ran into. I had even found videos he had posted after his expedition and gained significant insight into what it was like there.

It was bad—very bad.

Now my excitement for the idea of skiing solo to the Pole was founded in reality. I had no idea if I would be able to make a round trip out of it, as so many had failed. But I was confident that I would be able to pull off being the second American to solo to the Pole. I now had a possible goal as a serious expedition to put my efforts toward. But there were so many unknowns. For as much time as I had spent ski trekking, sled towing, camping in hard winter conditions in both the Rockies and Sierra, it seemed that Antarctica was a whole different animal. After contacting ALE, and securing their gear list, I was astounded at both the expense and the difficulty in finding everything.

"Sourcing gear for Antarctica can be quite a challenge," ALE operations manager Steve Jones told me.

"Yes that seems to be the case," I quipped.

Much of ALE's expedition gear suggestions were based out of Europe, I was going to have a difficult time finding it all. San Diego was not the right place to purchase Antarctic gear. Although both major retail outdoor recreation outlets in the city had plenty of equipment, much of it was not up to snuff for extreme polar travel. My ski boots were comfortable when it wasn't too cold, but the first year in Yellowstone had proven they were inadequate for polar travel. And, they constricted my feet. I had the largest size available and they were still not wide enough. My feet are wide, so finding well-fitting footwear was a major ordeal.

The only boots ALE recommended for long distance skiing were manufactured in Norway. People had used Baffin extreme cold weather boots with step-in bindings for short one degree ski trips. That is, people are flown into Antarctica where they are then flown to the 89th parallel, 60 nautical miles (69 regular statute road miles) from the pole. From there, they spend 10–15 days skiing to the pole. Though the boots are extremely warm, they and their strap-based bindings are inefficient for traveling hundreds if not thousands of miles. They do not hold the foot rigidly enough and tend to flop around, increasing effort and thus wasting energy. There was only one type of boot ALE recommended for their guides; and they, plus their peculiar wool liners, cost $1500. There were no US retail outlets where I could try on a few pairs to find the proper fit.

I was in a serious bind. Even though I was not planning on traveling to Antarctica in 2011, I needed to perform one last test trip through Yellowstone with every piece of gear I planned to use. I had learned that I did not want to use anything I had not tried in similar conditions. If equipment failed in Yellowstone, there was virtually no chance I would die. But in Antarctica, if something broke, failed or didn't fit right, the chance of injury or worse was much higher. But how would I have the boots fitted, other than flying to Norway? I had seriously debated this option. But it would have cost $4,000 to fly to Norway only to fit and purchase the boots. The supplier said that they would ship me as many sizes of boots as I wanted. But, they warned, the import duties and shipping multiple pairs would cost at least as much as a single pair. To solve the fitting problem, I drove to the few ski shops in San Diego, trying on as many ski boots as possible to best estimate the right boot size. After a week of pestering poor store clerks for boots I was not going to purchase (I felt bad about usurping their time), I ordered the boots from Norway. After a month and $200 in customs fees later, I had them. And, miraculously, they fit. There was room enough to put on extra socks but they were not so large that my feet slipped around. The biggest gear hurdle was behind me.

The skis, parka and tent were less troublesome. The one datum I learned from my first year in Yellowstone was that cross country skis were designed for a skier's weight. The old rule of using height to determine ski length was utterly bogus. The first clerk I bought the skis from used the height estimate and fit me with skis for someone weighing 180+ pounds. I don't weigh that much.

When I called one of the few vendors in the US who carried the skis ALE suggested, then received a recommendation based on height, I was immediately suspicious. After talking for a few minutes, I knew this guy had no idea what he was talking about. Thanking him, I hung up. As the Norwegian skis had no sizing instructions available online, I only had intuition to go by. Based on my bad experience with over-sized skis before, I was wary. Two days later, I called back and, thankfully, talked with a different clerk. I told the new clerk what had been recommended and he asked me my weight. The phone went silent for a moment. I told him I thought the original recommendation did not sound right and he agreed. Once we sorted out the proper size and placed the skis on order, I thanked the clerk and disconnected. As this was the only store in the United States with these special skis in stock, they were my only cost effective option. The only other choice was to make another expensive order through Norway.

By this time I felt confident with my expedition shopping, so I ordered a parka from Will Steger's company and had it dropped shipped to an Alaskan company to have the fur ruff sewn in. I wanted protection that a dog sled driver would want, as they face brutal conditions constantly. Again, these were items that were impossible to purchase in San Diego, including a real fur ruff for the parka. There is nothing better in the world than fur when facing into a 30 knot headwind in -25°F temperatures.

The tent was the least problematic item. For as many tent options available in the world, few are adequate for Antarctica and even less appropriate for a solo expedition. As I happened to be flying through Seattle, I was able to visit a few vendors and touch the tents I was considering. The best tents are, for esoteric reasons, unavailable for sale in California. As there are few cities in the western United States that stock polar gear, I was happy to have had a full day layover to purchase gear I would have otherwise needed to mail order.

As 2011 wore on into spring, I fielded a test of my idea on my closest friends Danny, Lance and Alfonso over drinks. I've known each for over 25 years, so I knew they'd give me their honest opinions. I revealed my plan to head to Yellowstone in the coming winter.

Danny, looked at me and asked, "Again? Don't you have something better to do with your time and money? Like go to the Cabo San Lucas or somewhere else warm and comfortable?"

"Yes. Again," I replied.

"Aren't you just a little tired of freezing your bum off?"

I said, "Well, that's not just the end of it. I'm doing this as a test run for something much bigger."

All three of them gazed at me with some incredulity. They knew I tended to do trips they thought were crazy. They waited patiently for me to float my idea.

"I'm using this as a training trek in preparation to go to Antarctica."

"Are you crazy? That's just insane!" both Danny and Lance said in unison as they flailed their arms. I sat and smiled. I learned that even my closest confidants thought the idea was crazy.

"Are you sure you want to do that? Going into the forest in winter is one thing, but Antarctica. How are you even going to pay for that?" Alfonso asked.

I laid out the particulars of the trip, emphasizing that no one had ever succeeded in doing this trip. Ever. This spawned a relentless barrage of questions as though I was on trial for some heinous crime. Danny, a lawyer, was adept at picking apart my plan and the logic behind it. That was exactly what I needed. It allowed me to test out the validity of my thoughts for the expedition and the answers I needed to have. In the past, I have tested ideas with my friends as a sanity check. I had learned that if my arguments convinced them, without raising too much doubt, I knew what I had in mind would work.

When I video conferenced with Wendy Davis, my friend of 12 years, and told her of the idea, her reaction was muted. On a smart phone, it was difficult to discern her eyes, but I swore they bugged out for a moment. She knew of my desire to go there, so it wasn't a total surprise. But, as she knew I had a penchant for coming up with some crazy ideas and executing them, she soon bought into it. I was glad to have her on board, as she had appreciable skill in managing details about travel that I would have otherwise missed. Since she had a wide network of contacts after working as an English instructor at Aeon in Japan for a decade, I knew she would sleuth out information and resources. I began to build my team.

I tested my idea on my brother and his wife. Their reaction was similar to my friends', though a little more subdued. I imagined they were more in shock. They, too, thought many of my trip ideas were pure torture. Their idea of a trip was comfortable travel to Hawaii. I saw the hint of fear in their faces, too. From the withering barrage of questions my buddies subjected me to, I anticipated Jason and Nicole's responses and allayed their fears. I saw their wide-eyed looks as confirmation that they did not wholly buy my reasons, ideas, training and backup plans. In their place, I would have felt the same reservation.

After I had leaked the project to them, I knew it was time to tell my parents before they found out via the grapevine. Standing in their modest kitchen, while talking about where I would travel over the summer, I segued into telling them I was working toward an expedition across Antarctica. Mom's eyes grew wide and Dad laughed.

"Are you sure you want to do that?" Dad asked. "It's not a place where you go to camp. It's much tougher than Yellowstone."

"Can't you go somewhere nicer? Like the Caribbean?" Mom said imploringly.

The tone of their voices was that of, "Holy cow, son, I want to keep you alive a little longer."

Both peppered me with questions. As they had both grown up in Wyoming, they knew how severe winter was and that Antarctica must be ten times worse. I was proud of my parents. They didn't break down, storm out or make a scene. We were a stoic family; emotional outbursts never happened. Everything happened as an undercurrent. For all the trips I had taken, I wondered how many sleepless nights I had cost my parents. That's the nature of being a parent: it is impossible not to worry about your children.

All the while, work had been enjoyable at the beginning of the year. It was a pleasant change. My nerves had calmed down after talking to the people in my life, and I had succeeded in purchasing the gear I needed for my test expedition. All was going smoothly. That was, until I received an email from Wendy telling me to look up a couple of Australian guys named James Castrission and Justin Jones, better known as Cas and Jonesy.

I was blown away. They were planning the same expedition I was, but in the 2011–2012 season, a year earlier than I had planned. My heart sank hard. I sat there with my face in my hands, sighing in disbelief. The centennial of the first expedition to the South Pole was this year, and I should have thought that there was someone planning to recreate Amundsen's journey in grand fashion. Apparently there was. After reading about them and their recent feat of kayaking from Australia to New Zealand, it was clear they had a massive leg up on me. I was barely purchasing gear. They had been working on this for four years. At first, I thought brazenly to ditch everything, sell it all off, and go this year. Annoying pride had bitten me. For some stupid reason, I wanted to be the first to accomplish this task. After a week of stewing about it, with lots of hours spent scouring the web and libraries for information, I cooled off. Though their chances were slim, they could pull it off. The difference between them and me was that I was going to do this solo. I grew excited about reading their preparations, efforts, failures and successes. If I was not the first person to do it, at least someone had the chance to crack this nut. I was excited that I still had a chance of being the first person to solo the trip.

That was, until I learned about Aleksander Gamme in July. He was attempting the exact solo trip I wanted to do. I was dumbstruck. People were coming out of the woodwork this year! Cas and Jonesy had a significant expedition under their belt but had virtually no snow experience. However, Gamme was a different deal altogether. He was a muscular guy, had tons of polar experience and, the coup de gras, he was Norwegian. Norwegians are the veritable masters of polar travel. I had learned that many records and firsts were established and held by Norwegians. This guy had a huge adventure resume. If there was ever a person to do it, Gamme was that person.

Now I was crushed. I thought about ditching the whole project right there. "Figure something else out," I told myself. In all of one day, I experienced elation, trepidation, disbelief, acceptance and finally disgust.

"Stop acting like a child," the engineer inside of me chided.

There was still a real chance that neither team would succeed. Regardless of whether they did or did not, I had to be in Yellowstone for my training trip while they were on their expedition. If I did not move forward with plans to test all my gear, I would not be prepared should I be able to go to Antarctica.

The explorer side of me was more rash.

"Sell everything and go this year," my explorer mind cried out.

Of course, I was infinitely far from having the funds for the expedition. I had not tested my gear in the cold. I was not ready. I resigned myself to continuing preparations for my trip while at the same time watching how others did this year.

By fall of 2011, I had all of my equipment, save skis for the sleds. Finding skis in San Diego was near impossible. Downhill skis were far too large, and there was not a cross country ski to be had. The two plastic sleds I purchased were relatively short, so I estimated that children's skis would fit. As I owned only one pair, I only had to purchase one more. After endless driving and phone calls, I found one shop in town that had skis. After driving there and scouting the store, I saw they only had new, adult length skis.

"Would you happen to have some old rental skis for kids?" I asked the manager.

"Yes, we do, though our selection is limited," he replied.

"That is fine. Nothing I see on the floor will work for what I need."

He invited me to sleuth around the rental room and to see if anything would work. After a little sleuthing, I found one damaged pair sitting on the rental rack. They were chipped, the wood core was exposed and there was a set of mostly ruined bindings attached.

"How much for these skis?" I asked.

The rental manager pondered them and said, "Twenty bucks."

Sold. If I had pushed the point, I could have walked out of the store with the skis for free, as they were all but destroyed and certainly inappropriate for rentals anymore. But, I did not want to waste the manager's good graces and bought them. As I had searched the city for two weeks, I was unsure I would find anything else. Compared to the expense in gas that it cost me to find them, this was nothing. Now I had everything I needed. My dad and I machined brackets and mounted them to the sleds. After only a night's worth of work, everything was ready. However, there was no snow to test the sleds on. Not wanting to end up in Yellowstone only to discover the design did not work, I devised a test. As we finished at night and the air was humid, I thought that the wet grass was a reasonable snow simulation. Casting about for a load to fill the sleds with, I hit upon an idea.

"Mom, could you come out here for a second?" I called into the house.

"What do you want me to do?" Mom asked, suspicious of my motive.

"I need you to sit in the sled while I pull it."

At first she flatly refused, but after some coaxing and demonstrating that the pulks (sleds in expedition parlance) were safe, I coaxed her into sitting inside the plastic tub. I gently tugged on the tow trace and pulled mom in the sled. It worked perfectly! Both dad and I shared a hearty laugh, as mom looked like a small child in the sleds. Now I knew I was ready to go to Yellowstone with all of my Antarctic gear to execute the best simulation I could.

All the while I was searching for skis and building the sleds, I had begun towing a tire through the neighborhood to train. I had trained inadequately the previous two years and had suffered for it. Most of my training was done either in the dark of night or early in the morning. Those were the only times I was able to do it due to my long commute and work schedule. I also wanted to evade the neighbors. I was fairly outgoing and weathered questions about the odd-looking activities I engaged in, but there was still a limit as to what I felt comfortable doing in public.

As much as I wanted to be with family and friends during Christmas, this was my only opportunity to break away and trek. Work had again turned troublesome, with all sorts of rush projects. Management said there was a possibility that I would not be able to go on the trip due to company overcommitment. I put in plenty of extra hours to ensure that the software I wrote was ready and that there were no troubles with it. I did not want to leave my coworkers in a lurch. They should not miss time with their families because I made a mistake.

After a 16 hour drive, I was in Jackson, preparing for my trek. After a few days of acclimating and testing out my rig, I was ready to push off into Yellowstone. I had done essentially the same trip the year prior, but this time I planned to ski all the way to Indian Creek and back. It was a round trip of 180 miles, an excellent short simulation of crossing Antarctica. That was, until I arrived to the south entrance ranger station and tried to secure a permit.

"I'm sorry, that's not possible," said the ranger.

"Why is that?" I asked her.

"Because there is not enough snow on the roads north of the lake.

We are still allowing wheeled vehicle travel up there."

For what seemed to be the hundredth time, my spirit flagged. As I had planned to travel along Yellowstone Lake and ski the reverse trip of that I had done in 2009, I had to formulate a new plan. The reason I skied that way was to sidestep skiing over the continental divide three times while headed toward Old Faithful. Then it dawned on me. If I was not unable to put together a longer distance trek, why didn't I take the more difficult trek and go over the mountains? Certainly there was enough snow over there.

"Actually, we can issue you a permit all the way to Old Faithful, but that's it. There is barely enough snow on the road between there and Madison junction."

"What are the other options?" I asked.

"We can issue you the permit to Old Faithful and, if enough snow falls, can modify it to allow you to make it to Madison. But again, that's it. You would have to be on the side of the road much of the way and, seeing as you're on skis, you wouldn't want to try it."

There I was: I either accepted the change and went with what was available or ditch the whole trip.

"Please write the permit to Old Faithful and we'll see how it goes."

"Okay. Also, do you have bear spray? With the low snow fall this year, the bears are still out."

My eyes grew wide for a moment. I had always relied on late December and early January as being cold enough to keep the bruins in their dens.

"Yes, I actually did bring bear spray."

"Why don't you take this spare canister, too," she said.

I stared at the black bottle with some disbelief, thinking I will now have to fend off grizzlies.

"Be careful, we've had plenty of sightings along the road."

Although ski towing was physically difficult, the mental aspect was much more so. I had learned from previous trips that my body had deep reserves. Tapping into and coaxing them into being required an substantial amount of will power. But, when I did call it up, my body grudgingly responded. However, if my mind decided it did not want to go any farther, that it was too cold, wet, steep, harsh, or otherwise, my body ground to a halt instantly. There was not one more step to be had. After snowshoeing across the park, I knew having bears around would require exhausting attention.

"Perhaps this is a better simulation of Antarctica than I expected," I mumbled once outside the comfort of the ranger station. There are thankfully no bears in Antarctica, though the icy continent itself could take my life.

It took me several days of hard ski towing to reach Old Faithful. The whole time my ski poles banged into the asphalt, as there was only a few inches of snow. This was massively different from two years prior when I sank up to my waist in snow while pitching the tent. While coming down the pass into the Upper Geyser Basin, the sound of wolves howling followed me all the way down. Each time I glanced back up the hill, I expected to see a cluster of eye reflections staring back at me. More than once, the howls were so close I could not believe their owners were not visible. Hearing this hurried me along to the Snow Lodge, dissuading me from camping. I had no desire to be wolf or bear food.

At the lodge, enjoying the rare experience of having people around me while on an expedition, I took advantage and cleaned up prior to eating in the dining room. I did not want anyone to suffer from my odor after being in the forest for so many days. It had not been cold enough to prevent my sweating. When it was extremely cold, I stayed relatively clean compared to when it was warm. This was a new experience to be too hot while ski towing. In previous years, it was cold enough that I could layer clothing effectively. Now, it was too warm. I could only take off so much. I had to keep a waterproof layer on most of the whole time. On the rare days that the sun was out and it was not snowing, I stripped down to my wool shirt to stay cool.

After staying at the lodge, I was ready to return to the trail. Having a comfortable place to sleep did nothing for either my mental or physical toughness. It was certainly no preparation for Antarctica. In Antarctica, there would be nothing but my tent as a shelter. On the way back over the pass toward West Thumb, I saw a trail of wolf tracks. I guessed they originated from the wolves howling at me down into the valley on Christmas Eve. The trip back to Flagg Ranch was uncomfortably warm, soaking my gloves. I had trouble with my ski wax, as the skis had 0°F wax and the temperatures hovered in the low 20's. This was not the cold simulation I had hoped for. But this was the best I could do in the time available away from work.

(Main) *Elk killed by wolves the day prior on Yellowstone Lake.*

(Below Left) *Snow was not deep in Yellowstone in 2011-2012, so the bears were not hibernating and were frequenting the Old Faithful area and West Thumb.*

(Below Right) *One of many whiteout storms in Yellowstone during the winter. This campsite overlooks Lewis Lake, one of the worst weather spots in the park.*

6

CRUSHED BY HISTORY

A FTER RETURNING HOME from Yellowstone, I was both excited and downtrodden. The expedition through Yellowstone was a suitable final test. But I returned to the same place I started from. What depressed me was that, after such a fun and challenging trip, I found myself back exactly where I had been when I left: at work, being the dutiful engineer. Now, more than ever, I pined to be on a real expedition. I now had the gear for a polar expedition and, as best as I could simulate, the training. But I had not committed to when I would go or how I was going to put it together. By the end of January, I learned that both Gamme, Cas and Jonesy had skied the round trip to the South Pole and back. As happy as I was for them, I suffered from a rash of depression. I asked myself why I had not done it before these guys made the attempt.

The depression also corresponded with how work was going. For as much as I enjoyed the technical aspect of my work, everything blended into gray. The cubical walls, the lighting and everything else had a dingy pallor. I did my best to lose myself in the deep world of embedded software. I had to put my mind completely into the job, otherwise I would continue stewing over my Antarctic project being completed by someone else. Hiding in work helped for a while, as it was a coping strategy I had used before with success. But in the end, it distilled down to seeing myself in this position for a long time, with no hope of advancement. It was a mid-life crisis and time for a new job. I knew the problem was at a head.

Finally, in early February, I told my parents that I was quitting my job. Mom looked as though she had been hit with a boxing glove and dad laughed with incredulity.

"At work, there was no indication from management that there was a plan for more reasonable hours, more contracts or increasing our staffing. We are treading water. At best," I told them.

"I can't believe you are just going to leave. They are paying you good money," mom said.

"I know. But if I don't do this now, it may never happen."

As soon as I let my family and closest friends know what my plan was, I felt freer than I had in half a decade. Everyone asked what I was going to do next. The answer became completely clear. I gazed at each and gave the only reply that came to my mind.

"I'm going to Antarctica. This year."

Putting in my resignation at work, I found myself faced with many decisions to deal with, some of which I was unsure of.

I knew one fact for certain: I needed to begin training—and quickly. Although I had been running and kept in shape, I knew that ski towing was difficult and I again needed to drag the tire along the neighborhood streets. That was easy enough to take care of. Soon, I was grinding tires along the sidewalks of Carlsbad. Although I covered half marathon distances in two hours, I knew that training at sea level did not improve my chances of success. It happened that my lease was over in June and, as without a job there was no way I could afford the place, I prepared to move out. I needed a place where I could store my gear, train in earnest and pursue sponsorships for the expedition.

To set my plan into motion, I contacted ALE and requested a formal quote based on my plans to ski from Hercules Inlet to the South

Pole and back. They obliged. And sent me an eye popping invoice.

"Wow. How am I going to pay for all this?" I said out loud as I read the email.

San Diego is an ideal place to raise funds from, as it is a major metropolis and has plenty of companies to potentially partner with. In contrast, it is one of the worst places to train for Antarctica. The weather is nearly perfect and the city sits at sea level. Conditions in Antarctica are the exact opposite. Weather is always unpleasant and the elevation at the South Pole is over 9,000 feet. My pressing problem was to figure out where to train.

As I knew Kelly and Nancy in Jackson, I thought it would be the perfect place for training. But, it was the worst choice for buying expedition supplies and there are relatively few companies as potential sponsors. I knew the town lacked resources. If I needed gear immediately, I would have to pay for next day air. I needed to order supplies early, leaving nothing to the last second. That problem was surmountable with enough time and patience for shipping everything in. The town was small enough that I could go knocking on doors to solicit sponsors. That advantage was also its weakness. Only a tiny fraction of companies and people were willing to sponsor this type of expedition. It was a numbers game.

I had arranged to stay in Jackson over the summer and into the fall to train for the expedition. That stress was eliminated. But the stress on my parents saddened me. I felt guilty for exposing their son to dangers so far away from home. Their child would not be able to stop by for a Sunday dinner. But there was no other way to do it. And, they heard the commitment in my voice. There was no way anything short of a tragedy was going to stop me from attempting an expedition no other American had done before.

The last week in San Diego was full of hurried preparations and visiting with friends and family for the last time. I had arranged to rent a one-way trailer so I could haul all the supplies I needed to Jackson. Between the time I quit my apartment and left for Wyoming, I stayed with my parents and kept them company. I was glad to have spent that time with them and relished it. We also videotaped interviews of them to create an expedition promotional video. While we did that, I learned that they did not know all the dangers I faced. After listening to the responses dad gave from the questions I asked him, mom was visibly shaken. When we were done filming, mom walked out of the room.

"I don't know if I can do this. I need some time," she said.

"Mom, try not to worry. It will all be okay," I replied.

She said she did not have any idea how difficult and dangerous Antarctica was.

Several days later, I drove to Jackson and settled in as quickly as possible. There was so much to do and I had to start working on it. Although I had visited Jackson countless times, it was only for a few weeks at most. All of those times, I was out photographing, backpacking or visiting with relatives. Now the place took on a whole new appearance. This was where I engaged the community and garnered as much media attention as I could. One of the first advertisements my girlfriend and expedition manager Kelly Gaffney made were t-shirts with my expedition website on it. She also had a blue ribbon silk screened on to signify my raising awareness for prostate cancer. As my dad had survived that disease, I was happy to be promoting the work of the National Prostate Cancer Foundation. The cause was personal and valuable to me. Had my dad taken the foolish manly man approach and refused to take a simple blood test, who knows if he would be alive today.

Whenever people approached me about the expedition, I made sure to tell them what I was raising awareness for. I told them of what happened to my dad. To my surprise, so many people told me that someone they knew had battled prostate cancer. Some had won and others had lost. I always told men to go have the test. It was a simple blood draw. For the women I talked with, I asked them if the men in their life had been checked. I was happy to hear so many had. I told the few that had not that the test is at least as important as a mammogram. My sales pitch went like this:

"He will scrape a knee or elbow in a pickup game and lose more blood than this test takes. You don't have to go for an embarrassing exam. If nothing shows up—great! Go out for a drink and celebrate. If something does come up, talk to his doctor and figure out the right course. It's terribly stupid to die from so preventable a disease. Ninety-five percent survive if the cancer is diagnosed early enough. Those odds are much better than the lottery!"

That little speech hit home with more people than I anticipated, making me happy. It was foolish to lose a person to inaction.

As summer wore on, I became stronger and was able to tow the tire farther and faster each time. Tugging that tire for hours on end was punishing. It had been a long time since I had been in Jackson in the summer and I had forgotten how warm it was there. Ninety degrees was warm in San Diego, but in Jackson with the thinner atmosphere, the sun beat down on me. I wore a hat, slathered sunscreen and drank plenty of fluids. Even then, the sun assaulted me. So many times I fought through cramped muscles. If they kept failing me, I was never going to build enough strength for the expedition. I took salt tablets and invested heavily in electrolyte supplements and drinks. So many times I was unable to see through my glasses from the sweat pouring down my face. Towing tires was also rough on my clothing. I shredded several pairs of shorts and destroyed an expensive set of boots. Normally those clothes would have lasted me years. Nothing I had done previously chewed through boots so quickly. At least the three tires I destroyed were free and replaceable.

Eventually, I reached the point of being able to drag the tire seven miles a day along the bike trails circling town. One issue I learned from towing a tire in Carlsbad was that I became an incredible distraction to drivers passing by. Although the sign I carried and shirt I wore were excellent for raising awareness of the expedition, I did not want to endanger anyone. I stayed far away from any intersections where someone could be distracted by my tire towing. There were a couple of close calls in Carlsbad when people gawked at me while approaching a red light. The screeching tires told me I must be more careful and stay away from busy locations. Garnering attention was exciting but causing someone to be injured by the distraction forced me to be conscious of where I trained.

For all the calories I expended running and towing a tire, I had to gain weight—and a lot of it. I estimated I needed to gain 15 to 20 pounds on my relatively light frame. That weight, in turn, would melt off during the expedition. Although I had begun to add weight while still living in San Diego, I was having a difficult time doing it. I had been at the same weight since my early college days. Normally, a high metabolism was a wonderful advantage, as I ate whatever I wanted and never had to worry about becoming an overweight programmer addicted to soda. But building fat reserves for a polar expedition was a real challenge for me. I took to eating fast food at least once a day if not more. Breakfast consisted of eggs, bacon, cereal, toast and jam. After that, on the way into town, I stopped by a fast food place and ordered another full breakfast. In spite of all the eating, the pounds refused to stick.

My only solution was to purchase weight gain powders and drinking gallons of sweetened tea each week. As much as soda would have added weight, I did not want to down the massively empty calories. My body was under stress and I had to consume as many valuable calories as I could swallow. I tracked my workouts with a fitness app for my phone that allowed me to keep record of my intake and exercise. It helped me become more aware of what I consumed. However, the app also calculated that I was not eating enough to hit my weight gain target by October. I was flabbergasted. For as much as I was consuming, the exercise regimen was burning it off and more. I started carrying food with me where ever I traveled and ate constantly. I felt like the poor obese kid whose parents let him have a candy bar every day.

As much as I struggled to gain weight, so was I having a difficult time drumming up sponsorships. Being a complete unknown made the task close to impossible. Although I was skilled at engineering for creating devices, my marketing and sales skills were mediocre. As neither of these subjects was taught during any undergraduate or graduate technical degree, I was at a disadvantage in raising the kind of cash I required to make the trip possible, let alone successful. One ALE staffer told me that when he guided his first expedition in Antarctica, it was futile for him to try to raise funds.

"Do you have anything like an Everest under your belt?" he asked.

"No, I don't have anything even remotely close to that," I said.

"Well, if you did, finding sponsors would be a little easier."

He continued, "I found it was much easier to gain sponsorship after I returned from my ski-the-last-degree trip to the Pole."

That did not build my confidence about my chances of raising the funds. Although I had banked money away in anticipation of a layoff at work, it was not to pay for the expedition. I thought about the modest retirement fund I had been dutifully saving. Dipping into that was not the wisest choice. That option was held in reserve as a last hope. Flipping burgers was not how I aspired to spend my 70s. For now, I put that thought aside and hoped I would be able to stir up some concrete cash.

(Main) *Video interview for a multi-part series by KUSI television in San Diego for my Antarctic expedition.*

(Below Left) *While towing up the Old Pass Road in Wilson, WY, I loaded rocks in the tire and measured the drag force. Beyond 60lbs, my tendons ached at the end of a towing session.*

(Below Right) *Towing my tire around Carlsbad, CA. I received many bewildered stares from drivers.*

7

So the Expedition Begins

TRAINING IN JACKSON was paying off, in spite of the heat of summer. I garnered considerable interest with the sign attached to my tire, including that of the media. People stopped to ask me questions, and I would share my story with them. Though using the pathways alongside the road was magnificent for advertising, I needed to train on more difficult terrain. I had been thinking about towing the tire up Snow King, the town's local ski mountain.

The trail was rough and gained 1600 feet elevation over 1.4 miles. I knew that I must step it up, otherwise I would not be ready for dragging sleds over random sastrugi. [Sastrugi are jagged grooves, fins and blade-like ridges of ice formed by wind erosion in Antarctica] Now more than ever, I had to push myself harder to toughen my mind. If I was going to be able to fight through skin-freezing headwinds on the way to the pole, I needed to be able to drag a tire up a minor mountain, even when I felt light-headed and shaky-legged.

Towing over rough trail was especially difficult, as the tire snagged on rocks and roots, requiring me to go back and free the tire incessantly. "This was good," I thought. This was probably a far better simulation of dragging a sled across Antarctica than towing on a smooth bike path, based on what others had told me and the photos I had seen. The surface of the Antarctic ice was far from smooth, so the towing experience on the trail up Snow King should mirror that. The path is heavily trafficked, so it did not take long before I bumped into other people. Reactions to me were varied. Some people were honestly interested in what I was doing, so I told them about the expedition and that it was to help raise awareness for prostate cancer. Other people glanced at me but, as I neared them, they made every effort to pretend I was not there. I suppose it did look crazy. One question that surprised me was, "Are you doing penance?" After being asked this several times, I realized that it did indeed come across as penance. Soon I answered, "Yes, in a way," every time.

One of the people I ran into was Amber Hoover, wife of Mike Hoover, a film producer who had gone on a climbing expedition to the Antarctic peninsula. She invited me over to their home to talk and share ideas and experiences. As I had never met anyone who had gone on an expedition to Antarctica, I was thrilled. Towing a tire in places frequented by people had finally paid off. I launched the expansion my network of people who would help me be successful.

Kelly and I drove over to visit Mike and Amber to acquire some first person insight into what I was going to be facing. Over dinner, we learned some of the brutal challenges that Antarctica presented. Mike even told us that one of his expedition members died in an ultralight plane crash on the continent. I was saddened to hear about it and taken aback. It was not that someone died on the climbing portion of the expedition. Mike said it happened while the pilot was out surveying their route through a crevasse field. They weren't exactly sure what happened, as their other pilot saw the ultralight fly erratically and then plummet to the ground. By the time they found him, the pilot was dead. Mike admonished me that the expedition would not go as I thought and, as such, to be extremely careful.

He also said, "You had better be ready to be trapped in your tent for three days. Unbelievable blizzards will come out of nowhere. You would not even be able to go outside and take a leak."

The moment he said that, my mind flashed back to what happened to Scott's expedition, in which everyone perished only 11 miles from their next food cache. I was confident that the five different GPS units I would be carrying would not all fail at once. But, it was easy to go outside during a raging blizzard, walk a few feet away from the tent, look back and be unable to find it. Mike said it has happened and to be cautious about it.

"You don't want to freeze to death when you're only twenty feet from your tent. That would be a damn shame."

I appreciated his warning. Yellowstone had given me some tough blizzards and ground whiteout conditions, but I had never been in a storm so violent to render a conspicuous red tent invisible ten feet away. I had not been to a frozen place so bleak that there was nothing but ice for hundreds of miles. As excited as I was about the expedition, Mike's perspective on the realities I would face down there was arresting. I knew the place was tough from the videos and movies I had watched, but never did I imagine dying a few feet from shelter, blinded by flying ice and snow.

"Do you have a good memory?"

"Yes, pretty good," I replied.

"Good, because you're going to need it."

I asked him what he meant by that. Mike told me to imagine seeing nothing but an infinite plane of ice cast against a blue sky.

"Eventually, your iPod music will bore you."

"I plan to bring audio books instead. They'll keep my mind engaged."

He nodded and agreed that was a wise choice.

"You will have plenty of time to think about past events that have not occurred to you in 20 years. You are going to be alone out there and your mind will start to wander to places you completely forgot."

Meeting Mike and Amber was a stroke of luck. He gave me insight into what a long expedition was going to be like. As I had never been on that long of a trek, there was no way to anticipate what I would likely feel or experience.

I had received an eye-opening email in late September. Another polar explorer provided me with a few words of wisdom. She said about my training that a month before the expedition, I had better be doing two sets of back-to-back eight hour towing days. I thought I was training long enough by towing for six hours, every other day. The demands of finding sponsors, managing equipment purchases, and making media contacts cut into any additional training time. Even though Kelly was helping me as my impromptu expedition manager, she was not experienced in doing this, so I was mostly on my own. As a complete rookie, I did not have a massive network of people to help me with media, equipment, training and nutrition. As the calendar marked the beginning of fall, I was up late every night doing everything I could to keep preparations moving forward.

Another problem I was still battling to gain weight. By early September, I had gained about as much as I could. At a peak of 173 pounds, I was ten pounds lighter than I needed to be. But the amount of work I was putting into tire towing and running made packing on more weight impossible. I ate incessantly to keep the weight on.

By September, I had switched over to towing my tires up Old Pass Road, from Wilson to the Teton Pass. It was an old four-mile winding road, ascending 1,800 feet to 8,435 feet at the pass. As much as I reveled the challenge of towing up Snow King, the trail was too short for me to put in a solid continuous workout. Having somewhere I could tow for hours on end was a near-perfect simulation of the upcoming experience. When I arrived at the top, I loaded rocks in the tire to match the downhill with the uphill towing drag. The training had to be consistent, lest my muscles, tendons and ligaments not be tough enough. A luggage scale was handy for the task. With it, I could match the downhill to the uphill drag by placing rocks in the tire at the top of the pass. Also, I learned that my speed was not consistent when the pulling force exceeded 55 pounds. Even though that weight was easy to leg or bench press, pulling it took incredible strength. It was equivalent to carrying a case of paper with my core. The workout was brutal but necessary. I hoped I would not run into conditions that raised the towing force much above that. My tendons and muscles ached at the end of each training session. It was a delicate dance to become stronger yet prevent injury.

I planned to leave for Chile on October 25th. The final two months passed by in a blur of phone calls, internet orders, tire towing and equipment testing. Between contacting sponsors, media, and suppliers, there was little time left for keeping up personal relationships. This bothered me, as I knew it was impossible to do this without so many people supporting me.

"I'm sorry, I don't have the time to meet up for drinks," I apologized countless times.

People were understanding. I promised to make it up to them when I returned. In the back of my mind, there was a slight but persistent ballad of guilt. There were little, unanticipated issues that I kept running into, too. For instance, I knew I needed to bring at least three different pairs of gloves in addition to removable liners. As much as Jackson is a mountain ski resort, I found it difficult to purchase the cold weather gear I needed. The retailers in town would not have their winter gear out until two weeks before I departed. That was far too close for comfort in case they did not stock what I needed. For some gear, I learned that ordering them with two-day air shipping was cheaper than purchasing in town. As much as I wanted to help local business and the people I met, Jackson prices on many items were beyond my budget.

At the end of September, I took a road trip to Salt Lake City. I needed to ship a pallet of food to Punta Arenas a full month in advance. Otherwise it would not arrive in time. This trip made it possible to visit ALE's United States office to gain some last minute insights. Chris Nance at ALE also suggested bringing two cameras. That way, if the main one died, I would still be able to document the expedition for sponsors and be able to capture enough media to edit a documentary about it. As I was a photographer and cinematographer, this made sense to me. A D-SLR was way too heavy for this trip, so I had to purchase a compact yet high-quality camera. Researching these, too, consumed inordinate amounts of time. I was picky about my cameras. I did not want to find myself in the middle of Antarctica and realize what I had brought would not give me the image quality I needed.

While making all these preparations, Kelly was formulating preparations of her own. She had planned a surprise party for me on October 14th. My aunt phoned me, ostensibly to help her move some heavy containers around her condo. Being the dutiful nephew, I complied, as dinner was still hours away. That all was completely normal. Then Kelly sent me a text saying I should bring Nancy over so we three could have dinner together. Again, there was nothing out of the ordinary. As we arrived back at Kelly's place, her driveway had turned into a parking lot. Becoming suspicious, I studied my aunt and she shrugged. We walked into the house.

"Surprise!" sounded from all rooms in a chorus of excitement.

It was so cool! No one had ever thrown a surprise party for me on any scale like this. Virtually every person I had met through Kelly and Nancy was there to wish me good luck at my going away party. I was beyond shocked, embarrassed, and happy at the same time. All of these people were so thoughtful to venture out and wish me good luck as well. I felt overwhelmed at the outpouring of support so many people gave me. It was wonderful to chat with people I met over the summer, spend the evening with all of them. Kelly even produced a video slide show for everyone to watch, a precursor of the expedition and all the fun and difficult times yet to come.

With only two days after the party to pack everything and drive to San Diego to prepare to depart for Antarctica, I had written multiple packing lists to ensure I did not leave anything behind. For all the mistakes to make, leaving anything behind in Jackson due to carelessness was not one of them. Shipping supplies next day air in a panic was a spectacular way to waste money. Everything had a place in a plastic tote, duffle bag or box to carry with me. I had rented a trailer coming to Jackson, and now I would do the same returning to San Diego. All of my winter gear was silly in the summer with temperatures in the high 80's, but where I was headed was 110 degrees colder than that. Kelly was able to take a few days off, so she drove south and helped me make final preparations for the expedition at my parents' house. The 16 hour drive to San Diego passed quickly, as so many thoughts of the upcoming expedition swirled through my mind. It was impossible to contemplate on much else.

Once in San Diego, Kelly and my parents helped me distribute all my gear into four different bags to stay under the 50 pound airline weight limit. We made every effort to keep the gear as light as possible. We even cut off tags from each piece of clothing. At first Kelly and mom did not consider the time was worth it, but by the time all tags were removed, they added up to a full quarter of a pound. If they did not see scale reading 0.25 LB, they would not have believed it was worth the effort.

One piece of gear I had been able to save weight on was the shovel. I had a few different snow shovels I had used on different trips and, though they were fairly light, they did not extend far. This forced me to be on my knees to shovel snow, increasing the chance of frostbite on my knees. I had found a new shovel that was a few ounces lighter yet extended so I could stand up while shoveling. While reviewing the equipment checklist, mom had begun searching the web for equipment reviews. She said that the shovel I bought had not received sterling reviews. That caused me a little concern, so I read the write up but did not find anything dire written about it. The description was vague and uncertain, as though the author was doing more of a rant than speaking about any specific problem. Being obsessed with the weight, I wanted to shave off every ounce possible. What could go wrong? I tested the shovel, stomping and twisting it, and it seemed to hold up. This was one of the few items I had not used before leaving, but I was confident it would be okay.

We packed, shifted and re-weighed everything right up to the night before leaving for Los Angeles. Kelly helped me double check that everything that was on the equipment list was in the checked bags. All the while, dad filmed us making preparations. It was not every day that my parents' entire living room was stuffed with expedition gear. We all had an enjoyable time at it, shifting, adjusting and lifting until every bag was ready to go.

My truck was laden with people and expedition gear as we sped to Los Angeles. Though I had driven to the airport many times over the years, this time felt different. It was as though I was leaving the country, not to return for many years. I had seen a movie sequence with this type of scene, where the son, driven by wanderlust, enjoys the final trip with family and girlfriend before departing for parts unknown. Now I felt I was living that movie. The drive to Los Angeles was thankfully uneventful. We stayed overnight at an airport hotel, avoiding any traffic crunches in this car choked city. There was no way I was going to miss my flight on the biggest expedition of my life because of traffic.

While I was checking in for my flight, both my parents grew quiet. I knew what they must be thinking, worrying about their son going off on some crazy trip. I kept reassuring them that it would be okay and that I had plenty of ways to communicate. Kelly did not appear as worried, but she was simply better at hiding her stress. I was all smiles because, for as excited as I was, I suppressed an undercurrent of worry and did not want anyone to know it. I forced myself to imagine this was like any of the other international flights I had taken.

"Remain calm and cool, Linsdau," I told myself.

I did not want to appear a giddy teenager, blabbering on and on to everyone about what I was embarking upon. My parents and Kelly must have been screaming in their minds for me not to leave. I did not want to cause them even more concern than they already were.

Hugging and kissing everyone goodbye one last time, I threaded my way through the security gauntlet and onto the airplane.

A day later, I materialized in Punta Arenas, Chile, with all of my bags. One of my major worries was lost or delayed luggage. One of the warnings ALE gave about taking gear was to hand carry a bag with the ski boots. Most every other piece of gear could be cobbled together or purchased in Chile, but the specialized boots I required were available in one city. And it happened to be a city in Norway. It took some haggling with the gate agents to convince them to allow me to carry on both a backpack with boots and a cloth grocery bag with all of my electronics. These were something I could not stand to have lost in transit.

On arriving in Punta Arenas, I had developed a sniffle which quickly turned into a cold. My shoulders slumped. How could I catch a cold before such a major trip? Though it was not uncommon for me to catch a cold during an international trip, I hoped to escape it this time. If I were sightseeing, I would not have cared. But for Antarctica, I had to be in top physical form, not a sniffling wretch. After hiring a taxi to the hotel Condor de Plata, I searched out a pharmacy and purchased some cold medicine. As I wandered the aisles, a glaring omission on my gear list hit my brain with sledgehammer force.

"You idiot. How could you forget that, too?"

Not bringing cold medicine was foolish enough. But not having aspirin on my medications list was outright stupid. Yet there I was, paying five times what it cost in the States. The clerk handed me the stock of extra drugs after I passed her a pile of Chilean pesos. I immediately choked down the antihistamines. Now, if only my food was here.

One of the vagaries of shipping food into Chile involved all the agricultural and livestock importation laws. Chile is strict about keeping their crops and animals free of disease from imported products. As a consequence, I needed to palletize and ship eight boxes of food in their original cartons. Although the pallet was shipped a month prior to my departure, it arrived in Punta Arenas the same day I did. I was astonished that the shipment spent a week in Los Angeles and then a week in Miami doing nothing. I was glad I had followed Peter McDowell's recommendation of shipping early, as everything barely made it.

Now, all my food was at the hotel and in boxes. It took two and a half days of repackaging to prepare everything. I compressed the dehydrated food into quart-sized plastic bags, eliminating a full three pounds of packaging and several cubic feet of volume. The hotel staff was tolerant, allowing me to convert their dining room into an expedition food preparation factory, with plenty of space to work. They were kind enough to loan me two postal scales other expeditions had left to weigh out food. I was able to measure my calories precisely. I did not want to run short on my daily rations from haphazard packing.

Another ration I purchased was a mass of butter. I took a taxi to the free trade zone outside Punta Arenas, and visited Abu Gosche, the

Chilean equivalent of Costco. The prices of foodstuffs was far better than in town, even including the taxi ride. This mattered because I ended up purchasing 140 blocks of butter. Each block equated to two sticks of American butter. This butter made up a sizable portion of my caloric intake, so it was crucial to have it. Fat has twice as many calories per ounce as proteins or carbohydrates, so my diet was laden with fats to keep the food weight to a reasonable level. The clerk inspected the basket full of butter disapprovingly.

"I'm sorry," she apologized. "Our check registers are unable to handle more than 60 copies of any one item. I hope that is okay?"

Laughing, I replied, "No hay problema. I am sure this is not normal. I am going to Antarctica and need this for food."

"Ah!" was her only response.

With wide eyes, she shook her head as she stared at the 70 pounds of butter. I was not sure if she thought I was crazy. She put on a smile, rang up the multiple purchases, and made as little eye contact as possible with a nutty guy buying a shopping cart full of butter. I smiled and swiped my credit card for $380 in fat.

By now my cold was not deteriorating but disconcertingly not improving, either. Other than walking over to Unimarc for lunch and dinner at their cafeteria, I did not explore the city at all. I needed to tow a tire to keep fit, but I was exhausted from my cold. As much as I wanted to run around, I knew it was far more important to recover by resting and taking it easy. By the time I finished packing my food, I had to organize my supplies and sleep. I did not have energy for much else. On October 28th, a cough replaced the sniffle. That was always a ruinous sign for me, as I rarely coughed when fighting a cold. I hoped this had not morphed into bronchitis, my archenemy. So many times in college I had colds develop into lung infections. I did my best to rest.

Some of the ALE staff had begun arriving at the hotel, so I enjoyed the chance to meet some of the people I would work with while I was down there. They were a unique lot, several having worked multiple seasons at Union Glacier. I was glad to have stayed at the Condor del Plata, as it was the most common place for expeditions to stay and the staff was understanding about late phone calls and oversized baggage being dragged through their corridors. As much of the ALE staff stayed at the same hotel as I, we chatted for a bit, making me sense the excitement of the trip.

ALE notified me that we were on call after October 29th, the first possible flight window, and to be ready to go at a moment's notice. As the weather in Antarctica is fickle, every opportunity to fly down there has to be taken. Last year's expeditions were delayed a full two weeks due to weather, something I hoped to avoid. I received status phone calls in the morning and afternoon with no other news than to remain ready. There was a real chance that the weather would open tomorrow and we would be flying. I had to remain near the hotel and be ready to go. As I felt under the weather, I happily complied with this request.

The morning of the 30th came and went. At noon, I received a call telling me to sit tight and not wander off from the hotel. As I was ALE's only client taking the first flight down, I did not want to be the buffoon, causing everyone trouble by being late or missing my flight. It was not as though there was a daily schedule departing from Punta Arenas to Antarctica. The ALE staff was jittery and excited, sitting in the hallways and common room, regaling the first-timers with stories of previous years and how conditions could be.

One of the staff said, "Are you ready for this thing? It's pretty big."

I replied, "Yes, I think so."

"Well, mate, I think I would be more than ready for this size of an expedition."

Knowing what I was facing, I said, "You always think you know you're ready until you actually get out there. Then that thinking faces reality."

He nodded with a slight smile. ALE called me later that evening and told me to linger at the hotel in the morning, as it was likely we were going to be flying. Had I felt better, the excitement would have prevented me from sleeping. But as I was fighting a cold and cough, this was one of the rare times when I was able to sleep prior to embarking on a major trip.

Right at 9 a.m., the hotel staff let me know there was a call waiting for me.

"Hello Aaron! We have a good weather window, so we are going to get everyone to the airport. If you can, please be ready to go in 45 minutes."

They weren't kidding when they said there would be little warning. To preserve my butter stock, I had crammed the 140 bricks into the hotel freezer and my room's little refrigerator. To ensure the butter was solid in the room unit, I lowered the thermostat as low as possible, creating a thin sheet of frost on the contents. Now that I had less than an hour to pack, I quickly rushed down and jammed the mountain of butter into a pair of duffles I had purchased for this purpose. It felt awkward lugging bags loaded with 70 pounds of butter I kept frozen until the last second to prevent spoiling. Also, I was told to wear all of my Antarctic clothing on the flight, as when we landed I would be stepping right into a freezer. Cleaning up my room and grabbing my bags, I headed downstairs and joined the waiting ALE staff. In 15 minutes, the bus drove up, we loaded in and it whisked us to the airport. We passed through the metal detector and security screening, as the Russian charter flight followed international rules. It felt uncomfortable to be sitting in heavy clothing for an hour while the aircraft was fueled, but I wouldn't be able to change into my gear in mixed company while on the plane.

We rode a bus out to the massive Russian Ilyushin-76 transport aircraft sitting on the tarmac. Before walking up the boot polished steel stairs to the door, everyone was required to step in a pink anti-microbial wash. This helped prevent the introduction of any non-native species into Antarctica. The aircraft contained one large transport truck and multiple pallets of gear in cargo netting. All of us were crammed along the side of the fuselage on flip-down, carpet covered plywood seats. They were the modicum of luxury for a five hour flight. Each chair had a seat belt, so there was at least some semblance of the feeling of safety. The all-Russian crew was courteous while they explained the aircraft's features. I had never flown in the cargo bay before, so it was a new experience. With all the pallets of gear jammed against our knees, there was not much room to stretch out.

"This is a very loud machine. You will need these," the Russian loadmaster remarked as he pressed foam earplugs into each passenger's hands.

He was not kidding. I now appreciated the sound damping effort put into commercial aircraft. The roar was indescribable as the four engines powered up and, using 25 barrels of fuel to take off, lifted us away from Punta Arenas and on our way to Antarctica. As soon as the flight crew signaled it was safe, people started milling through the hold and sleeping on the shipping crates. With everyone draped all over the aircraft, it was more of a refugee transport than a high-end expedition flight. The flight navigator invited us to wander in and peer through the glass front of the aircraft as we passed over Tierra Del Fuego. The vertical view induced vertigo. I could not help but think that if one of the panels broke, I would experience my first and final skydive.

During the whole flight, it was impossible to see anything but clouds over the southern ocean. I hoped to catch a glimpse of the worst seas in the world, but they were obscured. Gazing around the cargo hold, I noted the Russians had foresight in their design. There was a hot water tank for coffee and tea near the crew door, making the otherwise industrial experience more civilized. The ALE staff fashioned tasty sandwiches and provided snacks for everyone on the flight. For whatever reason, the thought of having food on such a long flight had completely slipped my mind.

Ben Cooper, the ALE medic, took me under his wing and gave me a few pointers about what to expect when we first arrived. He was cordial and no doubt knew this was my first rodeo. He talked about some of the medical issues people ran into, especially coaching me regarding hydration and keeping up my energy.

"It is very easy to become dehydrated down there before you know it. The air is drier than on a commercial aircraft, so make sure to drink lots of water."

With the noise of the aircraft and our earplugs, we had to lean close and yell over the din to be heard. I asked him about some of the other problems he'd seen in previous years. He said there was always something unplanned. Even though people were careful, there were what he called "crevasse incidents", so I needed to be mindful of where I went to avoid becoming an incident. The whole camp was on a glacier, so the area was riddled with crevasses.

He also said, "Be careful when you step off the ladder onto the blue ice runway. It is extremely slippery, more than you can imagine. I've seen people excited to see their friends and hop off the ladder, only to slip, fall and break their arm."

I made a mental note of that. I did not want to have my first step on the continent end in tragedy. Blue ice is so compacted that it contains little air, developing a cobalt blue tint.

When we were an hour out, the staff donned their insulated overalls, heavy shirts and boots. They had been able to pack their cold weather gear separately so as not to overheat on their way down like I did. But since I was not feeling perfect, I was happy to be warmer.

Soon we were putting on our seat belts for landing. There were only tiny portholes in the doors, so it was impossible to see outside during the final approach and landing. I felt the jet shift slightly to the left and then to the right as we touched down. Presumably, the pilots were adjusting for whatever wind blew down the glacier and for putting their tires down on a solid sheet of blue ice. It seemed to take forever before the airplane rolled to a stop. We must have taxied for a minute, though it was difficult to tell being unable to see outside. The crew let us know it was -4°F outside with 30 knot winds.

"Please be careful going down the stairway, it is windy and very slippery."

Ben leaned over and, with a wry smile, said, "Welcome to Antarctica!"

The crew opened the door and all I saw was blinding white outside. It was impossible to see until my eyes adjusted, as the inside of the Ilyushin-76 had been so dark. I walked up near the door and felt the icy wind pushing inside as the cargo bay doors opened.

It was time.

(Above) *Flying as cargo in the Russian-built Illyushin-76.*

(Left) *Looking serious in Union Glacier as I contemplate the next three months ahead of me.*

(Below Left) *Only a small portion of the 90 bags of dehydrated food I had shipped down to Chile and then on to Antarctica.*

(Below Right) *A shopping cart full of 70 pounds of Irish butter. I ate one of these blocks every day while on the expedition.*

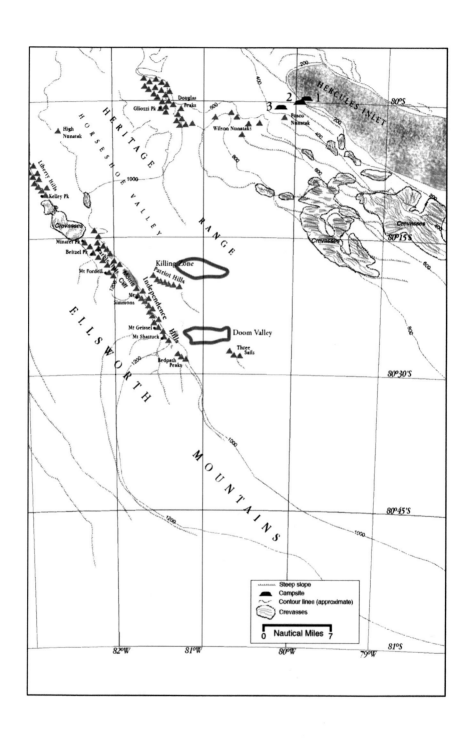

8

A Cold Antarctica, Days 1-3

STEPPING OUT OF THE NOW DORMANT Ilyushin-76, 30 knot winds tore into my thighs. Although I had plenty of clothing layers on my chest and head, I only had one layer of wool long underwear and my shell pants. This setup had handled cold winds at -20°F on my previous trips without issue. But the wind and cold down here were another matter. As the staff and I gingerly walked away from the imposing transport jet, I shuffled my feet to prevent slipping and spun rotisserie-style to prevent any one side of my body from freezing. I leapt into the transport van fitted with massively oversized tires. Once inside, I vigorously rubbed my thighs, praying my skin was not already injured.

As we careened toward camp, I did my best to protect my head from crashing into the van's ceiling. The road to the camp was rough. More than once, the van's passengers levitated. With my precious electronics bag in my lap, I was happy to be a human sardine. At camp, I was invited over to the cozy mess tent for a late dinner. The food was scrumptious. After eating unexciting food for a week in Punta Arenas, the fare was delectable. Fresh bread, pasta, meats, a slew of vegetables, and a glass of wine all made for a wonderful introduction to Antarctic culinary arts. During dinner, the international staff shared what they were doing here and where they were from. Several said they would offer to help me pitch my tent. Each, after a moment of consideration, then laughed and said I needed practice setting it up by myself. Laughing, I nodded, knowing they were right. I thanked them profusely as I ambled to the tent. On the way, I visited the toilet.

"Enjoy the sheltered toilet while you can!" bellowed an anonymously dressed staff member. It was impossible to identify people when they were fully dressed. We were indistinguishable. As I pitched the tent for the first time, I had to prepare all the bowlines and taut line hitches on the guy lines. This was much easier to do in a controlled camp rather than configuring everything on the Ronne Ice Shelf. Using these knots made adjustments and removal quick and easy in the field. My Boy Scout training came right back to me as though I had reviewed the Boy Scout Handbook hours before.

Not sleeping soundly that first night due to the 24-hour sun, I awoke groggily. Without much sleep and being ill during my time in Punta Arenas, I now sported a persistent cough.

During breakfast on Halloween, Ben Cooper, the company medic, looked at me with a modicum of shock when I told him the cough started prior to departure from Punta Arenas. Ben's eyes opened wide for a moment but then resumed their British calm. He said that most everyone suffers from a cough upon reaching Antarctica while acclimatizing to the stunningly cold dry air. There was little he could offer in way of remedy. After talking for a while longer, the topic of where I learned Antarctic travel from arose.

"Did you only learn to do this from a book?" he asked.

"In part, yes," I replied.

My response elicited more than one raised eyebrow from the people at my table. I had learned many skills from books, especially while earning my engineering and computational science degrees. The approach seemed completely logical to me. My table mate's shocked response did not surprise me, either. I had become accustomed to people looking at what I did with disbelief. This response always disheartened me, but I learned to cope with it.

As an embedded software engineer, the geek within me became excited to learn that ALE utilizes ground penetrating radar to scan the road each season to assess the crevasse danger.

"Please do not ski too far off the road, as we cannot guarantee your safety," I was told.

If I were to ski too far off the established track, there was a chance of falling through an unidentified crack in the ice. Several of the staff pointed out the black flags south of the camp, near the mountains, and alluded to "crevasse incidents" in previous years. The descriptions were ambiguous, obscuring the exact details. ALE respected and protected the privacy of their clients, keeping blunders and mistakes relatively quiet.

With a squinty grimace, I simply nodded and acknowledged the warning, replying that I would not even attempt to go where I was warned not to. Sensing that others had received the same warning and then had gone off on their own anyway, resulting in problems, I made it clear I was going to follow their instructions.

"There is no way I am going to prove myself an imbecile by falling down a crevasse at camp," I muttered to myself.

While mounting up the skis with nuts, bolts, washers and brackets, I endeavored not to drop anything on the snow, lest my limited supply of parts should disappear forever. The constant refrain of not screwing up flitted through my thoughts. Being a polar rookie, I was not eager to fall prey to avoidable simple mistakes. Those blunders, I've learned on previous trips, can turn a relatively rough situation into an injurious or even potentially lethal one. Though I had plenty of spare parts, I didn't want to dig into that stock until absolutely forced to. The luggage scale illustrated the stunning difference in drag force between plastic sleds directly on snow and those mounted to skis. Fully loaded, the single sled on skis only required 12 pounds of pulling force, while the unmounted sled required a whopping 20 pounds. The 40 percent reduction in pulling force would surely be a world of difference to me.

"The drag reduction is pretty impressive. How well do they track, though?" Tim Hewette asked.

"You know, I'm not exactly sure. That is not something I could test," I admitted.

He was impressed with my taking measurements and being somewhat scientific about them. But now that he had mentioned the tracking issue, I felt the seed of doubt being sewn in my mind. Had I missed some subtle yet critical point about travel here?

As I skied along the air strip, I moved on and off the sastrugi to see what the difference was. Though the pulling force with a three-quarter load felt easy and I felt strong skiing, my persistent cough wore on me. Annoyed that my body had not yet adapted to the jetliner-dry air, I sipped water to keep dehydration at bay. After skiing away from the campsite a half mile, I glanced back and my eyes flashed wide. At this short of distance, even the aircraft were diminutive in scale against the mountains. Without the GPS to verify the distance, I would not have predicted I'd skied this far, as I'd never been to such a flat, featureless place which distorted the perception of distance.

Back at my tent, I sorted gear and portioning out what I was going to take on the expedition. My nerves pulsed with apprehensive energy. As I popped my head out of the tent, staff walking toward the mess tent waved at me and used the overhand shovel hand sign to indicate it was time to eat. Waving back, I stuffed my loose gear in the tent and followed them in. I met Ben Cooper at the entrance.

"Don't wait around too long or you'll be asking for a job as a dishwasher," he said.

Smiling, I entertained the idea only for a moment. Washing dishes would be easier than dragging 330 pounds of gear across Antarctica.

After what Ben said, watching the entire staff work together to clean up after the meal made me feel embarrassed for not rolling up my sleeves to help. I knew that I needed to spend the time preparing myself and resting. One of the staff saw the look in my face and jovially said, "Just think, Aaron. This entire crew is here to serve you. At least for now." Catching several of their glances, I sheepishly grinned. Never in my life had I so many people working to make sure I had the best chance to succeed. Normally it was the other way around: I worked to ensure someone else's success.

On November 1st, Tim Hewette asked if I was ready to fly to my starting point today if the weather held up during breakfast. I said yes, I would be ready for a 9 p.m. departure. That way I would have a hearty meal in me before resorting to my calorie-laden but not so tasty rations. He made preparations with the air crew for the flight. They invited me over to review the flight plan and asked if I wanted to fly over to Redpath Hills and Three Sails to ascertain a better overview of the conditions. Declining, I said I'd rather fly over the known crevasse fields near the Wilson nunataks to see the dangerous start from the air. I knew it would be late in the day when we would touch down, so I didn't want to be up too late pitching the tent and establishing my first camp.

Sitting in my tent most of the day except for lunch, I shuffled gear, perfecting where each piece of gear was to be placed each day. I needed to be confident that I could find everything with my eyes closed. Even though I did a simulation at home, the heat in San Diego made wearing the cold weather clothing impossible. Rehearsing how I would open, light, and close the stove with gloved hands was critical. Opting to use flint and steel to light the white gas (naphtha), I performed one more test of both stoves to confirm they lit properly. I eschewed lighters and matches because of the altitude and moisture. The last problem I wanted to have was a fuel leak from the stoves being damaged in transit. It was better to figure this out while still at Union Glacier than when in the field. A broken fuel line would not only threaten my unsupported status but my life.

After dinner, I packed my gear and tent into the sled bags. Examining my checklist, I gasped. Where was my food thermos for rehydrating meals? A rush of panic filled me. I knew it was in my gear in San Diego and I had double checked it in Punta Arenas. Inexplicably, I found it in the ski bag, which was to be left behind. Chuckling to myself, I shook my head to think I'd nearly left it. After suffering errors in the past, my checklist proved its worth. I was now ready to go. I dragged my fully loaded sleds to the aircraft and the remaining baggage to the storage tent to be left for three months.

A few of the staff strode over to bid me good luck and quickly returned to their duties, as the wind was punishing, not making long goodbyes enjoyable. Tim and Ben, along with the flight crew, loaded the sleds and bags into the aircraft. As everyone wore face masks against the wind, it was difficult to tell who was who. Thanking Ben for his help and advice, I bounded up the ladder into the Twin Otter, followed by Simon.

After their flight checks, the crew powered up the plane. I saw Ben standing outside, watching us take off. I waved to him and he waved back as we taxied toward the icy runway. With a strong head wind, we were quickly in the air. Sensing a stomach churning twist of the plane, we circled around to peruse the camp and headed off toward the drop off point.

My jaw dropped as the crevasses farther down Union Glacier entered into view. There were eight evenly spaced cracks, wider than the twin engine aircraft I was in and longer than then entire length of ALE's camp, roughly 200 yards long. These gaping holes presented a formidable barrier. I was astounded by their size. As we circled the Hercules Inlet, the two crevasse fields I was warned to go between became visible. Though these were not as numerous as those on Union Glacier, these were far longer and much darker, indicating their depth. These threatening maws reinforced Steve Jones's admonitions to follow the suggested, though indirect, GPS path.

The aircraft heater made the passenger compartment unbearably hot, as I was fully dressed in my expedition gear. Apologizing while asking the crew to turn the heater down, I said I did not want to cause them discomfort. They happily obliged, cutting the heater. I became nauseous from the combination of being dressed for sub-zero temperatures in a warm aircraft cabin and simultaneously bucked back and forth from the wind turbulence. A smile returned to my greenish face as the cabin cooled down. Stuffing my head in a bucket to evacuate my last enjoyable meal was not how I wanted to begin my South Pole expedition.

Landing on the Hercules Inlet, the crew brought the airplane to a momentary stop, then pushed the plane forward again, breaking the skids off the ice created by the friction of landing. Should they not do this, the plane would freeze in place. The crew told me it was -35°F with a 35 knot wind outside. Sitting there, I watched Simon stand at the door, ready to open it on the pilot's command. The crew hopped out of the aircraft, checking to make sure everything was okay, and then opened the cargo door. What little heat the cabin retained was sucked out as quickly as an airlock opening to outer space. The copilot attached the ladder and beckoned me out of the Twin Otter. Facing backward, I descended the ladder.

Expedition
Days 1-3

Hercules Inlet, Ronne Ice Shelf
Wind 35 knots at -35˚F,
Dropped off by Twin Otter at 10 p.m.

Thursday, November 1, 2012, Day 1
Padding down the ladder and onto the ice, as I touched the ground I was nearly knocked off my feet by the 35 knot winds. It was good I had all my gear on because the cold cut through and chilled me as we unloaded my two plastic sleds and huge supply bags. Quickly clipping them together, I moved the train out of the way of the aircraft so the crew could prepare for immediate departure. The wind made speaking to each other difficult, having to lean into each other's ears as though we were at a rock concert. Simon walked around the airplane and took a few photos, as did I.

Once the crew had the aircraft ready, all three stood to face me and bid me good luck. We quickly shook hands. As I stepped back away to a safe distance, I pulled out my camera to photograph and video the takeoff. Simon hopped in the main compartment and latched the hatch shut. The crew mounted the cockpit and slammed its doors shut, fighting the wind the whole time. In moments, both turboprop engines fired up and the airplane shuddered to life, rocking in the wind. I set my camera to record a video of the plane taking off. The battery indicator plummeted from four to two bars in 30 seconds, though the camera was warmed and freshly charged. I hoped this was not an omen of future challenges.

The Canadian Kenn Borek airplane scooted forward while ice chunks, chiseled free from the skids, picked up speed and blew past the aircraft. The vertical stabilizer flung to port, swinging the lumbering machine into the wind. Though I could not see anyone inside the windows due to glare, I waved anyway. The plane seemed to wiggle its wings, waving back to me. The crew powered up the engines with a terrific roar and, after traveling only what seemed to be fifty feet, took off into the air. As the plane lifted off, the camera battery died, retracting the lens with its last gasp of energy.

Standing there for a few moments, watching as they gained altitude, dread flashed over me.

"What have I gotten myself into?" I asked the endless void staring back at me.

I recollected myself, took my eyes off the plane as sunlight glinted off its windows and turned to my sleds. Standing in the wind made me shiver, even though I was fully geared up. My mind snapped back to attention. Not wanting to waste a second longer, as it was already 10:45 p.m., I unzipped the sled bag and extricated the tent. This was easy as everything was done in full daylight. Carefully latching the main tent lines to the sleds with carabiners, I lay out the tent to push the aluminum poles through the sleeves. Lying on the nylon to keep the wind from tearing it out of my hands, I staked down the additional tent lines and, with the greatest care, shimmied off the tent and held the remaining free line.

The tent exploded into shape.

My tent-turned-parachute yanked the sleds downwind. Holding onto my line for dear life, I watched as the main support lines snapped as taut as steel cables. The stakes arrested the sleds' forward motion. Pulling back my line, I guided the tent to the ground. All lines held. Everything had happened in a shocking instant.

Pressing the stakes into the styrofoam-textured snow, I secured the windward side of the tent. Walking around and grabbing each flailing line, I pulled them tight and staked them to the five hundred foot thick sheet of ice floating on the Weddell Sea. Within minutes, I had passed the first test: securing the tent and not helplessly watching it blow away. There was no way I was going to suffer the indignity of calling ALE for them to drop me a second tent on my first night out.

The snow carried by the wind created a ground blizzard effect, immediately burying the windward edge of the sleds and stuffing snow in between the tent fly and inner shell. To prevent more snow from building up inside, I dug up blocks of snow and sat them on the edge of the tent's fly. After several minutes of chunking off snow and placing it on the fly, a security perimeter reduced the roar of the flittering nylon to a more livable thunder.

Dragging the piles of gear into the tent, I immediately pulled out the sleeping bag to allow it to reconstitute from its compression sack and then freed the feather-filled air mattress from its cocoon and worked to inflate it. After several minutes of effort, my first expedition bed was ready. I was tired and all I hungered for was sleep. Stuffing the water bottles into the bag to prevent freezing, I stripped down and donned my thinnest wool shirt and long underwear. Even though it was frostbite cold outside, I knew my body would overheat and sweat inside the behemoth four-pound feather mass of a sleeping bag.

As I squirmed into the bag and zipped it shut, I lay there wide eyed, irrespective of my brain and body's fatigue. Laughing out loud, I hooted and hollered. Here I was, in Antarctica, beginning my solo expedition. After seemingly endless preparations and training, this was it. An honest and cheerful smile creased my face, for I knew that no matter what adversity visited me, I crossed the starting line and returning was not an option. A thrill of endorphins rushed through me as I thought about the payoff of all the hard work, preparation and support from so many people to turn my dream into reality, for it would have been impossible to be here without them.

Calming down, I wriggled until comfortable and felt my eyelids droop. Tomorrow, and the many days after, promised to be an unequaled experience.

Camp AC01
79°58.732'S 79°48.656'W
Straight-line distance to South Pole: 601 nm

Friday, November 2, 2012, Day 2

A partially overcast sky greeted me on waking up. As my brain spun into consciousness, my mental iPod kicked in, playing Miranda Lambert's, "The House That Built Me." Thoughts of my parents and brother flitted through my mind, alternately making me tear up and laugh as I prepared for the day. Poking my head out of the tent, I was whipped back to my current reality, decades and thousands of miles away from my childhood. A glove-deep pile of spindrift snow filled the entrance of the tent, between the outer and inner walls, even though I had stacked snow blocks upwind of the tent. The sleds were completely buried by snow driven by the 35 knot winds ripping at my nylon home. The sound was akin to sleeping three feet from a freight train passing by at full speed. Even though at -10°F the wind swirled around me, the sun's ferocity, positioned above the horizon at what would have been two hours before sunset, was palpable.

This day's navigation was critical, much more so than any of the others. While shooting between two nunataks, mountain peaks poking out of the snow, I needed to target specific waypoints to dodge the crevasses while escaping the coast. This GPS path would take me between the two largest crevasse fields. ALE advised me to keep the course but also to carry my satellite phone and beacon on me until I passed Patriot Hills in case I fell into a crevasse. Scary! To alleviate such thoughts, I entertained myself by yelling into the wind, telling the danger to stay away and my compass to be infallible. With no one for miles, I had no concern about appearing to be a raving lunatic.

Even though I drank a liter of water last night and gulped down another three liters during the day, my urine was a dusky yellow, the first sign of dehydration. The books I had read only cursorily mentioned managing hydration. It was a balancing act of making sure I wasn't drying out, heading toward shoe leather, while at the same time not overworking my kidneys and having to stop every half hour.

Keeping the drinking water liquid was an immediate problem, too. Putting the six one-liter bottles in the sled bags wasn't keeping them liquid. They all began freezing, both inside and on the cap threads, threatening to make the life-sustaining fluid inaccessible. During test runs in Yellowstone National Park in winter where I experienced -45°F temperatures, I learned to keep one bottle wrapped in a spare jacket for easy access and the rest inside waterproof bags inside my sleeping bag to prevent freezing. Having a water spill inside the down sleeping bag would be catastrophic, with no way to dry it. At these temperatures, uninsulated bottles turn to slush in half an hour. Also, I had to be careful to dry the threads of the bottle lids each time I drank out of them. Otherwise, the ice welded the lid shut, compelling me to use the cave man technique of banging the lid on the sled's edge to break the lid free.

As I only drank three liters today but made six last night, I opted for making five tonight to cut the weight down. While waiting the hour and a half for the ice to melt, I kept myself busy brushing snow off my boots and extricating my sleeping bag. Boiling five liters of water took too long and wasted fuel. So, after pondering it, I reasoned that three of the bottles only needed to be warm liquid, as they needed all to be in the sleeping bag to prevent overnight freezing. The other two, used for rehydrating food and warming up the electronics, had to be near boiling. Heating the water to the proper temperature required constant attention, leaving me only a few minutes of real down time during the evening.

Tonight I busied myself taping the back of my heels, as after one day of skiing, even with triple socks, they were badly abraded. At least the problem wasn't a surprise, as I had tested out the boots in Yellowstone. Another layer of duct tape on the ankle area of the kartankers [thick wool boot liner] eliminated significant shredding damage from constant motion. Other explorers told me to anticipate spending considerable time to repair both myself and my gear. Thus far, they'd proven to be right.

Camp AC02
79°59.271'S 79°55.741'W
Distance: 1.3 nm, Time: 2.5 hours
Distance to South Pole: 601 nm

Saturday, November 3, 2012, Day 3

Weather dictates everything in Antarctica. Today was a case in point. The wind whipped along at 35 knots at 6 a.m., and by the time I started trekking up the massive slope leading away from the Hercules Inlet at 9 a.m., the wind had completely died. Initially, I thought calm conditions and an overcast sun were the perfect conditions for ski towing. How wrong I was. Even with the air temperature at -5°F, it did not take long before I was cooking. Cautiously, I removed a layer of clothing, as I wanted to avoid burning my skin from both the cold air and the solar radiation. After all the warnings I received about freezing skin, horrid sun burns and snow blindness, I was overly cautious. Becoming this hot fogged my goggles, which in turn formed a thick cake of ice, blinding me. To alleviate the problem, I switched to glasses, which fogged in short order from my rising breath. This made for a long day. To be able to see through the ice on my glasses while still protecting my eyes, I pulled the glasses two inches away from my face, increasing my field of vision enough to be able to see where I was stepping without risking snow blindness. It was irritating to be fighting this problem so early on, but I made do with the tools at hand. Learning to surmount whatever Antarctica threw at me was one of my goals and, when I figured a way to solve the problem, smug satisfaction crept onto my face.

Had I been able to pick up some speed to generate my own breeze, it would not have been so nauseatingly hot. But, trudging up the first hill, passing the Wilson Nunataks, dragging 320 pounds of gear, all while walking, was not conducive to making terrific speed. In fact, after checking the GPS, I found myself having only covered 0.3 nm in the first hour of travel. Frowning at the GPS in wonderment, my mind generated several scenarios of why I was moving so slowly. Certainly, walking up this hill was not helping my speed. But in my training, I pulled the same drag force up a far steeper hill back in Jackson at 6,500 feet elevation. My breathing was labored and, being overly hot, I did not feel well, so I paused every ten minutes to take a mini-break. After swapping from skis to boots for travel, I chose to walk because the undulations in the ice surface made skiing a stumbling experience. The boots punched into the hard-packed snow giving me traction. Had the surface been hard, smooth ice, I would have been seriously cursing the recommendation not to bring crampons to escape Hercules Inlet. My biggest concern with stumbling on skis was falling down and hurting a knee or breaking my wrist. To be only a few miles into the trip, avoiding crevasse fields, only to have my expedition terminated from an injury weighed on my mind. The thought was not crippling, but it certainly made my steps tentative.

Even though I followed the suggested GPS coordinates to circumvent the known crevasse zones, several smaller ones, only a few inches wide, coated the slope in a random spider web pattern (79°59.30'S, 80°00.086'W). Poking my ski poles into these crevices opened short cracks which were an astonishing electric blue. Even though the snow and ice were perfectly white, it looked as though I had punctured finger-thick blue neon holes. While staring into them, there was no discernible bottom, only where the bright blue cascaded to navy blue and then nothingness about a foot below the surface. The sunlight reflecting off the snow was dazzling, making peering deeper into these cracks impossible because of the contrast. I was warned about a solo Canadian skier who fell down a crevasse in 2003, only a day or two into her trip, and was only saved because she had a satellite phone on her. Trapped at the bottom of the abyss, she was able to contact ALE and they were able to scramble a plane and rescue her. With that warning in mind, I carried both satellite phone and beacon in a waist pack for such an occurrence. To reduce the constriction from the extra belt, I took the pack off each time I rested. This all was working fine, so I thought. While setting up my tent at day's end, I felt around my waist for the pack and found it missing. At first, I thought I'd tossed it into the sled. Rummaging through the sled, I quickly realized the bag was lost. That wonderful sinking sensation of going over the first drop on a roller coaster hit my stomach hard.

Both primary satellite phone and beacon were gone.

Quickly, I thought back to when I took my last break, or at least the last time I remembered having the pouch. The realization struck: it did not matter how far back those two devices were, I absolutely must have them. Last season, Aleksander Gamme had to ski a 2.5 mile round trip to retrieve the GPS he had dropped. Although his having made such a mistake as a professional made me feel less like a rookie, I placed my face in both my hands and shook my head. How could I be so stupid? Never having worn a waist pack before, I had not trained myself to check it every time I stood up. Being clad in bulky clothing made it difficult to detect anything missing.

"But there is no excuse Linsdau," I told myself.

So, I plucked out my GPS, marked the campsite, mounted up the skis and raced downhill, following my tracks. I broke the unwritten rule about leaving without an emergency shelter. The tracks disappeared more than once, much to my consternation, making me stop and wander to rediscover them. Soon, I saw an indistinct blue blotch farther down the hill. There it was. Quickening my pace, I scooped up the bag and turned back to head for camp. Even though I had only covered a quarter mile downhill, my tent appeared tiny and insignificant in the icy rubble. I was glad to have GPS-marked the tent. Had a blizzard struck, I would have been without shelter and lost in the biggest wilderness on Earth.

Safely back in the tent, I cursed myself for being stupid. I emptied the pouch and stowed it. It was irritating anyway. I'll carry the phone, with leash, in a zipped pocket. Everything was so new and there were so many distractions that it was easy to make such a costly mistake. The last time I left something valuable, a camera lens, in the forest was over a decade ago. I recovered it but learned to always look back after standing up from a break, as I did when I had stood up from the sleds. However, as I thought over what had happened, I visualized that the pouch had been hidden behind the sleds, so my check had been incomplete. From now on, after I drag the sleds forward a few feet, I craned my neck back for a check every time, preventing any more screw-ups.

Tonight was the last time I put a stick of butter into my dinner. The dehydrated meals were so filling already that the butter exceeded my stomach capacity. Even though I'd trained and overeaten for months, I was still unable to wolf it all down. So now the plan was to eat half a block, 4 ounces, of butter for breakfast and the rest during breaks over the day. Eating solid butter was not too unpleasant. It was like chomping into a block of cheese at these temperatures. It was firm enough not to crumble but not tooth-breaking hard, either.

I also dialed in keeping the electronics warm to keep the batteries alive. Putting the satellite phone and beacon power pack in my jacket while sitting in the tent did not warm them up enough. Even though they were in there for an hour, they were still cool. This put the battery life in jeopardy. As I had no desire to kill the batteries prematurely, I figured out that by placing the phone on top of the first hot water bottle, I was able to eek out more bars on the battery indicator. Keeping the battery level up cut some stress. I worried that if clouds obscured me for a week, the solar-powered devices would start dying even with spare batteries. As I planned to be out here for a long time, every precaution was necessary to keep the expedition moving forward.

Camp AC03
S 80° 01.055' W 80° 11.396'
Distance: 4 nm, Time: 7 hours
Distance to South Pole: 599 nm

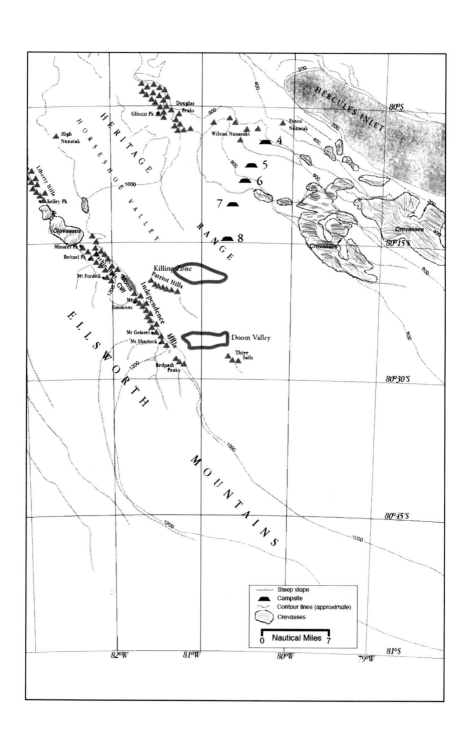

9

Days 4-8

Sunday, November 4, 2012, Day 4

IT WAS COLD, clear and windy. The barometer was at 27.8 in Hg. My face felt windburned because I only wore glasses and not the protective mask which fogged up the goggles. As I was not keen on traveling blind, I didn't have any other choice. My goggles were entirely fogged, so I had to choose from blindness, windburn, sunburn or frostbite. Crud! I thought I'd bombed the distance today based on how I felt, but I was not even close. Leaving camp at 10 a.m., I skied for eight hours and stopped at 6 p.m., yet I had traveled only three miles. I kept bonking out and had terrible trouble moving, as though I had run a marathon before even leaving the tent.

Over the years of trekking, I've learned that when the first thought of food passes through my mind, I become hungry in 20–30 minutes. If I didn't eat when I thought about food, I bonked by the time I was hungry, and then it turned into a vicious cycle. My energy levels reduce to a crippling level. I was able to override this emotion and force myself to march on in spite of my body crying out. If I were to stop every time hunger hit, I would only stand all day and eat. I was constantly on the cusp of bonking.

The foot beds in my boots were wet and I was sweat soaked when skiing uphill from the coast. Once I crested the hill, past Wilson Nunataks, and was over the slope, I cooled down considerably but had little energy all day. Even though I should have been mostly over my cold, it felt as though the cough I was fighting was deteriorating instead of improving. During this hill climb, I learned it took over an hour to feel the energy from the sticks of butter I ate. Thus far, thoughts of food coursed through my mind every hour, making for distracted towing. The snow surface was extremely hard today, making skiing dangerous. I constantly slipped and wished I had boot cables or ski crampons. Even though others said I should stay on skis to help avoid the danger of falling through a crevasse, falling down and breaking an arm from slipping on skis was not an enviable alternative.

I started to develop a timetable for making camp at the end of the day:

Stop at 6 p.m.
6:18 have the tent set up
6:28 have the tent fly buried with snow
6:38 unload the sleds into the tent
6:45 melting snow for dinner

It took so much longer to pitch a tent when it was cold. Though the time it took was discouraging, in oversized boots and gloves, it was difficult to move any quicker.

The GPS showed I had already climbed to 2,200 feet, meaning I was progressing on to the plateau, which was over 3,000 feet in elevation. Pulling this amount of weight up such a steep hill proved to be stunningly difficult, tougher than pulling tires up 1,800 vertical feet on Old Teton Pass Road.

Camp AC04
80°04.296'S 80°18.709'W
Distance 3.48 nm, Time 8 hours
Distance to South Pole: 596 nm

Monday, November 5, 2012, Day 5

My whole body ached when I awoke, so it was a slow morning. I didn't start skiing until 10:30 a.m. Todd, an ALE guide, had told me that this expedition was difficult for the first 10 days before everything smoothed out. As this was only day 5, I had a long way to go.

Damn, I felt I had traveled twice the distance I did today! Skiing uphill gave the false impression that I'd gone farther than I had. The surface was completely wretched today. So was the weather. It was total white out conditions with 20-30 knot winds out of the SSW to the SW. Right now I was heading south, so the wind was off to my right all day. The staff at Union Glacier told me the wind did not gust. Instead, it felt like the wind outside a moving vehicle, consistent and rarely varying.

During the white out conditions of the day, I fell off some sastrugi and slammed my side. Even though there was no damage, the incident made me feel the need to walk rather than ski through these ice sculptures. If I were to have taken some of those falls on skis, I could be nursing a sprained wrist or worse. Falling off a short block of ice while blind and attached to 320 pounds of sleds would not end well for my body. With the whiteout, it was like I had strapped on semi-transparent white plastic over my eyes, attached a rickshaw to my body, then started walking through a construction zone on a street with broken asphalt and sizable potholes, all at -15°F with 20 knot winds.

For some reason, American patriotic music played in my head all day. "God Bless America" was the constant refrain in between my struggling with the pulks flipping over. It kept me going and, if nothing else, entertained. I hadn't sung this song in a decade. Yet it surfaced here out of nowhere.

I'd become more adept at using the crumbled styrofoam snow as toilet paper. As long as I used the proper scrubbing speed, it was tolerable. I tossed each piece of ice after one pass. With only two squares of toilet paper per event planned, I was careful with my supplies. It was having my backside hanging in the burning wind that put the hurt on. The sensation of developing frostbite on my hips and bum cheeks scared me. Also there was the problem of having a carabiner dangling from the harness while taking care of business. More than once, the frozen aluminum rested against my skin, feeling as though it was pulled out of a lit grill. The metal was so cold it felt like it was heated by a torch.

After 1 p.m., I thought more than once about being in the shelter of my tent. My mind's justification system of why I was here ignited, attempting to convince me that what I was doing made no sense and that what I was doing was foolish. It wasn't hunger or thirst that drove these thoughts. I presumed it was the frustration of the conditions and making poor progress that picked on the weakest center of my brain. Any time justifying an activity comes into my mind, I have to tell myself, "It's okay, you'll walk farther tomorrow. The weather will be better. You're tired, everyone will understand why you're having such a tough time."

When this miserable mental monologue rears its ugly head, I know something was awry.

During a break at 3 p.m., I parked the pulks next to some sastrugi, maneuvered them so they were stem to stern and managed to lie on their leeward side to hide from the wind. The ski pogies [fleece hoods placed over the ski poles for hand protection] served as insulation from the snow, allowing me to lie down on my hip and shoulder to relax for a minute. It wasn't exactly comfortable but it sure beat sitting on the sled in the punishing wind. I felt weak because I wanted to hide from the wind, even though it was a primary part of the experience here. One of the thoughts that crossed my mind was that if an aircraft flew over and saw me lying down beside the sleds, the crew might think something happened to me. I guessed I looked pretty sorry from the air.

Through all this, the end of my day drew upon me. I was utterly punished. The whiteout was so absolute that I became disoriented. Tossing and swirling the fluorescent tow rope across the snow surface, I ascertained the rough surface shape and where the pits were. It was as though the line was magically hovering in space. Even then, I kept stumbling over sastrugi and other snow features I couldn't see, for want of a few shadows to reveal the pitch and roll of the land.

I waxed the skis on both sleds, as I felt the red sled skis were dragging. This was the third day since I had last waxed them. The coarseness of the ice crystals tore through much of the wax base on the skis in a matter of days. Checking the supply of glide wax I brought made me wish for another tin, even though I had brought two. Although waxing the skis in unpleasant weather was annoying, the effort will pay off in tomorrow's towing sessions.

I spoke with Mom and Dad by satellite phone for a half-hour yesterday. It was wonderful to talk with them! They were ecstatic to hear from me, as if they thought they wouldn't hear from me the whole time. I planned to call every Monday to make them and myself feel better. Dad said skiing up to the polar plateau was going to be the worst and he was right. This steep grade was brutal. It was like dragging a refrigerator up a mountain road. The towing force was near my maximum capacity. There were flat parts where I moved quickly, only to be forestalled after a few quick steps. I felt free of the glue I skied through only for mere moments.

I answered a few questions from people via my phone-in blog. Kelly let me know what the questions were and I answered them in my broadcasts. It was a relief not to waste time typing. All I needed to do was talk for five minutes and my daily audio message was finished.

Camp AC05
80°07.268'S 80°27.155'W
Distance: 3.5 nm, Time: 7 hours
Distance to South Pole: 593 nm

TUESDAY, NOVEMBER 6, 2012, DAY 6

Thus far my body was not dialing into the heavy expedition load. It felt as though I had absolutely no energy. I skied thirty steps and then was forced to stop, as though I was badly out of shape. A cold, dry environment was nothing new to me, yet my body acted as though I had not worked out in a year. The incessant cough worsened as the day wore on. The flour-fine dusty snow made breathing difficult. I felt as though there was an alien choking me from the inside. It both frustrated and discouraged me, as I was able to drag an equivalent amount of weight with not nearly this much trouble while training in the Rockies. That was far higher than I was now, so it wasn't an altitude issue. Although I thought I recovered from my cold in Punta Arenas, the cough had progressively deteriorated and now sapped my energy.

When the wind died down and I caught glimpses of the Ellsworth Mountain Range with the still far-off Patriot and Redpath Hills, my spirits surged, even if my body didn't. I was here, in Antarctica, excited to be making my way through the toughest continent on the planet. With my supporters cheering for me back home, I grinned even though I gritted my teeth while dragging the load up a steep hill. Once the weather calmed down in the afternoon, I pushed harder and picked up a few more miles. From what ALE said, this whole area was extremely difficult to pass through, as the wind and deep snow had hampered explorers before.

Now that I've been here for a week, much of my bravado had diminished, and now it came down to making forward progress in the face of poor mileage. I knew conditions would improve once I escaped out of the coastal mountain region, but it was difficult to envision that happening when my skis, boots and sleds bogged down in the perpetually deep snow. Even though this was part of the experience, it was a real ego buster not to have shot out of the gate as fast as I would have preferred. In a way, it was a humbling experience. For all the training I had done, it did not prepare me for illness nor dealing with heavy snow and strong winds.

My body was adjusting to the absolute lack of humidity in the air. All day I fought a parched throat, so I downed water in an attempt to adjust my hydration. With the cold air, the only consequence was that I stopped frequently to water the landscape. Having been through this before, I knew that it would take time to sort myself out. It was far safer to have too much water in me, even if it slowed me down. Once serious dehydration sets in, muscle and stomach cramps follow soon thereafter, making me downright miserable.

Having watched training videos of other teams in the Arctic Circle, one of the vital emphases was on drinking before thirsty and eating before hungry. With those warnings in my head, I made sure to stop frequently and take care of both. However, it did not make for efficient travel. I was still running on fear in this huge, empty place. I knew that if I kept to what I knew, the expedition would work out. Extending my previous travel distance from hundreds to over a thousand miles was another matter in my mind. It was difficult to not contemplate the big picture but rather to focus on the immediate. Since there was nothing for me to do but push through, worrying about events out of my control only sapped my energy. I thought about my successes up to this point, thinking about what I had gone through to reach Antarctica. This reduced the feeling of being overwhelmed.

Far away in the United States, thousands of miles away, it was election day. And I didn't miss the barrage of campaign ads at all. As much as I was glad I live in a country where I can participate in the process, I was so wrapped up in my own personal battle that a presidential election was rather irrelevant. Suddenly this place felt like the moon: raw, inaccessible and fully detached from the world. I was out here all on my own, slowly making my way toward the South Pole.

Camp AC06
80°09.704'S 80°34.451'W
Distance: 3 nm, Time: 5 hours
Distance to South Pole: 591 nm

WEDNESDAY, NOVEMBER 7, 2012, DAY 7

I wore my goggles most of the day and suffered through the infernal fogging. Depending on how I oriented my head, the fog would reappear and disappear in a minute. When I faced dead into the wind, the goggles turned opaque, making it impossible to see. One time when I stopped to adjust the harness, I faced away from the wind and the goggles quickly cleared, as though I had turned on a defroster mechanism. Thrilled to see again, I turned into the northerly wind and pushed forward. Within two minutes, the goggles fogged over again. For reasons unclear to me, my orientation relative to the wind completely dictated how much or little fog there was. I expected them to stay clear in the wind, as it should have carried the heat away. Yet that was not the case.

Having read about other explorers suffering from the same problem, I made sure to bring spare lenses and glasses. When I stopped to change from goggles to glasses at 1 p.m., I had to take off my outer gloves to unzip the glasses pouch. Quickly my right pinky finger felt as though it was on fire. I thought I had frozen it. It hurt worse than smashing it with a hammer. I stopped and rested on the pulks, retracting my fingers into the palm of my glove to rewarm the pinky. After several moments, feeling started coming back, allaying my fears of frostbite. Angry at myself for coming close to suffering a cold injury, I berated myself. I have been in so many cold places that I should have known better and felt embarrassed. Others, with far more polar experience than I, had suffered worse. Being frostbitten because I desired to switch glasses quickly was not the story I wanted to tell when I returned home.

The pulks kept falling into holes, necessitating constant retrieval. It was advantageous each one only weighed 150 pounds, as I didn't want to wreck my back yanking them upright. Those who bring down a single sled weighing in excess of 400 pounds must do some impressive lifting. I wondered how I fared in comparison with others who were attempting the South Pole round trip this season? Had they surpassed me in distance already? Thinking about what others had done and how I stacked up weighed on my mind. I knew my mileage was terrible, but there was little I could do to improve it. Between the sleds constantly falling into holes, my incessant fatigue and having the wind blow the sleds backwards, I was at a loss for a method for moving more quickly. I was satisfied that the sleds were gliding, as when I righted them after falling in a hole, they immediately slid sideways, forward or backwards, depending on the slope. However, I was blown away that the wind was so strong that, upon stopping and loosening the harness traces, I felt the sleds tugging at me because the wind shoved them backward.

Surely this had to seriously hamper my forward progress.

While pitching the tent, one of the stakes bent in half. Damn. The lightweight stake was an efficient design for snow, but the drilled holes for weight savings made the stakes weak, always bending at those drill points. Of all the issues to run into: ruined tent stakes! As the tent was not self-standing, having no stakes means having no tent. This was a surprising first for me, considering how superbly the stakes worked in Yellowstone over the winter. Then again, I had not tried to smash them into solid snow or ice. It was disheartening to be running into equipment failures at only the end of the first week of the expedition. I felt pathetic about my mileage, regardless of how my body felt or the incredible force of the wind.

Camp AC07
80°12.687'S 80°41.715'W
Distance: 3 nm, Time: 8 hours
Distance to South Pole: 588 nm

Thursday, November 8, 2012, Day 8
The weather had deteriorated from yesterday, right along the lines of the area forecast. Now there was a ground blizzard and a whiteout, making it impossible to see anything. Never having been in such perpetually rotten weather, I decided to play it conservatively and wait to see if the winds abated. With the knowledge that other professional teams had lost their tents in similar storms, I didn't want to be the fool and watch my tent blow irretrievably away. If that should happen, I would have to bundle myself inside one of the sled bags or fabricate a shelter until ALE could drop a tent. And, if they did that, my unsupported status would be wiped out. I was way too attached to the idea of completing the round trip, so I was being overly careful.

My thumbs and index fingers had split wide open, bleeding, when I woke up. The stinging was familiar, as I suffered from it many times when camping in the winter. I knew it was a result of improper hydration, and it was depressing to be facing the same old problem. Normally, my solution was to drink copious amounts of water, but thus far down here all that did was make me stop frequently to relieve myself.

Not wanting to waste my entire travel time with my pants unzipped, I throttled back my water consumption. It was clear I had not achieved the magic balance. I broke open a tube of super glue and patched myself together, careful not to accidentally glue two fingers together.

Not until noon did the sun finally pierce the gloom, so I rapidly bundled up all my gear and started towing. Even though the wind blew hard, I knew I had to be outside making miles. This wasn't a summit attempt where the strategy was to wait for the best weather, I needed to travel as hard and as much as possible. I remembered the surfing bumper sticker "Eddie Would Go" as I exited the tent and pushed my way through the storm. The phrase referred to Eddie Aikau, a legendary Hawaiian surfer, who surfed regardless of wave height or conditions. I needed to emulate Eddie if I was to even have a chance of repeating the feat of Aleksander Gamme last year.

As the clouds opened up even more, a 22° sunbow appeared circling the sun, igniting up a brilliant pair of sundogs [brilliant spots of light on either side of the sun along the sunbow]. They flitted in and out of the low clouds. Then a large sun pillar rose off the horizon, making for a spectacular sky display. These usually mean there was ice in the upper atmosphere, indicating a possible storm. I hoped that wasn't the case, but I enjoyed the shiny sky spots for what they were worth. Too bad my camera was buried deep inside the sleds for protection. I wanted to have it on me, but when the battery died from the cold so quickly, it was frustrating to be carrying an expensive paperweight.

Once the clouds closed up, plunging me into another blinding whiteout, the temperature plummeted, badly chilling me. The disorientation of being in a complete milky white forced me to stop and stare at my sleds, as I had moments of dizziness, causing me to stumble. Having only an hour remaining of skiing scheduled for the day, I did not want to take the time to stop and readjust my clothing, only to have the temperature change again, forcing another stoppage. Instead, I forced myself to dream of the hottest places my body has withstood. Bathing in a near-boiling Japanese onsen, hiking in the crushing sun of Death Valley, and sweating profusely in a 170°F Budapest steam room all came to mind. Meditating on each of those experiences warmed up my hands and feet. Even though I was not skiing harder, and the wind and temperature were the same, my extremities slowly lost their chill.

I recalled reading about a technique Himalayan monks used by envisioning tubes, leading from their core to the outside their bodies, spewing fire. Using this thought process, they were able to stay outside overnight in sub-freezing temperatures in little more than their robes. Since the monks were doing nothing other than kneeling in the punishing weather, I could only imagine the concentration required to keep heat flowing through their body, keeping hypothermia at bay. I was hauling a heavy load and generating heat, and yet still fell prey to the cold. It took every ounce of untrained concentration to drive heat to my hands and feet, all the while endeavoring to effect forward progress and not fall over in the whiteout.

Somewhere in the back of my mind, I mused about the purported vehicle tracks somewhere out here. To think that there was something out here that would impart the slightest advantage overwhelmed me. Thoughts of warm baths evaporated in the fog of fantasy. If only I could find the road, would I be able to ski the 12 to 16 miles per day I needed to round trip across Antarctica? I felt guilty about even considering it and yet, after being here over a week and having gone virtually nowhere, I sensed an urgency. Too, I had less and less energy each day and the coughing had progressively worsened. Knowing that I didn't work my hardest to achieve my goal would be the worst result I could conceive.

Right at 5:45 p.m., 15 minutes before my stop time, I saw what was an impossibility. Right there, in a tiny pocket dug out of the ice, was a patch of sand. With a complete whiteout enveloping me, the grains appeared as though they were hovering in space. As the wind had picked up and I wanted to hide from it for a moment, I dragged the sleds windward of the pocket and then lay down to hide. Upon lowering myself to the ice surface, the wind disappeared and relative calm returned to my ears. Thinking the wind had stopped, as there were no cues that it was blowing, I poked my head back up, only to have it shoved backward from the wind pressure. No, it was still there.

These 20-odd grains of sand were so remarkable that I lay on my stomach unmoving and stared at them for several minutes. As there was nothing other than myself, the sleds and utter whiteness to look at, solid objects mesmerized me. At first I became terribly excited and thought they were meteorite bits that I could scoop up and take home as a souvenir. Then, after having a moment to mull it over, I realized the wall of mountains 12 miles to the south was the source of this wayward grit. Never before had bits of rock been so captivating. After a few more moments of study, I rose back up and finished off what remained of the day's skiing. The image of that little pocket of sand was burned into my mind, as all I could do was dwell on it until I fell asleep.

Camp AC08
80°14.106'S 80°45.107'W
Distance: 2 nm, Time: 4 hours
Distance to South Pole: 586 nm

(Above) *While north of Patriot Hills near the Wilson Nunataks, I had to build a 6 foot thick snow block wall nearly every night to shield the tent. Winds were routinely at gale force, making camp preparation difficult and dangerous.*

(Left) *Wind sculpts fascinating sastrugi out of the hard-packed snow and ice on the polar plateau. This pencil thin piece of ice had been carved out as the wind picked up and tore through the sides of the small lump.*

(Below) *Standing next to the Twin Otter aircraft that dropped me off at the Hercules Inlet, I began shivering in moments. The wind was 35 knots and the air temperature hovered at -35°F, making for a wind chill of -78°F.*

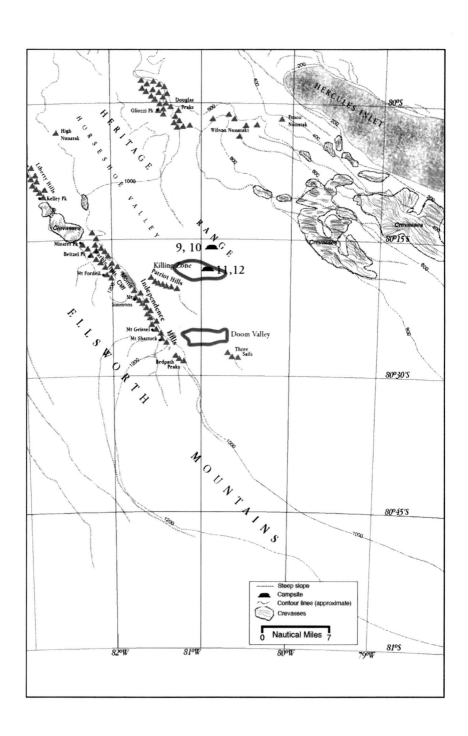

10

Days 9-12

Friday, November 9, 2012, Day 9

ALTHOUGH I DID COVER MILES, they were not amounting to enough to make the distance I needed for a round trip in the time available to me. There were so many times during the day that I skied for 15 minutes and then halted completely from either lack of energy or incessant coughing. My body had deteriorated markedly and I knew I was in trouble. This was not the ultra-dry air of Antarctica sapping the moisture from my lungs but rather a full blown lung infection. Last night I only slept five hours, as fits of coughing kept waking me up. By the morning, I woke up sweating, even though I was chilled. I knew I was in trouble.

Several times during the day, I was reduced to being on my hands and knees, trying to expel the mucus out of my lungs and into the snow. So many times I would start hacking and had to bend over to breathe. That's when I knew the problem was grave. At least the snow absorbed all the grossness I coughed up so I didn't have to look at it. To reduce the bacteria in my face mask, I boiled the mouth piece in an attempt to kill any additional microbes that were living in the foam.

I only wanted to deal with the infection in my lungs, not having anything reintroduced from an external petri dish of neoprene and foam.

During the scheduled call with ALE tonight, I spoke with Deirdre Galbraith, one of the ALE doctors, about what to do. My spirits were high because I knew I had drugs to kill virtually anything that had infected me, but I was frightened to think that I had contracted an illness and was in the middle of the most unforgiving place on Earth. Her suggestion was to start an antibiotics course immediately. She also suggested changing the dosage schedule to even out the level of drugs in my system to kill off the bacteria faster. I must have sounded rather desperate to her.

When the situation went sideways, I kept a calm and reserved demeanor in my voice. I suspected the doctor saw right through it. I imagined the doctor saying to herself, "Here's some guy who has never been on such a major long-distance expedition nor ever been to Antarctica and he's ill. Good luck, buddy."

In the States this would have been only an irritation. I would have taken a few days off work, rested, and been on the mend in no time. Recovering under duress was entirely another matter. It was impossible to rest adequately on a multi-month Antarctic expedition.

"If at all possible, you should take a rest day to recover," said the doctor.

"Okay, that is rather difficult to do out here, as I'm sure you know," I said.

"Well, that may be true but it might take weeks to recover if you are unable to rest."

"Weeks?!" I blurted out.

"Yes, that's pretty common for this sort of infection. You need time for your lungs to heal."

Suddenly my male ego faced the reality of the situation. If I did not recover quickly and start making my way, this expedition was all going to be for naught. Fighting through and making the hero effort was pointless if I ended up having to be evacuated. I had heard of another explorer having her cold turn into pneumonia, forcing her to abandon her expedition. I did not want to suffer that same fate.

Camp AC09
80°16.918'S 80°52.000'W
Distance: 3 nm, Time: 7 hours
Distance to South Pole: 584 nm

Saturday, November 10, 2013, Day 10

I woke up wasted, but the cough was markedly reduced, so I spared some energy for a smile. The infection was being exterminated and I was healing. After eating what I could, then taking another antibiotic pill and cleaning up, I collapsed right back to sleep, unable to fight my fatigue. The doctor was right. I must sleep and take at least one full rest day, otherwise there was the chance that not only would it take longer for me to recover from this illness but also my cough could devolve into pneumonia, forcing me to end my trip after it had barely begun. Though I have machismo inside of me, I knew it would be foolish to push farther. It was far better to take the day off so I would feel much better tomorrow.

With the storm still raging outside, it was as well that I rested. The winds buffeted the tent violently, enough to throw snow blocks off the door flap, allowing spindrift flour-like snow to fill in the vestibule and the space between the tent's inner and outer shell. I was so tired that I didn't care. Not caring made me feel spineless, but I knew that no matter if I packed more snow blocks around the tent, they would only be blown away in turn.

For much of my engineering career, I created and made devices bend to my will, forcing them to work as I needed them to for whatever project I worked on. Now, I was here in Antarctica with tiny bacteria swimming in my lungs, bending me to their will. The irony made me laugh, though the noise inside the tent was so loud I barely heard it. Then the laugh turned to a minute-long coughing fit which precipitated gagging and choking. I suppressed humorous thoughts to keep from laughing, lest the microbes living inside me make a comeback from my weakness.

I thought about how my skis and the sleds performed yesterday. Even though it was easier for me to ski over the ice lumps and sastrugi filling the landscape, the sleds handled them terribly. After waxing each set of skis, the drag reduced considerably, as expected. However, when the sleds slid over hard ice, they slipped laterally, both left and right, pulling me off course. They were remarkably easy to pull on smooth surfaces yet vexingly annoying on sloped domes and sastrugi. I wished I had my luggage scale to take some quick measurements, though I did not have much time to run experiments out here. The thought of improving efficiency plagued me. Was it better to reduce drag force or have the sleds track better? I loved the ease of pulling with the sleds on skis. But the sleds wandered off course repeatedly, requiring more effort anyway. As I fell asleep, my engineer's mind dreamt of a fully instrumented system able to provide quantifiable measurements for the sleds' performance over countless miles.

Camp AC09
80°16.918'S 80°52.000'W
No movement today
Distance to South Pole: 584 nm

SUNDAY, NOVEMBER 11, 2012, DAY 11

Even though it had been two days since I started antibiotics to kill the bronchitis residing in my lungs, it was going to be a while before I felt fully up to speed. Though the cough was much better, it was still present and the energy sapping effects of the waning infection was tormenting me. In my mind I was decidedly happy. I was still out here battling my way forward, though slowly, making progress toward the Pole. The infection could have deteriorated into pneumonia, so I focused on a positive: recovering from my first major problem. Waking up and feeling better lifted my spirits, but as I wriggled in the confined tent, the pressing lack of energy sapped away my happiness. Having been through this problem before, I knew that it usually took at least two weeks to recover in the best conditions before I started running and training again. This weighed on my mind, as it was impossible for me to stay in one place for a week. I had to keep moving forward.

Once I was able to exit out of the tent, 30 knot winds assailed me and kept my mind off the dying infection inside of me. I concentrated on not losing the tent or injuring myself. I learned that, if nothing else, my body made a splendid paperweight, capable of keeping the tent from blowing away. Though the weather was a welcome distraction from the despair circling the periphery of my mind, it was not a pleasant one.

At first I thought I moved admirably. But then my body let me know it was far from recovered. I was able to ski for a solid hour but then needed a 20 minute break. The next two hours felt progressively slower, as though I was either skiing up an indiscernible hill or the sleds had magically gained significant weight. As neither was a hill apparent nor had the gravitational constant of the universe changed, my only conclusion was that my body was spent. The exhaustion made my mind go blank. I pushed forward with everything I had until I completely stopped, dumbly staring into oblivion, seeing nothing. From starting off with high spirits to now being wasted after few hours of towing, I knew that I needed to take it easy or I'd end up even more ill.

So, I pitched the tent and, ignoring the persistent wind, focused only on making camp. More than once I stopped, knelt down and caught my breath as I placed stakes. The discouragement was palpable, but I knew it was only from extreme fatigue and the inability to draw in enough oxygen to keep my brain happy. As soon as I lay down inside the tent on the foam mat, I fell unconscious.

I snapped awake, aware that I had shifted at night and my legs were freezing because they were on the ice rather than the foam mat. Checking my watch startled me. Three hours had passed without me waking once. Shaking the sleep out of my eyes, I was determined to gain another mile.

Though I was able only to pick up three-quarters of a mile when I reached the stop time of 6 p.m., I was mildly happy with my progress. Given that I had zero energy, regardless of what I ate or did, I was surprised to have traveled over two miles. I pondered what had others done when they had faced serious illness on the plateau. Did they stop until they were recovered enough to continue or did they suffer through the illness? As I made camp for the second time today, thoughts of earlier explorers assailed me. I felt pathetic for putting in all this effort only to be defeated by a microscopic bacterium. Even though the illness seemed completely out of my control, I wondered if there were measures I could have taken to prevent it all together. I used ethyl-alcohol hand sanitizer to kill germs and was careful to wash my hands. Was it the stress of preparation and rushing about combined with sleepless nights leading up to my departure from the States?

Camp AC10
80°19.167'S 80°58.284'W
Distance: 2.5 nm, Time: 4 hours
Distance to South Pole: 581 nm

MONDAY, NOVEMBER 12, 2012, DAY 12
This was the first day I experienced what Scott and his men might have suffered when they met their fate 101 years before I set foot on Antarctica. The rage of the storm outside was unbelievable, nearly an 11 on the Beaufort scale of wind, right below a hurricane. Although I wanted to go out and cover more miles, the weather made it not only impractical but downright dangerous. The tent was designed to withstand 100 mile per hour winds. This gale was its first real test.

After hiding out from the wind until 10 a.m., I crawled outside to see what was happening. The moment I exited the tent I was rammed onto my side, as though a car had hit me. Not wanting to give up, I pushed forward and struggled into the wind to see what it felt like. Leaning massively, I was barely able to trudge ten feet at a time before being blown backward. After fifty feet of walking south, I realized there was nothing to do but return to the tent and bide my time. Turning about, I was shoved back to the shelter as though I was slammed by a breaking ocean wave. As the sleds were fully buried, I had little concern for them being damaged. It was only the tent and myself that had me worried.

During the day I chomped on the massive stores of butter to

conserve my other food supplies. Although I still had two and a half months of rations, I wanted to be careful with them. As I had apportioned 1.5 blocks of butter per day, I didn't worry at all about eating too much of it. Those bricks of fat made me feel secure in knowing I would not starve, but it was going to be a heck of a time hauling it. I started thinking that I had brought too much butter.

The cough from the lung infection had improved but it was still present. As I lay on my side, listening to the storm roaring outside, I still hacked and coughed. Rolling over on my back seemed to help the cough, but then it became more difficult to breathe. The infection brought back tinges of the asthma that had plagued me as a child. Even though I had done a reasonable job of keeping it suppressed with heavy aerobic exercise, situations like this still brought back that chest pressure.

Near 1 p.m., the sound of the wind changed from roaring to something unlike anything I had heard before. I ventured out and found that the wind tore through three of the six feet of snow blocks I'd placed on the windward side of the tent. My throat closed up in a rush of adrenalin panic. Holy cow!! I was nearly blasted off the continent. In a hurried frenzy, I rebuilt the wall in hopes of saving myself from being destroyed. I knew the tent was supposed to handle this kind of weather, but I didn't want to discover where the limit was.

Once the wind shield was repaired and bolstered, I rested until 3 p.m. in hopes of escaping my camp and making a few miles. I had no such luck. The wind was too severe to even open the door. And, I started hacking and coughing each time I opened the zipper. Somewhere in the back of my mind, I felt the beginnings of disheartening depression about being trapped, unable to travel. I immediately quashed the thought, instead concentrating on the enjoyable time I was having, irrespective of being stuck. Even though it was difficult thus far, it was all part of the experience and it was exactly what I wanted. I thought about listening to an audio book but nixed the idea. I enjoyed being alone with my thoughts, like the explorers a century before.

Camp AC10
80°19.167'S 80°58.284'W
No movement today
Distance to South Pole: 581 nm

(Main) Near Patriot Hills, where ALE had their old camp, the weather was perpetually bad. I deployed the solar panels in hopes of being able to charge up my satellite phone battery, without success.

(Below Left) The kitchen area was always configured the same way every day. Being efficient and not fumbling around looking for items was important. Wasting minutes meant less relaxation and regaining strength for the next day.

(Below Right) I was having a good time but I did not feel well at all in the beginning of the expedition. Coughing took the place of sleeping many nights.

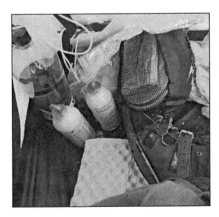

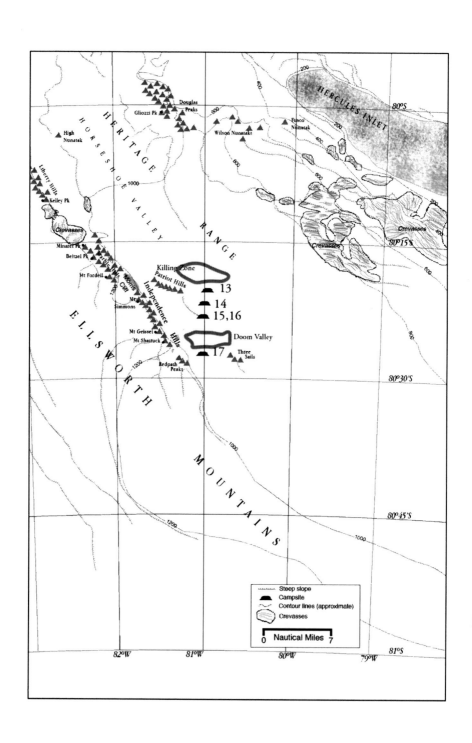

11

DAYS 13-17

TUESDAY, NOVEMBER 13, 2012, DAY 13

ALTHOUGH I HAD STARTED to feel marginally better and was not coughing any more, I still had the energy of a lackadaisical teenager. I rose, rearranged gear, then lay back down on the sleeping bag. 15 minutes later, I reawoke, aware that I had passed out from fatigue. The illness had sucked the energy out of me. Although my spirit craved to fly across the sastrugi toward the South Pole, my body was completely unwilling. This was a rare experience for me, as I am one of those annoying morning people who loves to rise early, thrust his hands skyward and proclaim whatever day it was to be wonderful. How I wished that person would reappear, shaking off the remnants of this respiratory bacteria and kicking me into moving.

At this point, traveling in whiteouts seemed to be the entire Antarctic experience. I knew that these conditions would not last forever, but since I'd been in a whiteout since November 9, it was difficult to perceive this area any other way. The snow must have filled the spaces between the sastrugi because sometimes I was able to ski remarkably fast and then, a few feet later, would sink along with the sleds into a pit that consumed them and my skis. At least for today, it seemed to be an on again, off again problematic relationship with the snow surface. The snow softened up to the point that the sled skis would dig into one side, bury the runner and dump over the sled. There was nothing else to do but stop, ski back, yank and lift the sled onto smooth snow, and resume skiing. As I was still unable to breathe well, the fatigue damped any irritation that welled up inside, thus preserving energy for coaxing the sleds forward rather than wasting it on anger.

The satellite phone battery was close to dead. There was no sun in the forecast tomorrow, either. Although I warmed up the phone in my jacket, the LCD was still sluggish. That suggested the warmth in my jacket was inadequate to keep the phone at the proper temperature. To fix this problem, I packed the phone against one of the hot water bottles and kept it there until the phone felt warm to the touch. Though it took a half hour, the phone seemed to operate better and the battery regained another bar. I was glad to have learned why I needed to keep batteries warm as a young engineer. That training paid off. Until there was sun to recharge the phone, I had to do everything I could to make the battery last.

Camp AC11
80°20.600'S 80°59.366'W
Distance: 1.5 nm, Time: 4 hours
Distance to South Pole: 580 nm

WEDNESDAY, NOVEMBER 14, 2012, DAY 14

This was the second day I woke up more energetic and ready to cover more miles. But, I was denied, slowly postholing for much of the morning. That is, when walking through deep snow, my boots sank into the snow, looking like someone dug holes for a fence post, hence the name postholing. Doing this dramatically increased the walking effort. The GPS showed I was walking at 0.3 MPH and skiing at 0.4 MPH in this deep, ultra-dry snow. My shoulders sagged. I would never reach to the pole at this rate, let alone ski a round trip.

Too, I was stunned at the speed differential. Skiing was plain easier in these conditions, even though my skis constantly slipped backward in the fluffy powder. The ski skins, glued onto the bottom of the skis, normally provided traction. They were smooth and slide easily when rubbed one direction, but were rough when rubbed the other, making it possible to grip snow. But with the drag force I was battling, the skins held onto the top few inches of snow but the layers below broke apart, making forward motion close to impossible. The energy required to tow was astonishing. More than once my legs experienced complete anaerobic burnout, as though I was lifting weights. This was the worst-case muscle use because it was unsustainable, requiring constant rest. The effort cut my speed to virtually nil.

Looking back, the sleds were more like anchors, churning up mounds of snow. The snow was softer than what I had encountered in Yellowstone, something I had not anticipated. More than once, I glanced back and saw the sled bow completely buried, even though I had loaded the heaviest weight in the back, theoretically giving them upward lift in front. In a way, it was funny. They appeared to be submarines pursuing me, barely breaking the snow surface. Even with my skis pre-compressing the snow, the sleds sank. I thought of taking a photo but realized there was nothing to see, as the sleds were buried, it was a complete whiteout, and there was blowing snow.

Also, the whiteout made efficient navigation impossible. I had to use the chest compass holder. I had been using the watch compass up to now, as the wind kept flipping my dangling compass into my face. Though the chest-mounted compass was annoying, it was far easier to use in windy whiteout conditions. Using the watch cost me 20 seconds per check, whereas the chest compass took five seconds. As there was nothing to sight and ski toward, I checked my bearing every few minutes. More than once, I veered off course by over 30°, as the soft snow, wind and blindness made me stagger. The sun disc finally peeked out at 3 p.m., giving me shadows to navigate by, reducing my navigation errors to a tolerable +/-10°. By 4 p.m., farther out targets became discernible, making navigation a snap. The clouds near the sun were beautifully iridescent; I had been waiting to see that. Then, at 5:45 p.m., the whiteout returned right before time to make camp.

Two guides at ALE had said that a deadman placement of tent stakes wasn't necessary in Antarctica. Today I found the case where that advice was invalid. The surface I had been traveling on for the last two hours of the day was a mottled mixture of ice chunks and soft snow all obscured by a delicate shell of ice. When attempting to place my stakes, they met either an impenetrable surface or complete mush incapable of holding the tent. As I probed, there seemed to be no happy middle ground where the stakes broke through but held fast. So, I reverted to making deadman placements, where a hole is dug, then the stake is lain flat inside it, then covered with a mound of snow and stomped on. The compression warms the snow up slightly, solidifying it, freezing the stake into place. Once the snow sets, the stake can only be removed by digging it out. The deadman placement has never failed me in any condition I've ever encountered. The only downside was the extra time they took to remove when striking camp. After seeing ALE's camp and their use of aluminum tent poles for stakes, I should have asked about them. They seemed to be the best option, better than what I brought. Having those would have saved me from more work and bent stakes. But I had to work with what I brought. One stake was already damaged. I needed to make the others last, so I was careful how I jammed them into the ice.

With the sun higher in the sky and the clouds cleared off, it was easier to position the solar panels to supply enough power to recharge the satellite phone. The most crucial equipment maintenance activity to take care of each night was to plug the phone into the solar panel charger. I did this even before lighting the stove to make water. Staying in contact with the world was a top priority. Had I been unable to call, I would have caused an emergency response to a non-existent problem. Six days had passed since I had last been able to use the solar panels to charge anything. I became stressed because the primary phone was down to one bar on the battery. Once it was dead, I'd have to activate the backup phone, something I desperately hoped to avoid. Since it was my backup, there was nothing else to fall back on. Of all the gear that I could deal with or live without, the satellite phone was not it. I needed it to call ALE daily to keep them informed of my whereabouts and status. If I failed to contact them for over 48 hours, they would notify my emergency contacts and proceed with a rescue and recovery effort. If an expedition has three ways to contact the outside world and it hasn't been heard from in two days, the chance that something has gone wrong is exceedingly high. I did not want to trigger an emergency response only because there was no sun to keep my phone charged.

While writing in my journal this evening, I poked my head out of the tent to check on the snow wall to verify it had not been torn apart by the strong winds. While dusting snow off one of the sleds, a coughing fit hit me. All I could do was hack and cough for the better part of a minute. Unable to breathe, I stripped off my face mask and faced down wind. Suddenly, I was wracked by uncontrollable spasmodic coughing, knocking me to my hands and knees. Gulping air, I stared blankly at the snow. Then, my whole body was jolted and I was blinded by an extremely hard cough. A few moments later, my vision returned.

There, in the pristine snow, was a bright little patch of blood.

Never having this happen before, I first thought of some disease I contracted while in Chile. Multiple worst-case scenarios whirled through my mind. I rolled over and laid on the cooling snow for a minute, composing myself. The coughs subsided and I started feeling better, other than the crimson spot in the snow. As I slowly recovered from the bronchitis, my lungs had been badly weakened and this was the result. After the shock wore off, I crawled in the tent, put my gear away and wriggled into the sleeping bag, hoping whatever injury my lungs had sustained would repair itself overnight. At the time, it made sense not to mention this to ALE or my support team to prevent panic. Should I cough up more blood tomorrow, then I would inform the ALE doctors and figure out what to do. I did not cough at all the rest of the night and tasted no blood. Breathing slowly to calm myself, I drifted off to sleep to the mantra of never giving up.

Camp AC12
80°23.066'S 81°01.929'W

Distance: 2.5 nm, Time: 8 hours
Distance to South Pole: 578 nm

THURSDAY, NOVEMBER 15, 2012, DAY 15

Antarctica has literally been a blast. Going now on the third week, ten out of those fourteen days have been horrific weather, either whiteout or 40+ knot winds or both. Being unable to charge the satellite phones for the last seven days, I've limited myself to communicating only with ALE. My expedition manager, Kelly, knows that I will not be in voice contact or blogging until the phones can be charged again. The satellite transponder let me stay in text message contact with her and my sponsors, as it posted my messages to a website so anyone could follow. The electronics required constant attention to keep communication alive with the outside world, so I needed to be stingy with the batteries. My reserve stocks were limited.

Still not feeling healthy, I woke up terribly fatigued and decided to rest another hour to regain my strength. With the wind assault, ground white out and soft snow, I made little progress; it was a mental fight every day to extract myself from the comfort of my sleeping bag. Had I not became ill, my spirits would have been far higher. I knew that the emotional effect of illness was dragging on me. Leaving the tent, striking camp and moving forward made me feel much better. That was until the headwinds started pushing me backward. If I stood any way other than directly into the wind, I was shoved sideways repeatedly. Coupled with deep snow, I made terrible mileage.

In my mind, I entertained a conversation with a virtual weather company about the conditions. I imagined yelling into the phone to the operator on the other side of the line confirming my "weather order." It sounded like this:

"Hello? Hello!? Yes, is this Hell, Inc? Good. I'd like to ask about my weather order today. Yes, order number Linsdau-Antarctica-Day-15. Great, can you confirm the request? Maximum pain and punishment package? Right... Okay, what was in that again? White out, 40 knot sustained winds with 50 knot gusts? Okay... Fogging rather than antifogging goggles came with that? Awesome? At least one-foot-thick snow drifts, mixed with randomly hard-packed ice. Gotcha. Wind straight in my face? Ya. And this all has to be delivered in an uphill section so I can't see where I'm going, with steep sections followed by slick ice to prevent easy sled towing? Okay, was that all that's in the package? Oh, you did throw in the undiscoverable air mattress leak and no sun for satellite phone charging, with the ice in between the two goggle lenses. Are you sure I ordered this? .... Yes, yes, I see. Thank you for checking!"

I felt like I was on the Biggest Polar Loser show all day. The wind was so strong, I worried about being able to strike or pitch my tent without losing or destroying it. As much as my subconscious did not want to leave the tent, there was no option but to do so. I had to move. Cold and wonderfully tough conditions were exactly what I wanted. Unless the winds were 50+ knots, I needed to ski and make progress.

The polar cough was still with me, though it slowly improved daily.

I moved slowly and drifted off course because my goggles fogged between the lenses. Again. Even the fancy goggles I purchased specifically for this expedition were not immune to this problem. I switched to glacier glasses, waited for them to fill with ice, then hung them off the end of my face. They protected my eyes from freezing in the wind, but the gap between the glasses and my face meant I could still see a few feet ahead of me. As there was a ground whiteout, there wasn't much else to do than blindly follow the compass toward the next waypoint. Not seeing was infuriating at times, as it slowed me down. I could either ruminate about the annoyance or keep moving forward. It was a valuable lesson: keep concentrating on the activity. There was no reason to focus on the irritation because all it did was drag me down, wasting valuable energy.

Tonight I enjoyed chili mac with beef as my freeze-dried dinner. However, I quickly learned that spicy food was not the best on a polar expedition. Normally, I love to eat the spiciest foods I can find. But out here, I learned that bland was the better way to go. My stomach rolled 20 minutes after finishing dinner, not altogether stable from the manhandling of the antibiotics. As chili mac was one of my six dinner options, I hoped my stomach would be more stable in a few days. Because I randomly pick out my meals, my rule was whatever I grabbed was what I ate. Doing this prevented me from chowing down on the most desirable meals, leaving the less enjoyable for the end of the trip. Having the least desirable food during the most difficult part of the trip would be unpleasant. Thus, eating whichever food pack I randomly picked was a better way to go. Doing this cut away a source of stress. Though there was the chance of having the same thing three nights straight, the approach eliminated eating the same food for two weeks straight at the end of the trip.

Camp AC13
80°24.490'S 81°03.803'W
Distance: 1.5 nm, Time: 5.5 hours
Distance to South Pole: 576 nm

FRIDAY, NOVEMBER 16, 2012, DAY 16
A horrible noise woke me up at 5:30 this morning. At first I thought it was only the tent flapping in the wind. Then, once my eyes adjusted to the light, I realized the tent wasn't flapping, it convulsed like a team of football players had grabbed ahold of it and were intent on tearing it apart. Gazing out the north-facing window, I saw little. The south-facing window was buried, bowed under the weight of hard-packed snow. The noise was loud enough that it was impossible to even hear myself talk. Unzipping the door, all I saw was a wall of white. The ends of the sleds, a mere five feet away, were invisible.
"Whoa," was all I could muster.
Knowing that the winds had decreased in intensity during the morning before, I initiated the morning routine by eating my cereal with butter. As I poured the cereal, the motion of the tent wall vibrated the air in the tent so strongly that it agitated the granola dust out of the cereal bowl, as though I was next to a four-foot-wide speaker at a concert. Everything trembled. That was okay, I thought, because there was a six-foot snow block wall I had built protecting the tent. The air

compression was intense enough that I had to yawn and pop my ears during breakfast. It was frightening, but certainly this couldn't last long. Then, abruptly, visions of the snow blockade disintegrating in the wind filled my mind. Fear gripped me.

I needed to go outside and check on my tent.

After cleaning up and everything packed, I again unzipped the door and saw nothing but a wall of snow blowing by. I wondered if I would even be able to walk in these conditions. So, rather than pulling in the sleds to pack them out of the wind, I slithered out of the tent, zipped the door shut and crawled to the end of the sleds and turned around, 10 feet away from the tent.

It was barely visible. And I was being pelted with ice chunks, presumably from my shelter wall.

Thoughts of being lost and freezing to death only feet from shelter raced through my mind. I hurried back, yanked the door open and threw myself inside. It took some effort to close the door, as the wind kept tearing it from my gloved hands. Once I sealed it up, I looked around. There was a half-inch of dusty snow coating the contents of the tent. The door had been open for, at most, one minute total. Mike Hoover, the climber and filmmaker I met in Jackson, warned me of days like this. "You had better be ready to sit out a storm for three days," he said. His prophesy seemed to be coming true. There was no way I wanted to take the risk as a soloist of having my tent destroyed or have critical clothing blow away. Had I been on a team, it would have been a different story. Even if I were only to ski a mile, it was one fewer to travel the next day. If the sleds not been buried, they would likely tumble in this wind.

So I lay down and rested for two hours, waiting for the wind to abate.

At 11 a.m., it did. Somewhat. Peeping out of a gap in the door zipper, the ends of the sleds were visible, so I decided to give it a go and hopped outside again. The tent was visible, so I was not going to become lost. I decided to walk upwind without encumbrance to see what it was like. After a minute of stumbling, I looked back. I had, at best, covered 50 feet. Snow still blew far overhead and I estimated the wind was between 45 and 55 knots (51 to 63 miles per hour). It felt as though I stood in a pickup bed on the freeway. More than once, the wind shoved me and I fell onto my side. This wasn't working. Walking back to the tent, I saw the snow block wall had changed to a solid ramp of drifting snow. The sleds were entombed. Since I couldn't safely walk, I retreated to the tent and rested another two hours.

Then the sound of the tent thundering changed. The wind that had torn apart the snow block wall on November 12th was crazy, but it did not sound like this. Never having heard such a sound before; I wasn't sure what it was. The wind had strengthened over the last two hours and I was thankful to be inside, not having risked going out. So to entertain myself with how crazy conditions had become, I unzipped the shelter.

Chunks of ice flew by the open door. I could not see anything but the fronts of the sleds. Everything else was a wall of white. I didn't want to stick my head out for fear of being struck by windblown ice. I was able to shoot some video footage before the cold killed the camera battery. ALE had warned me the wind near Patriot Hills was bad, but I had no idea what bad meant until now. There was nothing to do but lie on the foam mat and wait to see how conditions changed, as going outside was out of the question. For another half hour, the wind screamed at what I could only guess was hurricane force. After some time, it cut back to a mere violent storm strength. Worried about the tent, I put on all the clothes I had and stepped outside to inspect the camp.

The sight shocked me.

The six-foot-thick snow block wall that had turned into a smooth ramp was now only a foot and a half thick and shot full of holes. I had doubled the thickness after the experience on the 12th and the wind had blasted through twice as much this time. The wind had taken a smooth surface and torn it apart, exposing the holes in the blocks which were now being obliterated, too. That going down the roller coaster sinking feeling hit me. What if the wind had lasted much longer? Inspecting each, I saw the tent stakes were half unburied! Unbelievable. They had been fully submerged in the snow, flush with the surface. The wind-blown snow must have swirled around the lines and blasted away the surface snow. The stakes were close to flying out of the snow.

Words again failed me and a general panic struck. Had the stakes been broken free, would the tent have blown away with me? Not likely, as it was half buried in snow anyway. But those flailing stakes would have lacerated the tent and injured me. I staggered back to the tent door, grabbed the shovel and furiously packed snow blocks over the stakes to re-secure them. After doing that, I spent another half hour in 55 knot winds rebuilding the snow block wall on the windward side of the tent. Should violent winds return, the now hole-laden snow wall would have certainly failed on the next assault. Several times the wind nearly ripped the shovel out of my hands. I had to be careful and hold the shovel downwind, as I did not want it to flip up and strike me in the face. Another explorer had warned me about his goggles being shattered by a flailing tent pole in the wind. I did not want to learn what a wind driven shovel would do.

Back in the tent, I yelled out loud in satisfaction at having survived what was probably a hurricane burst of wind, by myself, in the Antarctic wilderness. I hoped not to have to keep this siege defense up for several days as it was by far the worst weather I had ever experienced. Unfolding the foam mat again, I rested from the fatigue of hurriedly building my own miniature Great Wall of China.

I decided to call this area the *Killing Zone*, for had I left at my normal start time, I was not sure what would have happened to me when hurricane-force winds struck.

At 3 p.m., I roused myself and tried to depart for the fourth time. Even if I was to ski a mere two miles like I had done in days previous, I wanted that distance cut from the total trip. It was worth the effort, as lying did nothing for me. Again, I crawled out and was struck by winds that blew me around, making it impossible to walk, let alone tow. At least the snow wall held and the stakes remained buried. There was nothing else to do this day but return to the tent and rest. Since I was still far from being recovered from the residual effects of the lung infection, I felt this day was a gift, forcing me to rest and recover before continuing on the journey.

ALE was not surprised I had not moved, as winds in their camp were remarkably strong. Patriot Hills was known for horrid conditions and now I knew why. I had to do everything I could to break free of the area as quickly as possible, lest even worse weather befall me tomorrow. Only having moved a pathetic 31 miles in two weeks, I knew I was in deep trouble. Being unable to move camps only made it worse. Tonight, after I completed the satellite call to ALE, I inspected my log and saw that there had been 10 days of continuous terrible weather. Still, I felt upbeat because I knew it was still possible to recover the massive mileage deficit. The deleterious fatigue I felt from the bronchitis did not help, but I was happy to be here, living out my dream. After weathering this storm, I felt confident the miles would start picking up if nothing else went wrong.

Camp AC13
80°24.490'S 81°03.803'W
No movement today
Distance to South Pole: 576 nm

Saturday, November 17, 2012, Day 17

After being blasted with hurricane force winds yesterday, conditions were relatively calm this morning. Curious to see what happened outside to the snow block wall and the guylines, I dressed and stepped outside. The landscape had transformed. The sleds were invisible, buried under a foot of hard-packed snow. To the lee side of the sleds, there was what looked to be a 15-foot-long snow drift tailing away, like a smoke stream in a wind tunnel. All around the tent, there were now foot-high sastrugi where, prior to yesterday, there was nothing but flat snow. And these sastrugi were not soft but hard-packed, as though they had been here for weeks. I wished to have been able to film a time-lapse video of the sastrugi appearing out of nothingness. I was certain I would've had an award winning short film.

It took two and a half hours to dig out and pack the tent. There was a foot of hard snow packed surrounding the tent, holding it firm until

I cracked the last pieces of ice away. I wanted to yank the tent free of its icy sarcophagus. But I knew there was the chance of tearing the tent. As it was my home for a couple more months, I treated it gingerly. The way it looked, had that storm continued into today, there was a chance I and the tent would be completely buried. The snow chunks covering the sleds were the size of a child's torso. I was glad to have a shovel, as I could not have broken camp without it.

The relatively flat land I set camp in two days ago had now turned into an endless stream of two-foot-tall knife-edge sastrugi all the way to the horizon. I wished there had been a visible point of reference so that I could have taken before and after pictures. After two hours of skiing, the ice gave way to soft snow. Slowly, the fluff piled up from an inch to over a foot deep. Soft snow was the worst case scenario for towing a pulk. Even my skis sank, the tips snagging on the soft snow, dragging me down. This was the one moment, thus far, when snowshoes would have been a wonderful choice for travel. Based on my testing in Yellowstone, they took 50 per cent more effort and cut the equivalent speed compared to skis. With the snow this soft and deep, I was barely able to pull the sleds. I spent more time slipping than I did moving. I pulled out the GPS and did a quick comparison. The skis gave me 0.55 miles per hour. Walking resulted in 0.84 miles per hour. As much as I did not want to believe it, postholing was more effective than skiing, completely contrary to my experience on day three. Walking took more effort and energy, yet it resulted in more miles. I both loved and hated postholing. After two weeks of travel, all I could do was drag the sleds like a mule. Even though I generally don't resemble one, at this point I felt like one.

Step after step, I fought to ski southward. Every foot moved brought me one closer to the pole. Yet, it was not fast enough. But there was no other alternative other than to keep stomping through the dusty soft snow. I put my head into the wind and kept pulling.

After 3 p.m., the soft snow dissipated, giving way to hard snow and finally to sastrugi again at 4 p.m. Then, the sastrugi grew in height to what they were near this morning's camp.

"Good," I voiced out loud to no one.

I remounted my skis and moved forward. Forging on for several more hours before making camp, I tried to recover the miles I had lost in the soft snow. After the slog earlier today, it felt invigorating to stride out on the skis. The land was relatively flat so, at 6:30 p.m., I was able to stop and build camp.

And then my knees buckled and I fell face forward and lay on the ice in exhaustion.

After I gathered myself, I still felt the residual effects of the lung infection and the fatigue from hours of postholing. After a minute of rest, with my face comfortably planted in the snow, I picked myself up again, dusting myself off. It was time to set camp.

While pitching the tent, I cut out snow blocks to secure it. I excavated chunk after chunk of snow, the same way as I had for two weeks. Then, it happened.

I felt metal snap in my hand. The shovel broke. And with it, the ability to prepare water and protect the tent.

Raising the shovel, I examined the blade hanging from the handle by a sliver of aluminum. I felt nauseous. Fear coursed through me. I screamed pointlessly into the wind and fell to my knees, my whole body shaking with fury and fear.

"No. No. No," I kept saying, my voice choking out a sob.

I bowed my head and finished the job, snapping the blade off.

This had to be a defining moment, I thought.

"If this was how it is, then fine," I said.

There wasn't a moment to waste, the die had been cast, and now this was my lot. I stood up, opened the sled bag, stuffed the handle in, returned to my knees and dug like a dog. In my mind, nothing had changed. I still needed to reach the South Pole and return. So what if it took longer to do everything at camp? I had already suffered a lung infection and was still alive. Certainly I could cope with a shovel blade as a primitive scoop. I knelt down and chiseled away at the snow.

As soon as I was in the tent, I inspected the shovel remnants and figured out a way to reattach the handle. If only I had a drill. Reflecting on what I had, the multi-tool file appeared to be an adequate, if slow, means to dig a hole. Using the sharp edge of the file, I figured I could dig out a hole large enough to accept the handle pins. It would take several days, if not a week, to perform the repair. But with the spare ten minutes available each night while melting snow for water, the task was no more daunting than crossing a continent. Until I repaired it, I would have to kneel to shovel, freezing my knees while digging. Now wary of even snapping the shovel blade, I stopped prying with the blade. Instead, I only chopped and then lifted with it, never again prying. That's what broke the handle off. I had to avert the added misery of breaking the shovel blade, so I was cautious with my scrap of sheet metal.

ALE asked if I could repair the shovel or had a spare. I let them know I was still able to manage with what I had; I told them yes, setting camp only took longer. They made note of it and asked if there was anything they could do for me. At the moment, I said no. But, as it looked now, I would need a replacement shovel and other help if things didn't improve.

Camp AC14
80°28.593'S 81°03.582'W
Distance: 4 nm, Time: 8 hours
Distance to South Pole: 571 nm

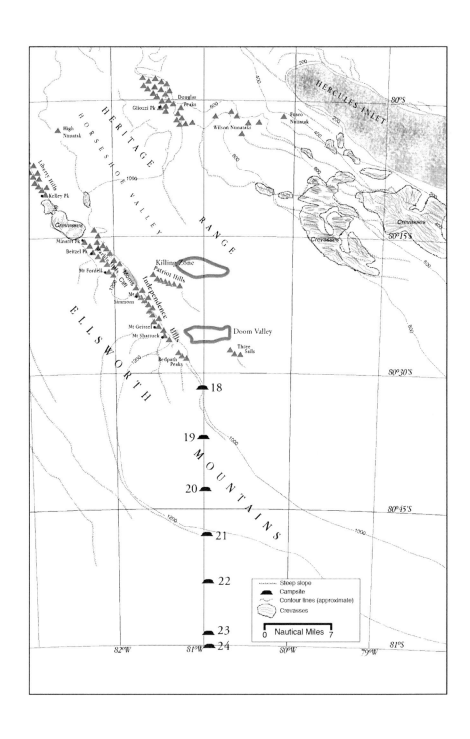

12

DAYS 18-24

SUNDAY, NOVEMBER 18, 2012 DAY 18

AFTER TWO WEEKS in Antarctica, the bottoms of my feet looked like they belonged to a desiccated corpse. These dead areas weren't in patches but rather the entire bottom of my foot. It was covered with dead yellowish skin. Disgusting. Staring at them, I was embarrassed that I had allowed them to deteriorate, as I had gone to great lengths to keep myself halfway hygienic, irrespective of conditions. Using the rough rasp on the multi-tool, I started filing and ground off much of the dead skin. As much as I wanted to expose the flexible, soft skin, experience taught me not to be too aggressive. Doing so would make my feet too sensitive, making skiing painful. Also, my right heel was cracked and it stung. I opened the anti-fungal cream and coated my heel. I guessed the prickling pain was not only from dehydration. My fingers had also begun bleeding from cracks. That, I knew, *was* from inadequate hydration. Although a combination of super glue and hand cream held my finger tips together and kept them soft, the only preventative treatment was to drink more.

Whatever was wrong with my intestines still plagued me. The high-powered antibiotics I took to exterminate my lung infection also killed healthy digestive bacteria. As a consequence, I had not been right for over a week. This impacted my energy level, aside from the weakness still present in my lungs. Even though I had survived the bronchitis, the residual effects afflicted my weakened body. Without a proper examination, there was no way to know what was wrong in my digestive system. And, even with an examination, there was little I could do about it. My body was depleted from the disease and only time was now going to improve my health. To quash whatever had infested my gut, I took an intestinal antibiotic. There was the chance doing that would make the problem worse, but I did not want to end up crippled from nausea.

After cresting a hill I'd been traveling up since sighting Patriot Hills, I felt confident. The surface firmed up and the sleds moved better. Far in the distance, I saw the escarpment between Patriot and Redpath Hills. It looked like an imposing face. From video I had viewed, I knew it to be steep and was worried about crevasses at the top. I did not want to deal with the hill or my worries. Far to the southeast, the Three Sails peaked up on the horizon. Stopping, I put my arms out in triumph. I relished the view of these three peaks, years after reading about and seeing photographs of them. It was invigorating to see real waypoints after so much work to arrive here.

Inexplicably, after I towed for an hour, they disappeared out of sight, as though I was headed down a hill. Staring back, I realized my path had indeed taken me down an indistinct hill. Staying east of Redpath Hills brought me into the first valley I had encountered on the trip. The further south I traveled, the steeper the hill became until the sleds ran into me from behind, imperiling both them and myself. I realized I was headed into a massive hole with a difficult escape.

A heated flush of panic washed over me. What had I placed myself into? Was it even possible to escape from this hole? I adjusted my bearing and tried to keep on a constant contour, not wanting to lose any more elevation. Soon the slope became so steep that the sleds now slipped sideways, rolling over uncontrollably. They dragged me sideways. Forward motion was impossible. Looking right to the west, I saw the Redpath Hills were completely obscured by the now insanely steep slope. The incline was so great that I nearly had to climb with my hands to escape. Looking left, to the east, I saw another massive wall rising up, at least as steep as what I fought now. The southern wall of the valley appeared more approachable. At least my route took me up the easiest incline. All while moving forward, I repeatedly dodged my errant sleds until they crashed and rolled over.

Thoughts of calling Union Glacier and asking their input on this predicament crossed my mind. Checking the GPS, I saw that the suggested path took me at least another day's travel east of Three Sails before heading southward. Great. Another day wasted not on the bearing I needed to follow. ALE did not mention any crevasses in this area, so I decided to head directly south now. I didn't want any more diversions. Too much time had already passed. Reaching the hill and staring up made me feel a sense of doom. How was I to climb that hill? I proposed a name for this place, for the sense of foreboding it gave me: *Doom Valley.*

[*Doom Valley*: 80º32.953'S 81º01.003'W]

Following the GPS coordinates to the east slope of *Doom Valley* was, in retrospect, a better choice. But, now inside of the valley, there was only one route: to the south. After reaching the bottom, I scanned for an easy escape. There was nothing to do but grit my teeth and yank the sleds uphill. This was my first physical test after escaping Hercules Inlet. Time after time, the pulks rose up on sastrugi and flopped over. More than once, they rolled over and tumbled, dragging me backward. I was yanked onto my back with my skis in the air.

Forget this!

Pulling off my skis, I strapped them to a sled and continued working my way up the hill. It felt like being on a leg press for hours on end. It felt as though I was back in the California Sierras, hiking up the famously steep passes. No matter how much I walked, there was no end in sight. I knew this was only a visual effect which simply messed with my mind. Having experienced this illusion countless times, I shook my head to clear it, then stared at the slope twenty feet ahead of me. As long as I kept what was ahead of me in my center of vision, concentrating on the next obstacle, thoughts of the whole expedition did not overwhelm me. Even though the mileage I needed to cover was beyond my current comprehension, I knew that concentrating on these smaller problems would, eventually, turn into real progress.

After seven hours of clawing up the hill, I had not reached the top. In fact, not anywhere near. The Redpath Hills had reappeared above the western wall of *Doom Valley*, so I knew I had climbed. Looking back, I was shocked by the sastrugi rubble I had crawled over. The sled skis snagged constantly, but that was okay. It beat having them slide backwards. By the end of the day, I found a 10 foot by 10 foot site for the tent. I collapsed right there. I had never done seven straight hours of leg presses. Though I was spent, my legs were not throbbing or cramping. Dragging a fifty-pound tire up a 10 percent grade, at 8,000 feet, had paid off.

Camp AC16
80°32.954'S 81°01.011'W
Distance: 4.4 nm, Time: 8 hours
Distance to South Pole: 567 nm

MONDAY, NOVEMBER 19, 2012 DAY 19
Hydration was still problematic. I had not figured out exactly how much water to drink. Some days I was fine, but today again I woke up parched. Yet, I needed to relieve myself frequently, the sure sign that I'd consumed way too much. The problem was that my parched throat compelled me to drink more, only exacerbating the condition. This was something that I have learned to suffer through until my body adjusted. Because I roasted some days while freezing others, keeping a proper hydration level required never-ending management. Due to the freezing cold air, urination was the only way my body removed fluid waste. Not sweating caused my body to shunt all fluids to my bladder.

This morning while inspecting the foot bed liners, I noticed the mylar thermal lining on the bottom was cracked. I relied heavily on that material to reflect back the infrared heat from my feet, keeping them warm and insulated from the 1,000 feet of ice I stood on. Although the heavy ski boots had three layers of insulation to keep me separated from the snow surface, it was inadequate. Another polar explorer, Eric Larsen, had suggested adding an additional layer of insulation to the boots. Even though it seemed like a smart idea, the additional volume threw off the delicate alignment of my feet to the contours of the boot. Even though it would have kept my feet warmer when I was forced to walk, the imbalance it caused was not worth it. While on skis, my feet never chilled, as the skis and bindings built a thermal barrier between me and the ice.

The cough from the bronchitis was still present, but subsiding, while a runny nose kept me busy. I tried to keep myself from devolving to a disgusting mess. For the past couple of days, I used snow as a nose tissue. With the right technique, snow absorbed the drainage without freezing my nose or burning my skin. Though the result was repulsive, my skin was not damaged. Tissues always chafed my skin. And, I did not have enough toilet paper to waste. After battling allergies all my life, this was one trick I had learned that protected my nose. All I had to do was break through the mental block of shoving a pile of snow in my face every five minutes. These mini-breaks devastated my travel speed, but I needed to manage the runny nose. If I kept wiping my nose with my glove, it would chafe, crack, and then bleed, exposing me to possible infection.

After several more hours of slogging uphill, I finally reached the lip of *Doom Valley*. I was so excited that I whooped and yelled a mighty, "Ha ha ha!" like a madman. Escaping the pit allowed me to speed up and start moving aerobically after what seemed like two straight days of leg workouts. After being stuck in frozen super-sized ant lion trap, I was thrilled to escape. And, the best part was there were no apparent crevasses like I was warned about on the pass between Redpath and Patriot Hills. While traveling on sastrugi, it was easy to see why other explorers warned me to stay on my skis. They prevented crevasse falls. After reaching the polar plateau via *Doom Valley*, I wished I had taken the wider path and gone toward Three

Sails, had I known how extensive the valley was. The topographical maps of the area did not adequately describe the valley's depth, nor the steepness of the western and southern slopes. My hope was that by documenting this location, future explorers would not fall into the same trap. Though the sleds rolled over constantly, I told myself not to be frustrated. This was part of the experience. I knew that every time I skied back to right the sleds, it meant I had moved forward toward my goal, however incrementally.

After working on the shovel, I estimated would take at least a week to repair it. A tiny pinhole appeared in the aluminum blade. Progress. But it was still far from being usable. I spoke with dad and mom on the satellite phone tonight and let them know about the shovel failure. Mom reminded me about the poor reviews she had found on the shovel I chose. During the rush of packing, I blew off her warning. And now, I paid for that.

The lesson was don't ignore your mom.

Camp AC17
80°37.356'S 81°00.117'W
Distance: 4.5 nm, Time: 8.5 hours
Distance to South Pole: 563 nm

Tuesday, November 20, 2012 Day 20

I was not fully recovered from the lung infection. As much as I enjoyed challenges, illness in Antarctica was my most difficult ever. Skiing for longer than 15 minutes had been impossible. My energy failed, leaving me bent over and panting. It felt as though I'd never trained, being winded and wiped out.

Suffering from a grumbling gut and unpleasant toilet action did not improve my energy this morning, either. Thinking I had contracted an infection out of my food stuffs, I took a ciproflaxin as a pre-emptive measure, just in case. One of my biggest concerns with using this drug was a well-known side effect. With use over time, it weakened tendons, increasing the likelihood of tears. Every time I took these pills, I thought about one explorer rupturing an Achilles a few days away from reaching the South Pole. He was able to hobble to the finish line and pull it off, but it was a disastrous injury. I could not let that happen. Even though taking only one of these pills would not weaken my tendons, the thought still weighed on my mind.

During the day, I stopped and dealt with a hot spot on my foot. As there was little wind today, I hid my foot on the lee side of the sled and temporarily patched over the spot with duct tape. Stupidly, I had buried my first aid kit at the bottom of my supplies bag which, in turn, was buried deep inside the sled. Although I could spend the time to dig it out, I wanted to resume skiing as quickly as possible. The duct tape was accessible, so it made more sense to perform a quick fix. One skill I had learned from reading stories of Greenland's Sirius patrol was that it was best to keep moving to stay safe and warm. Once I stopped for any significant amount of time, my muscles cooled down, increasing the chance of injury and reduced my mileage. Too, if I had dug deeply into the sled, there was the chance of dropping an unseen item into the snow, never to be seen again. As I had already learned from that error early in this expedition, I was motivated not to make such a reckless mistake again.

One thrilling event was being able to see the moon today while on break. At first, I was not sure what I saw, as the moon blended into the sky when it was low on the horizon. Too, it never occurred to me that it was even visible. With the 24-hour sunlight here, I did not think it possible to see celestial objects, save the sun. It was peculiar not to see stars, for even in New York and Tokyo, a few are visible. Yet, once I recognized it, there the moon was, happily hovering above the horizon. I took a photo of it, as there were clouds on the horizon. I happened to see it because I was sitting on my sled, facing north, and at the right time of day. After the previous whiteout days with winds whipping snow into the sky, seeing the familiar moon sailing across the sky revived me.

The ground whiteout, combined with my flagging energy, resulted in a paltry 4.5 miles of progress. Sitting in my tent, I gawked at the GPS. My shoulders drooped. For as fast I had felt myself go, I was crushed.

"I'll never even make the pole at this rate," I groaned.

For all the test expeditions I had been on, I had never planned on recovering from bronchitis. No one plans or expects to endure an illness during an expedition. Antarctica was the worst place to recuperate, too. Had I been in a stationary camp for a week, I would have been able to recover. But that wasn't the case. These were the conditions I faced and I had to make something out of them.

Those digits showing four point five elicited my first meltdown. It was worse than any I had gone through previously. I had become so wound up on why I wasn't making progress that I sobbed. I felt so horrible that I leapt out of the tent and puked up some dinner. Not much, but enough to tell me that I took this way too seriously. I'd never experienced this before. The emotions hit me with freight train power. Suddenly, out of nowhere, I broke down. It was awful. So many years of planning, dreaming and training all came down to an absolute inability to cover miles. After having spent over two weeks on the ice, I've not even made the first degree, a puny 60 miles. I crossed Yellowstone, 100 miles, in 10 days on snowshoes!

After calming down, I focused on successes. One accomplishment was being able to drill the first hole into the shovel blade, meaning I was halfway to being able to reattach the handle. With concerted effort, I had bored a hole allowing the handle pin to click into the blade. It was unbelievably exciting, considering my complete lack of proper tools. Yet, I was able to fabricate something that worked. This made me think that, though I suffered in other ways, I succeeded in modifying my gear like MacGyver, a technologically resourceful hero in the 1980s television show. With the few supplies available, I was confident that, if nothing else, I would be able to keep this expedition going on guts and ingenuity alone.

Camp AC18
80°42.044'S 81°02.055'W
Distance: 4.5 nm, Time: 8 hours
Distance to South Pole: 558 nm

WEDNESDAY, NOVEMBER 21, 2012 DAY 21

One of the problems I finally dialed in today was the proper order and rate at which to eat the rations. Kelly told me that she, too, felt ill if she ate immediately after resting from a heavy activity. So she suggested I rest a few minutes before powering down anything. This was all important to figure out, as the third week was when my body finally needed 6,000 calories a day. Since my expedition calories consisted of a fat-rich diet, I continually experimented to find the optimal eating order. After several modifications, it finally seemed to feel right. The energy didn't burn up too quickly, yet I felt strong after eating.

I ate the following in this order:

Lara bar, chocolate bar, Pro-bar, five shortbread cookies, shot blocks and then almonds. In addition, I ate 25 grams of butter during each break, completely consuming a full stick by day's end. If I felt run down at the end of the day, I had an additional three cookies in reserve.

With light winds, it was an optimal day to test different pacing, when to eat, when and where to take breaks. Up to this point, my hours were not consistent, so I squandered valuable skiing time. The pressure to keep going and do the best I could, irrespective of conditions, was intense.

Wind also contributed to navigational drift. Even though I sighted sastrugi to ski toward, the wind kept blowing me off course and making my targets disappear. In strong wind, I mentally adjusted my bearing to keep in a straight line. Ultimately, I needed to head dead south at 180°. But to reach the next waypoint, I had to travel at 164°. Chasing GPS coordinates that were off course kept my mind occupied. I needed to keep on a course that diverted me from my goal, yet that was the safest way to reach the Pole. And, when the wind picked up, I drifted up to a half mile west each day. The last way I wanted to travel across an entire continent was haphazardly, bouncing off this and that, adding excessive miles to the already daunting task. Travel required constant vigilance.

So far this trip was an insane trek through an alien place, unlike anywhere I had been. Although the training trips through Yellowstone had been a realistic training for dealing with cold, the park had no sastrugi or severe wind, nor had it required any navigation. I wondered aloud if there was anything else I could have done to be more prepared?

Camp AC19
80°47.439'S 80°57.390'W
Distance: 5.5 nm, Time: 7.5 hours
Distance to South Pole: 553 nm

THURSDAY, NOVEMBER 22, 2012 DAY 22

I woke up at 5:30 a.m. and prepared breakfast. Even though I set the alarm for 6 a.m., I was already a week behind schedule, so I had to make up mileage by getting out of bed before the alarm.

"You have to get out of bed any time you wake up after 4:30 a.m.," I said aloud to the tent. Otherwise I simply laid there, staring, neither resting nor traveling. I had already been here for three weeks and hadn't even broken across the first degree. Until I hit my first cache and dropped some serious weight, this was going to be one tough trip. Now I knew why other teams had cached early or at every degree. Dropping weight was such a boon that I yearned to set a cache at the first possible opportunity.

The most difficult part of rising that early was eating a heavy breakfast and not puking. The stick of butter in my meal of cereal, milk and sugar bothered my stomach. The calories were absolutely necessary. But for all the bulky breakfasts I ate, this one kept hitting me hard. Until I started skiing, I did not feel well. Kelly suggested that instead wolfing down the food in one sitting, I should take my time eating as I prepared gear for the day. That way, it did not hit my stomach in one shot.

Although I only covered 6 miles in 9 hours today, I felt better about it. After climbing a long hill for four hours, I was happy to halt at a pleasantly flat spot. With my hydration fully under control, and feeling better from the lung infection, my spirits rose. The problem was that, though I felt satisfied about the mileage, it still was far less than I needed. Given all that had already happened, I had to figure out a way to make the round trip happen.

While melting snow for water, I discovered the lid to one of the Lexan bottles had started leaking. It was ice free, appeared to seal and yet it dripped water. Unbelievable. Although these bottles had served admirably for so long, this one outright failed. It was fortunate that I learned to check bottles by flipping them upside down and squeezing them in Yellowstone two years ago. Even the slightest water spill in a down bag was a disaster. That's why I placed the bottles in water-proof bags before putting them in my sleeping bag. Accidents happen. There was no way I was going to suffer a dumb mistake like that out here. There were plenty of other problems to deal with as it was.

I had completed drilling out the second hole in the broken shovel blade. The handle was now reattached. After testing the repaired shovel, I realized that without the aluminum sleeve the two pins holding the blade were not strong enough. The blade still flopped around. It needed one more hole, with a screw through it, for strength.

"It will only take a few more days," I told myself. I said anything to keep frustration at bay.

Tonight I ate a whole dinner for the first time. Until now, it was always too much food. ALE inquired about my food supplies tonight.

"How are your rations doing? Will you have enough to make the trip?" asked the operator.

"Yes, I am doing very well on food. I have a few spare cookies left over every day," I said.

"Good. Very good. How are you feeling?"

"Much better, thanks! I'm feeling more energetic and made another mile today."

I knew I might need the leftover cookies, so I kept them stashed in case of an emergency. Now I needed to figure out how to withstand skiing 12 hours each day.

Camp AC20
80°53.634'S 80°58.123'W
Distance: 6.2 nm, Time: 9.5 hours
Distance to South Pole: 546 nm

FRIDAY, NOVEMBER 23, 2012 DAY 23

At 4:29 a.m., I argued with myself about resting more or waking up and moving.

"If you look back at your life and couldn't stand losing one hour of sleep a day to make up for a week of short mileage, why are you here in the first place?" asked my explorer self.

"Because I need rest to keep up the miles I'm making," said my logical self.

The two argued for a few more minutes. I rose out of bed. I felt strong.

By midday, I felt abysmal. Constipation felt like a punch in the gut as I skied through the day. Chilblains developed on my hips and thighs from being exposed to the wind for bowel movements. Today, even when my stomach hurt, chilblains worried me so much that I did not want to go out. The last two days of winds ripping my bum had burned my skin. I swore out loud. I needed to figure out a way to deal with it. I built a temporary shelter by placing the sleds upwind of me, creating a wind block. Then, I dug a hole with my broken shovel and then did my business. It was much more pleasant to be out of the wind. But still, I'd have liked to have a tarp or some shelter. When the wind reached 25 knots, it blew snow and frostbite-cold drafts around the sleds, making the air swirl from all directions. The wind exacerbated the chilblains, making them hurt, feeling as though someone took a razor blade to my hips and bum. I made a skirt out of one fleece jacket and it helped, though only a little. I daydreamed about old-school thermal overalls with a back hatch, then laughed at the thought. I used to deem them silly but now they were appealing. The problem was they were too hot for me. These were complications I didn't anticipate, as I've never been out on a completely exposed plateau with no shelter for hundreds of miles.

For the first two hours after leaving camp at 7:30 a.m., there was punishing sastrugi, then a long, four-hour climb to the top of a hill. On the way up, my right ski slipped, snagged and partially tore off the ski skin. One screw was missing and the other half-ripped out.

More swearing.

Even though I despaired, I was happy to have the one screw hold, as it prevented complete skin detachment. I tried to make a repair and reattach the skin but swiftly realized I needed shelter to do this. The glue doesn't bond at this temperature. And, with wind blowing ice onto the skin, it was impossible to reattach it outside of a tent. It was going to take a hot water bottle to melt and reactivate the skin glue.

This meant walking the rest of the day.

After burning out from walking for 45 minutes straight, I realized how much worse walking rather than skiing was here. It took more energy and provided less speed. Postholing was crushing. I couldn't believe how difficult walking on the packed Antarctic surface was. I admired those who slogged through and walked the whole trip, but I did not envy them.

All the while my mind ruminated about these issues, I was intent on moving forward, fighting in the relatively light 15 knot wind.

Then, it happened.

My rope traces yanked back on me. Hard. Glimpsing backward, I dreaded what I would see.

One bracket holding the skis to my sleds had broken while the sled slid through a last patch of sastrugi, right before the ground cleared up. The ski dangled in the wind, uselessly swinging back and forth. Shuffling back to the rolled over sleds, I inspected the damage. I saw it was irreparable.

I fell to my knees and wailed.

How in the world did this happen, out in the middle of nowhere, right before a long stretch of clear ground? I punched the snow and then tore off my mask in disgust, all the while yelling, "No!" into the wind. At the moment I was doing better and making progress, the metaphorical wheels flew off. I extricated my tools from the mortally wounded sled and disassembled the remaining brackets, freeing it of the flopping ski. I wasted energy yelling into the wind. The only reward was mild hypothermia from lingering too long.

The design was flawed from the beginning. I trudged away from the scene of the wreck. Without a bolt through the bottom of the sled, the bracket was doomed to break. It was likely the rig would have held together far longer with a bottom bolt than without, but having that hole would have increased the chance of cracking the bottom of the sled. That in turn would virtually guarantee that the sled would have split in half, forcing me to ask for assistance and costing a minor fortune to keep me going. My design was meant for flat, soft snow. The ski mounts weren't built to sustain the lateral sastrugi impacts. I never even thought about this in my planning.

I was crushed. First, the ski skin tore, making me stumble while walking through sastrugi. Then, two hours later, the lead pulk ski broke. I occupied the next hour walking and cursing. Eventually I calmed down, refocused on skiing and moved on.

Although the sled drag was worse, tracking improved. The sleds didn't pull as bad laterally, keeping more in line. Rather than being ten feet off my travel line, they held within two feet of my ski tracks. Thankfully, the drag was less than I anticipated. The realization dawned on me that everything would be okay, despite what had happened, helping to calm me down. It may not be as grave as I first thought. More than once, over the last three weeks, I had thought of removing the skis and using the bare sleds. However, I didn't want to risk reconfiguring my sleds and have them fail. Now that choice had been made for me.

Not wanting to stop short, I sledged until 6 p.m. to make up for the time lost removing the broken ski.

Later that night, ALE doctor Diedre Galbraith told me that chilblains can crack, bleed, become open sores and ultimately become infected if they're not managed. The scheduled satellite call became more of a medical advisory than a position update. I needed to be aggressive in their treatment. Kelly suggested making a set of crotchless boxers for wind protection during bowl movements. I became desperate to devise a solution for my freezing bum. To let my subconscious originate with a fix for the chilblains, I refocused on reattaching the skins.

Once I warmed up the ski and its skin, I started in on their repair. It took two hours to modify, heat, glue and screw the skins back onto the skis. Using a Swiss Army knife from my Boy Scout days, I drilled holes for five additional screws. Now I was confident that the skins would stay in place for the remainder of the trip. The entire tail of the skin was now steel. I should have screwed them down at the outset. Not having adequate experience, it never occurred to me the skin could rip loose. With seven screws securing the nylon, I'd be amazed if the skin tore again.

After I completed the ski repair, I began conjuring up a way to upgrade my polar thigh guards to keep my hips and bum from degenerating into one festering open sore. I lay there and pondered what to do. The chilblains stung my hips, making it difficult to sleep, giving me plenty of motivation to formulate a solid solution.

As Aleksander Gamme noted in his blog, his inner seamstress emerged in full fashion when he repaired his gear. I'd be that seamstress tomorrow.

Camp AC21
80°58.136'S 80°57.203'W
Distance: 4.5 nm, Time: 10 hours
Distance to South Pole: 542 nm

Saturday, November 24, 2012 Day 24

From beginning to pack to skiing away took 1.5 hours. Cold made everything slow. Thinking of ways to start moving earlier, travel faster, and cover more ground were constantly on my mind. Time was my only remaining resource to throw at making the round trip possible. There was nothing else to tap.

At least there's one accomplishment I was proud of thus far. I sewed a full double-lined fleece seat into my Polar Thigh Guards. It took six hours from my travel day, but it was worth it to prevent further chilblains. Whenever I faced downwind, my bum burned. That wasn't pleasant. It was only a matter of time before the diminutive sores developed into unmanageable chilblains. With this modification to manage toilet activities in the wind, I knew I'd feel better. It made sitting more comfortable, too. As I sewed most of the day, all I heard in my head was mom asking me if I wanted her to add a seat.

"Are you sure you don't want me to add it? It won't take very long," she said.

"No, thanks mom. I think this will work just fine."

Again, she was right. Classic.

On the satellite call tonight, I spoke with Hannah McKeand, the most experienced long distance Antarctic skier in the world. She was preparing for her sixth trek across the continent.

She warned me this was a land of rolling hills and said I should be able to do 1.5 miles per hour if weather was stable. While going up a steep hills, it was safer to take the skis off for better footing, then put the skis on after the ice flattened out. Instead of my hour-long sessions, she does sessions of 75 minutes and takes ten minute breaks.

"It's much better to travel slower and more consistently. A one-minute stop will result in a loss of 300 meters," she said.

"You're right about that. I've been thinking about it for a bit," I said.

"It's very important to be rigid in your schedule here, otherwise you lose too many miles."

"Okay, thank you very much. I will have to implement this tomorrow. I have fallen badly behind."

"We know. Good luck and keep it up. Cheers."

I will stick with six 75-minute sessions tomorrow.

After speaking with Hannah, Steve Jones came on the line. I finally received the call I had been dreading for several days. It was the, "Let's talk big picture," phone call. We discussed the round trip and quickly concluded there was no way I was going to make it at this point. That was clear. If I did not figure out a way to do at least ten miles per day, there's no way I'll even reach the South Pole now. He offered a free cache pickup at 82°30'S, as they're doing a pickup for another team. It should take me about ten days to arrive there at my current rate.

"Just be aware, the best you've done is six miles. It doesn't look good."

"Yes, I'm quite cognizant of that. I'll change my approach as Hannah suggested."

"Good. I hope to hear better progress in the coming days."

So far, the expedition math did not add up to an attractive picture.

Out of 87 possible travel days, 22 were used and I had 65 days of rations remaining. My current travel speed suggested I won't make it. A round trip was beyond a Herculean effort, especially since I was only now feeling better after the bout with bronchitis. I needed to plan for a 50-day run to the South Pole and accept that accomplishment. That meant I was loaded with 15 extra days of supplies, a whopping 33 extra pounds. Using Hannah's schedule, I hoped to fare far better tomorrow. Something drastic needed to happen.

Tomorrow I desperately hope to ski 10 miles. This will be done by skiing slowly with no stops, enforcing 10-minute breaks and being harsh on myself.

Camp AC22
80°59.344'S 80°57.108'W
Distance: 1.2 nm, Time: 1.5 hours
Distance to South Pole: 541 nm

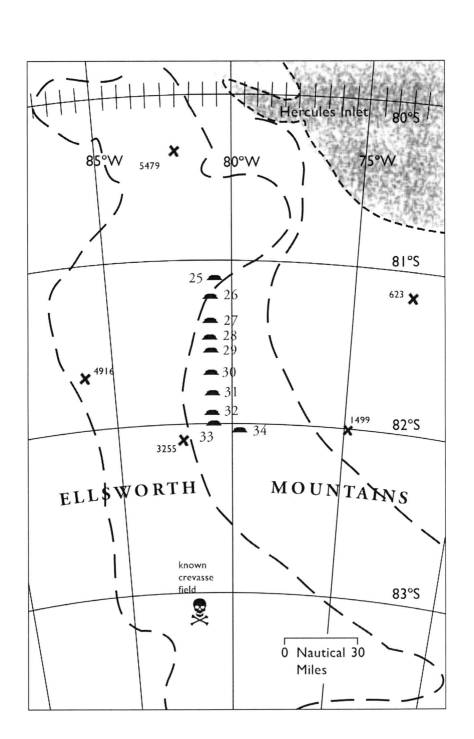

13

Days 25-34

Sunday, November 25, 2012, Day 25

THE SLEDS HAVE RECEIVED names based on their personalities, Charlie Red and Charlie Blue. The colors were for the sled bags. They were named after Charlie, my expedition manager's peculiar pug who was often reluctant to come out of his kennel, needing to be coaxed out. These sleds were reluctant to move and liked to stick in sastrugi pits, hence their names. With Blue's skis broken, I moved the 20-pound electronics and supplies bag to Red when loading the sleds this morning, making Blue as light as possible, keeping the drag force balanced. With that change made, I'll now do 75-minute travel sessions with 10 minute breaks. During the day, I was able to eat a food bar and chug my water in 9 minutes, only gagging once. It was not pleasant but it did work. How in the world Hannah McKeand takes 10 minute breaks was still a mystery to me. My efficiency needed a serious upgrade. I still had to shuffle water bottles, grab more food and relieve myself. After doing this trip five times, she must have it down to a science.

The major fear right now was that the skis on Charlie Red would break away. If that happened, I was not sure what I'd end up doing to manage sled drag. Gamme broke and then lost the skis on his sled, and I was sure others have dropped dead weight. They were a dead five pounds. It was tempting to dump the skis I've been carrying, as they broke off the sled on November 23rd. My idea was to keep a spare ski in case mine broke. Without tools, a vise and drill, it was impossible to replace the broken ski bracket.

I suffered a huge drift to the east [left] today. The winds were near 30 knots, shoving me far off course. I had adjusted my course windward to compensate. This time the wind misaligned my navigation, wasting valuable travel distance in lateral motion. While all this was happening, the song "Monster Mash" played in my head all day. I learned to embrace rather than fight whatever song stuck in my mind. As I have a decent library of tunes in my head, I had little use for the iPods I brought.

My first attempts to emulate Hannah's schedule failed because I needed to adjust my clothing to fit the new regimen, as I generated far more heat. After a half hour, I was on fire, even with strong winds and -20°F temperatures. But after making some adjustments, I felt more comfortable. I ended up towing with light clothing.

On breaks, I found five chugs of water upon stopping and then another four chugs after eating kept me from feeling parched. Each chug was roughly one ounce of water. I gagged on the cookies, but I chewed down the first food without issue. I'd forgotten to break up the second food bar last night, so I had to crunch it apart without breaking teeth. That wasted time and caused lots of gagging. The chocolate was tolerable. Butter caused some gagging. I learned to eat more like a wolf, not chewing my food. I had never anticipated having to relearn to eat.

A strange mental image developed in my mind during the afternoon. When I was skiing, each time I stopped off schedule, I envisioned a virtual self continuing to ski on ahead of me. That specter rapidly distanced itself from the real me, showing me how much distance was lost to wasteful stops. Instantly, I became determined to keep on schedule no matter what. After a few calculations, I estimated every minute stop cost me at least 100 yards.

Fifteen little stops added up to a mile lost. Every day.

Now, with all of these adjustments, I made huge mileage, over 30 percent more than I had in any one day over three weeks of being here. Hannah's suggestions made such a difference that it seemed unbelievable. Yet, I had done eight miles. Hopping up and down with excitement, I yelled and cheered into the wind. Here I was, with the advice of a seasoned expert, making real distance.

On tonight's scheduled call, Steve offered to fly in a plane, pick up some of my supplies and forward them to 88 degrees. This would likely be possible in three days. Or, he said I can slug it out to 82°32' and drop a cache for ALE to pick up later. Either way, I would lose my unsupported status. But, not making the South Pole was absolutely unacceptable, so I faced harsh reality. Based on how I did tomorrow would determine whether I asked ALE for support or keep forging on.

I also bonked out today, my muscles completely failing me. Was my magnesium or sodium too low? I had it dialed in for training, but without consuming 6,000 calories per day. If I double up the dosage now, the addition will take a week to show improvement. But as I cramped up sitting in my tent, I knew my muscle efficiency was poor. My body needed more electrolytes. I'll see how much I can push myself tomorrow to determine whether it was the new schedule making me flame out. I'd prefer to remain unsupported, though finding a reason to justify the extra punishment escaped me.

When I was preparing tomorrow's food, I pulled out the salami I brought and decided to give myself a sizable protein kick, something that had been relatively limited in my diet. The thought of tasty salami made me salivate.

That was, until I saw that there had been moisture inside the packages.

Dang.

At some time, when the wind stopped during the night some days ago, the sled bags must have warmed up and slightly melted the salami. It was unbelievable. Here I was, in the middle of Antarctica, with my food thawing out, even though the air was -20°F. Now there was the chance the salami had gone rancid and become infested with bacteria or mold. Forlornly looking at what was once tasty meat, I suppressed the urge to eat it. With everything else that had gone sideways thus far, the last problem I needed was to suffer food poisoning in the middle of Antarctica and require evacuation. That was not how I wanted this story to end.

Camp AC23
81°07.271'S 80°53.796'W
Distance: 8 nm, Time: 10 hours
Distance to South Pole: 533 nm

MONDAY, NOVEMBER 26, 2012 DAY 26

For as sunny and windy as yesterday was, today I awoke to a ground whiteout, heavy cloud cover and a 30 knot wind. It was going to be a tough travel day without the sun, making it much colder. This made my clothing choice more difficult, since, if the sun began to show through the clouds again, I would have too much on and overheat. Today I donned the vest under my parka but kept it unzipped. With the towing harness over my shirt, any clothing change necessitated a two-minute stop.

My new system of scheduled discipline disintegrated with an energy crash at noon. It was from pushing against the strong headwinds and then dealing with a toilet break at 3 p.m. I was destroyed. By 4:30 a.m. the next morning, I couldn't sleep any longer but tossed and turned until I rose at 5:45 a.m.

These rotten nights of sleep, stemming from the stress of figuring out what to do, now that the round trip was out of the question, were starting to kill me.

The whiteouts were emotionally frustrating and mentally straining. It was like having fogged up goggles: patently irritating. The 30-knot winds made it a total test of patience. The wind was strong enough that I would stumble when turning away from it. This all ended up being a recipe for a low-mileage day. Each time a strong wind picked up, the Kansas song "Dust in the Wind" played in my mind.

All day, I pondered on whether to lose my unassisted status by having ALE forward supplies and situate caches for me to ensure I reached the South Pole. During the scheduled call, Steve estimated that it'll be at least 40 days to the pole for me, but would a cache drop be that significant a difference? I fantasized about how to make the sleds hover. It was a childish dream. My only options were to pitch food or consume it much faster. By the end of the day, all that happened was that I was blown around by the wind. Even though I made forward progress, it felt more like stumbling in a general direction with no particular purpose.

Tonight, I worked on removing the broken bracket from Charlie Blue's skis but was unable to break the glue to remove the screws. My mounting job was surprisingly strong. I pried forcefully with the multi-tool but did not want to break it, as Todd Carmichael had done on a video I had seen. Once that tool was broken, I'd have nothing to work with in the event something else needed repair. It wasn't worth the risk. As a consequence, the sled was irreparable. There was still the option to keep the skis as backup. However, based on my tool's inability to extricate the bracket from the sled ski, I did not think it possible to remove the binding from my ski, either. There was the chance of breaking my multitool removing the screw. It was impossible without a heavy Phillips screwdriver. That was one tool I now saw as essential but didn't have. Now the sled skis were dead weight.

I sent Kelly a satellite text message asking how many Americans have made it unsupported and solo. If there have only been a few, I'll slog it out to see if I can still make something out of the situation, even if it only means a five-day difference. Had there been many Americans who had done this, I'd set a cache with ALE to make it easier.

Kelly said she had received two emails. One said to keep my days to 9 hours. "Past that, you really start to fall apart." That was certainly true. At nine hours, I was dead on my skis. The advice was both sage and timely, as I slept poorly. So, from now on, I made my normal schedule to be from 9 a.m. to 6 p.m. As long as I don't have to deal with too many field toilet activities, it will be a manageable schedule.

Another supporter suggested I write out, on paper, all the reasons to stay unsupported or to ask for help. That should help clarify the issue. At best, utilizing assistance will make me five days faster, though more like three. The thought was that, when I reach 80 years old, I'll regret not toughing it out, as this may be my only shot at this expedition. I hoped I would not regret it the moment I put in the request for help.

Camp AC24
81°13.960'S 80°57.183'W
Distance: 6.7 nm, Time: 9 hours
Distance to South Pole: 527 nm

TUESDAY, NOVEMBER 27, 2012 DAY 27

Sitting on a sandwich of the air mattress, Z-rest sleeping pad and sleeping bag, I ate my 27th breakfast of granola, sugar, whole powdered milk and butter. The random thought occurred to me that I learned how much this trip made me appreciate the people I have in my life, especially my immediate family. Every time I thought of them, tears filled my eyes of how I missed them. They're the best to me, even when I acted like an overdriven jerk. I hoped that this expedition would temper any vestige of the ingratitude of my younger years.

My brain and body were acting like a tachometer. When pushing it hard, negative thoughts crept in. And, I started suffering random annoyances, such as my bum and scalp itching, heels burning and thighs aching. Some mechanism, deep down inside of me, made every effort to slow down my progress. As soon as I slowed down or even stopped, all those symptoms instantly disappeared. Even slight forward motion brought these irritations right back. None of them had anything to do with actual skiing and towing, and yet they were real. It took superhuman effort to resist scratching, as I knew that scratching led to all-day irritation. Over most of the day, I experimented with dialing in the speed to keep the negative thoughts under control before they manifested themselves physically. However, this speed was still too slow.

The surface in the morning had been covered in soft shell snow, so both ski poles and baskets sank four inches below the surface, dragging me down. With an easier pace in the afternoon, I didn't feel as nauseated while eating. I had not gagged on the food for several days and was determined to ward off indigestion. Eating too much butter at each sitting seemed to initiate this problem, so I reduced the daily butter consumption from 1.5 blocks per day to one. If my adjustment worked, it meant that I had brought far too much butter. Learning to maintain the right speed to keep heat, hunger, irritation and pain all in balance required constant tuning. It was one of the most fun engineering problems I had ever had the chance to tackle.

With eight degrees of latitude remaining, there were 480 nautical miles yet to travel. To do it in 40 days, I needed to average 11 miles per day, mileage I've not even come close to achieving. As the pulk weight decreased, I should speed up. Other explorers reported increases in speed near the end. I wondered how much the altitude and body fatigue will eat into that. At least the dead silence from lack of wind in the evening was pleasurable to listen to. It was nothing like I'd experienced anywhere. Even in the Moroccan Sahara, where I'd camped years before, there was some sound reflected off the sand. Here, the snow ate it completely.

Camp AC25
81°20.869'S 80°58.807'W
Distance: 7 nm, Time: 9 hours
Distance to South Pole: 520 nm

WEDNESDAY, NOVEMBER 28, 2012 DAY 28

I woke up to a total, surreal silence again. Finally, this was the first night in a month that I slept completely through. The tent hadn't boomed me awake overnight through my normally impervious silicone earplugs. Though the tent was secure, the wind noise was incredible. Based on ALE's comments, their heavy clam-shaped and four-season dome tents fared no better.

The surface hardened enough to allow the sleds to glide today! After much experimentation, I had the loads adjusted for optimal performance.

Charlie Blue contained: electronics bag, sleeping bag, down sleeping mat, foam pad, food and butter, three liters of water and the miscellaneous bag with food thermos, duct tape, cup and any empty bottles. Any heavier and the sled would drag rather than glide. Based on the ski failure of Charlie Blue, I expect that when, not if, Charlie Red breaks, I'll be in real trouble. It contains all the fuel, making it heavy. The fuel cans will then need to be spread between the two sleds, making them susceptible to damage. If any of those cans cracks and spills fuel into my sled, it'll be an expedition killer. ALE warned me to be careful because fuel spills have happened to more experienced expeditions. I was always teetering on the bleeding edge of destruction in Antarctica. Stumbling through whiteouts was unavoidable, but the threat of the second sled's potential failure was emotionally taxing.

The sastrugi repeatedly made me fall over on my skis to the point I feared I would break them or me. So, for the first time in a while, I removed my skis and took to walking. Although I did not fall over, I slipped and slid constantly using only my boots. Without being able to see, it was as though I had been stricken blind, then was forced to maneuver through a construction site, all while towing 300 pounds.

More than once, I heard the dreaded "wump" sound above the noise of the wind, an indication that I was on a crevasse and it was ready to swallow me. The sound was similar to the start of an avalanche. Falling into a black hole was my principal fear. I could fight through everything else. Obsessing about falling down a mile deep crevasse wore my emotions raw. Every time I heard that sound, I sucked in my breath and readied myself to be smashed against ice. Being blind and in such a precarious situation was harrowing. After the third time in an hour hearing that noise, I put on my skis. Even though I fell and stumbled on the knife-edged sastrugi, the skis improved my chance of bridging rather than falling through a crevasse. At this point, all I could do was laugh. Each time I grew angry at my blindness, I lost energy, whereas laughter strengthened me.

Later I learned this sound was from a *drop slab* of snow where the top snow layer has hardened above a softer lower layer. When skiing across it, the top layer can break away to the lower layer, creating the "wump" sound. There was no physical danger but the sound was terrifying while skiing blind in a whiteout.

Gamme, Cas and Jonesy had warned me to stay on the skis no matter what. Apparently, they must have run into problems on their own traverses. Several times during the day's battle, I broke into tears, imploring the Almighty's help. In Landsing's *Endurance*, Earnest Shackleton did this, too. As he was experienced and had a tough team with him, I feel less amateurish about breaking. It was unnerving to be stumbling on skis over sastrugi I could not see. I imagined the sound of a crevasse breaking apart under me, swallowing me permanently. No matter how brave I tried to be, the worry ate away at me.

While walking blind, I tended to hit a sastrugi wall and then turn right to circumvent it. My reasoning was that the upwind side of each patch was sharply defined, whereas the lee side trailed off for up to 100 feet. It was easier to find that edge rather than wondering how far the leeward side of the patch was. Circumventing sastrugi patches ate into my travel like nothing else. Also, constantly heading upwind caused me to drift westward. To compensate, I adjusted the compass five degrees to the east to balance out the variance. Although it worked, the back and forth wandering wore me out.

Tonight I was able to talk with my parents on the satellite phone. My dad related how the Inuit (Eskimo) had used walrus ivory saws to build their igloos. I was astonished. Even though the ivory tusk was strong, it seemed that a bone saw would be brittle and fracture easily. Examining the remnants of the broken shovel that I have spent two weeks repairing, I realized that even though this was a tough situation, I wasn't laden with a bone saw. At least the aluminum blade could be beaten and readjusted if necessary. Once an ivory saw broke... I could only imagine the hardship for its owner.

Camp AC26
81°27.971'S 81°04.722'W
Distance: 7 nm, Time: 9 hours
Distance to South Pole: 513 nm

Thursday, November 29, 2012, Day 29

A light snow fell all night, leaving three inches of fluff on the ground. That, combined with an afternoon of full whiteout, made this an adventurous day. Whiteouts were better than fighting through gale force winds, but barely. Being blind was psychologically crippling and allowed my primitive mind to overtake my emotions.

My primitive mind was adept at being lazy. It made me prematurely hungry, thirsty and induced the need to urinate. My scalp, bum or hips itched, creating pains where there were none. It forced my emotions to run rampant, frustrating me with anything causing a stop. The worst problem was that it formed an upwelling of negative thoughts. I knew this part of my brain was persistent and have fought with it before, but never to this degree. I had a two-hour discussion with my primitive brain about travel in Antarctica.

I explained to my primitive brain that if we stop, we grow cold. My primitive brain doesn't enjoy being cold and neither do I. Consequently, I struggled through the last half hour and completely slogged for the last 10 minutes. It was rather strange now that I've become conscious of the duality in my mind. The primitive part of my body does anything to be lazy while my conscious self was aware that these "problems" were a psychosomatic reaction to wanting to slow down and take it easy. The conscious brain knows there's nothing wrong. It was all noise and mind junk in my head.

Imagining myself from a helicopter view, I saw myself skiing alone, towing two orange sleds, stumbling along in a total whiteout, muttering to myself the whole time, keeping up both sides of a conversation like a mad man.

But, knowing the sleds dropped two pounds each day from food consumption was a thought I clung to. I hoped to have a pleasant weather day soon and open up the speed. I've given Antarctica plenty of respect and worn layers of clothes to stave off whatever happens during the day, like drastic changes in wind. Now, the change in schedule caused problems. Unless I was on the edge of miserably freezing, I couldn't power up to tow hard enough, yet stay cool to keep moving during a full 75-minute session. I begged for the sun to appear tomorrow and the winds to lighten, allowing for lighter clothing, making it possible to ski hard, pushing myself to the edge of burnout.

My camp efficiency had improved. Staking the sleds, setting all the guy lines, securing the tent to them, digging up snow for both protection and water, placing those protective ice blocks on the tent, dragging the sleds to the door, then slinging all the gear in, and finally setting to work on firing up the stove now only took an hour. Tonight, after stopping at 6 p.m., I had water heating by 6:55 p.m.

Finally. I'd covered 100 nautical miles. That only left over 500 more to go.

Sadly, it only took me 10 days to cover 100 miles dragging sleds in Yellowstone, not the 29 days it took in Antarctica. The sleds were only 160 pounds in total at that time, though. I thought about Ray and Jennie Jardine and how they made it to the Pole with supply drops in less than 60 days using long fiberglass sleds with runners. Though other teams had used plastic Paris sleds, I surmised they were not loaded as heavily as mine. The drag performance of the sleds in snow must have an optimal operating weight. My rig must be way beyond it right now. I had several break-out moments when my speed ticked up today when the surface hardened. But for the most part, it was a slog. Disappointed with my performance, I dreamt up conversations people were having about me as the slowest and probably worst polar explorer ever. Even though this was my maiden voyage, I had several training trips but was unable to adequately simulate Antarctic towing conditions, much to my detriment. This made me sigh perpetually. I refused to give in to my body's craving to quit, failing everyone and myself after so much effort. It made no sense.

Camp AC27
81°33.263'S 81°05.175'W
Distance: 5.3 nm, Time: 7.5 hours
Distance to South Pole: 507 nm

FRIDAY, NOVEMBER 30, 2012 DAY 30

The wind was at 20 knots when I bagged everything up and took off. By the end of the first session, the wind rose to 30 knots. The intensity increased during my break. Snow blew high in the air rather than staying on the ground, indicating wind speeds of 40 knots and above. Had I known strong wind was going to strike, I would not have left the tent. Then again, I would have missed the miles and experience.

In hellish weather, I developed a mantra to keep me in a rhythm.

"I'm scared. Holy crud. I can't believe I'm out in this. Woo hoo! I'm scared."

This ran through my mind and escaped my lips much of the day. The concerted effort to keep skiing when the wind was at a 9 or 10 on the Beaufort scale was incredible. I had to keep my mind perfectly focused on skiing, balancing with the poles, otherwise the wind blew me sideways, forcing me to readjust and start again. My wish was to have video of me skiing in these crazy conditions, but when I pulled out the camera and powered it up, the battery dropped from fully charged to dead in one minute.

As long as I was moving, I was warm. With a fleece jacket wrapped around my waist, preventing chilblains in gale winds, I stayed warm. Though, by the end of a 15-minute break, I shivered uncontrollably. Keeping the pogies attached to the ski poles without them blowing away all day was annoying. I was surprised that I didn't lose them in the blasting wind. If that happened, I'd be forced to switch over to my mittens, rendering the alpine gloves useless in the wind. I liked having the fingered gloves because I was able to manipulate zippers, whereas the mittens left me with ineffective stumps.

In the afternoon, the wind dropped to 25 knots, causing me to overheat with all the clothing on, making the footbeds wet. At night, I saw my feet had become yellow and scaled. Keeping myself cool and dry became a major production. To fix the foot problem, I took the rasp of my multitool and ground the fish scales of my feet. It was gross. I hung my feet outside the tent but inside the fly to keep the dead skin out of the tent. One problem I noticed tonight from the wet foot beds was that the mylar coating had deteriorated to the point of cracking, making me wish I'd brought another pair. Though I didn't want to carry the weight, a backup pair would have been smart. In lieu of a backup, I cut several strips of duct tape and attached them to the bottom of the foot beds to keep them from shredding. The liners still had to last for hundreds of miles. During my audio blog post, I plugged Jackson Hole Boot and Shoe Repair for Bill Dillon's sponsorship of this expedition, as my shoe repair reminded me of the first-rate work Bill did on improving the fit of my ski boots.

My tent was coated in food crumbs, so whenever I first entered the tent, I would toss a few handfuls of snow inside to absorb the food remnants, then brush the whole mess out. The snow carried away the crumbs handily. I needed to do this every day to keep the tent clean. Noticing some mildew from residual moisture, I strove to keep the tent as clean as possible.

Camp AC28
81°40.685'S 81°06.810'W
Distance 7.5 nm, Time 9 hours
Distance to South Pole: 500 nm

SATURDAY, DECEMBER 1, 2012 DAY 31

Nearly kissing the mile per hour mark today thrilled me to no end. It was still not enough, but it was a vast improvement. As I thought it over, I wondered if dodging each sastrugi pile to prevent the ski-laden sled from crashing wasted distance. A larger fiberglass sled could glide over this junk easily. All sastrugi were difficult to ski over anyway, so I ended up dodging them constantly. The 20-40 knot winds made for another thrilling day, where I had to be exceedingly careful with my gloves and food, as the wind tried more than once to rip them out of my hands. Fortunately, all the gloves had idiot cords to prevent such an occurrence. An idiot cord is a nylon cord loop with a draw lock attached to the glove. These allowed me to adjust and retain the gloves, even if I dropped them. Still, I did not let them flop away from me. In a freak event, the cord could snap and there I would be, without a glove.

While brushing the snow off my boots at night, I had noticed a shocking problem. The soles of the boots had begun to split apart ever so slightly. I panicked. If the boots failed, the trip was absolutely terminated. The sole was made out of three layers of different types of rubber. Even though the separation was only a 1/16" wide and 1 inch long, I knew this would degrade into major damage. I had brought Seam Grip, a glue that was able to cure at -30°F. But I had no way to clamp the boot. To squeeze the layers of the sole together took significant force, so there was no way I was going to pile equipment on top and effect a repair. Casting about, I dreamt of tools far away. Then I remembered the brackets from the broken sleds. They had holes in them and I still had the bolts. Pulling the broken chunks of metal out, I experimented. In a few minutes, I created the proper angle with the brackets and, barely, compressed the sole back together. I had a solution! After smearing a copious mass of glue into the gap, I again positioned the clamp and screwed it down. Glue squeezed out of the split, meaning it had made a seal.

I pumped my fists in the air in satisfaction. Finally, I was able to make something go right!

With disaster averted once again, thoughts of giving up the unsupported expedition ran through my head. With Kelly, on the satellite phone, we discussed the options. There were not too many to choose from. Unless I was able to magically hit 12 miles per day in the next day or two, I was so far behind that there was the risk of not even making the Pole. The thought of that was anathema to me. These ceaseless days of gale force winds were certainly not helping, cutting at least a mile off of southward progress every day. Should those not abate any time soon, anything I did would not matter. While these negative thoughts swirled in my head, I did everything I could to boost my spirits. I visualized success, making the Pole, and enjoying myself. To liven up my mood, I thought of a fun way to express optimism in the face of adversity.

During today's audio blog post, I told my nephews about what it was like to be in Antarctica and to encourage them to do something exceptional in their lives.

"Hi Justin and Jake, my nephews in Imperial Beach [south San Diego]. I hope you are enjoying and listening to all of these posts. I'm having a good time in Antarctica even though it is tough going. The place is wholly alien. Here's what it's like: I'm farther from a grocery store here than you are from grocery stores in New York City. It's always at least 0 degrees Fahrenheit or colder. The sun warms up your back and the wind freezes your front. The sun keeps your tent toasty, but it will both sunburn and blind you in minutes without protection."

"There are no plants or animals anywhere near me. It's all snow and ice. You have to drink a gallon of water and eat both a bar of chocolate and two sticks of butter every day to stay alive. You get to camp every day, standing on a two-mile-thick ice sheet. My sleeping bag needs to be as big as your bed to keep me alive."

"Big storms and wind will tear through a six-foot wall of ice and snow protecting your tent in a half hour. It's scary."

"It's an amazing place, though you are always on the edge. I hope both of you get to have an adventure as big as this when you grow up. Whatever your dream is, chase after it with zeal. Don't give up. It's taken me 10 years to get here, one quarter of my life. More than a hundred people have helped me make this dream a reality. Don't wait until you are too old to do it. Remember, later in life you'll only regret the things you didn't do. Dare to dream, discover and explore. I promise it's worth it. I love you both. Out."

Camp AC29
81º48.326'S 80º58.821'W
Distance: 7.74 nm, Time: 8 hours
Distance to South Pole: 492 nm

Sunday, December 2, 2012 Day 32

Last night I took a break from waxing the skis, testing to see how long the wax would last from the previous day. There felt to be more drag, but it was difficult to tell. Thirty-five-knot winds meant it was impossible to sense if there was more or less sled drag anyway. Waxing the skis felt pointless. The wind was strong enough to whip snow off the ground making for frustrating navigation. It was impossible to see past a few hundred yards from all the snow flying by in the air.

After noon, the weather grew exciting, as the wind blasted past 50 knots, causing the snow not only to hover above the ground but to blow far above my head. I longed to be in my tent. When the wind reached gale force, I had no choice but to stop, turn around, and protect myself. Even with my parka fully zipped up and the fur ruff wrapped tightly around my face, I felt my cheeks beginning to freeze. There was not much I could do when the winds exceeded 50 knots, other than hang on. Although I was able to look south while facing the ground, I was blind to where I was headed. Unlike a whiteout, where I could use the compass to continually perform corrections, this Beaufort force 10 wind made navigation impossible.

I simply was unable to move.

Each time I turned away from the gale, I was rudely shoved northward, as though the continent told me to quit and go home. Several times I saw my sleds rammed backwards in their tracks. It was something that if I had not seen it with my own eyes, I would not have believed it. The bully beat me back. More than once I was compelled to stop and stumble back to the sleds, using them as a shield to inhibit the skin-freezing assault. I felt pathetic as I cowered behind the only shelter for hundreds of miles. I wanted to pitch the tent and call it a day. Yet I knew there was a real chance the wind would rip it out of my hands, sending it sailing away. My only option would then be to watch it tumble as tears streamed down my face. Instead, I opted to curl up in a ball against the wind when necessary, then ski when I could. I was going to move southward no matter what, in spite of the 50 knot winds.

By 3 p.m., my right quadricep cramped up, became sore and protested the strain.

By 4:30 p.m., my left Achilles throbbed as though my boot was not fitted properly. Pushing against the wind was beginning to tear my body apart. It made the sleds feel as though they were 100 pounds heavier. And to finally top it off, clouds occluded the sun, throwing me into a whiteout.

"You idiot wind! Stop it and let me move south," I screamed into the wind with contempt.

The roar was so intense that I could not even hear my own voice, the wind ripping it away from my mouth before my ears caught the sound. Even though I was blind, unable to see where I was headed, I pushed forward to gain another mile.

I refused to give up.

As my stop time of 5:45 p.m. drew near, the wind dropped mercifully below gale force, affording me the chance to establish camp. Following the procedure I had made to set both sleds apart, stake them down, then attach the tent to each while crawling over the shell to keep it from blowing away, I carefully set camp. Once I had the third upwind stake set, I wrapped my hand around one of the main support lines and rolled off the tent.

Boom!

It instantly popped into shape, flailing in the wind. The 290 pounds of sleds slid with tent attached until the stakes pulled the lines taut. It was near terror but a thrill. Pressing the stake attached to the line wrapped around my hand into the ice, I moved around the back of the tent to secure the other support lines. While doing this, another stake bent, the third one of this trip. As careful as I was being, it was impossible in this wind to gently stake the lines. Force was necessary. But being buffeted around, my aim was not true. I was not able to strike the stakes straight on, so another bent.

The wind took my curses away before they hit my ears.

Carefully, I reshaped and reset the stake. I made a mental note to ask ALE for some spare tent stakes. Though my tent was designed for hellish winds, the aluminum stakes were not cutting it. Rapidly unhooking the sleds from the tent, I dragged them around to the lee side, unzipped the tent, shoveled all my gear in and jumped in afterward.

Safety.

On my hands and knees, I collected myself for a moment as the wind increased in intensity. Glad to have made camp when I did, I set up the stove, transferred gas from the large plastic water bottles into the pint-sized aluminum bottle, ignited the fuel with three strikes of flint and steel and made water. The wind outside beating the tent made as much noise as the stove. Smiling, I laughed at the absurdity of what I was doing. This little nylon shell, in the middle of nowhere, against the baddest continent on Earth, was my shelter against gale winds.

This was the time of my life.

As soon as I had poured boiling water in the dust representing a dehydrated meal, I made my scheduled call to ALE and let them know that I needed my supplies forwarded. It was time to accept my fate. The operator said she would update me with cache locations and options to keep me within schedule and budget tomorrow. Now that I made the announcement, I felt instantly better. Knowing that I had given up my round trip hopes allayed my concern. After speaking with Steve Jones and having the 'big picture' talk, I knew it was over. ALE had lots of experience with similar situations. I trusted their judgment.

I calculated what I needed to drop, where to have the caches placed, and what my best guess was at my increase in speed. Steve said that he was concerned my speed had not picked up significantly even though I was 32 days in and dropped from 330 to 280 pounds. Each sled was kept as evenly loaded as possible. For all my effort, neither I nor the sleds were performing satisfactorily. I was amazed that I had consumed 50 pounds of food and fuel, yet was unable to pick up the pace. It was a rude revelation. Based on my testing at Union Glacier, it seemed the sleds performed up to a certain load and, past that, became boat anchors. Until my supplies dropped to the sled design weight, the drag force did not reduce appreciably. My hope was that dropping the weight would put the sled weight below that magic mark to where they moved easier. Once an additional 70 pounds were dropped from the sleds, they should be at 140 pounds. I planned to cache 33 rations and two gallons of fuel, leaving me with 17 rations and 5 liters of fuel, more than enough to reach the first cache.

Hopefully this will make all the difference. Otherwise this will be my biggest failure ever.

Camp AC30
81°56.899'S 81°03.006'W
Distance 8.6 nm, Time 9 hours
Distance to South Pole: 487 nm
Rations remaining: 51 days

Monday, December 3, 2012 Day 33

Sitting in the tent this morning, I placed my head in my arms and stared at my legs. Why were they not propelling me along as strongly as I had done during training? Knowing that I was not going to ski the round trip was becoming easier to accept, but still I yelled out in frustration. All I received back in response was the rippling sound of wind-buffeted nylon. Thoughts of catching a plane ride to the 89th degree and finishing out the expedition assailed me.

I felt inexperienced, inadequate to the task, and pathetic.

Yet, I knew I must keep going.

Contemplating one possible future, I saw myself comfortably lying in bed, thinking about how I could be out here doing my utmost to cover miles and move toward my goal. And, I knew the only thought in my head, should I do that, would be, "You would have been okay. There was no physical damage, only you battling your mind and your body's desire to give up." I had to keep the negative thoughts and emotions from overrunning me. It was so easy to stop and walk. The fatigue, soreness and gasping breaths would abruptly halt. Then, when I did reach home, I would stare at myself in the mirror and say: "Why did you stop? There was nothing wrong, only you pushing at the limit." Thoughts of bailing out of this expedition felt similar. So I knew without a doubt that should I decide to give up, regret would dig at me for the rest of my life. How many chances would there be for me to do this again?

Yelling at the tent, I received no response. It was time to accept what was and move south. There was no quitting. It was not an option. Only if I were injured or out of time would I possibly give up. Neither of those had happened. Once I dropped the supplies, my speed should ratchet up to 11–12 nautical miles per day, making reaching the pole possible. There was no way I was going to give up, catch a ride, and become a quitter. My dad did not have the option to quit when he was fighting prostate cancer. There was no catching a ride out of that one. Raising awareness for that was one of the reasons I was here and quitting would soil those efforts. Picking up the camera and using the LCD as a mirror, I looked myself in the eye and shook my head.

"Wake up and get out of the tent," I told myself. There was still a long way to go.

As soon as I did that, the dark clouds hovering over me cleared. The crisp air snapped my emotions back to calmness. There was no point in becoming emotional about this. Yet, it was impossible to control my emotions. Normally, I was unemotional to the point of having been nick-named Spock of Star Trek fame in high school. Crying out was all new territory for me.

During the scheduled call, ALE notified me that I should be on the 80°W longitude, 10 miles east [left] of my current travel path and position. I need to head over there because there was a large, known crevasse field 60 miles (100 km) south of my position on this latitude. So, even if I wanted to keep going and not drop the supplies, I was in danger anyway. I was excited to be completely off the known track, making my own way, where no one has ever been. It reminded me of Amundsen's expedition, venturing into completely unknown territory. Yet, if I kept on the way I was headed, this would end up more like Scott's expedition, something I desperately wanted to avoid.

The instructions were to drop all supplies at 82°04.171'S 79°57.082'W, 9.6 nm east of tonight's camp.

The first cache location would be at Thiel's Corner: 85°04.964'S 80°47.428'W.

The second cache would be at Hannah's cache, at the corner of old mechanized tracks: 87°19'S 82°32'W.

James Hayes, the ALE operator on tonight, indicated that a traverse road I was to hit doglegged east where I was to drop my cache, so there was no real help for me there. I asked about dropping some extra clothing I had never worn, warm layers that were unusable. He suggested against it, as the pole can be -30°F, so I'd need all the clothing I had. Even though I wanted to ditch the extra weight, fear of the unknown held me back. Even though I needed less clothing at -45°F in Yellowstone, a healthy respect of Antarctica kept me from dumping my extra jacket.

Once I dropped the supplies, I would have to be stingy with fuel and save my leftover food every day. I would boil no water except for the liter used for freeze dried food and the thermos. It was going to be tight. Near the caches, I should be able to speed it up, as I'd be much lighter.

The expedition was now about reaching the South Pole any way I could. Otherwise no one, not even I, would be able to comprehend the most expensive and punishing camping trip ever.

Camp AC31
82°03.736'S 81°05.201'W
Distance 7 nm, Time: 6 hours
Distance to South Pole: 476 nm

TUESDAY, DECEMBER 4, 2012, DAY 34

It was a difficult night's sleep, as I was excited to traverse east today and drop 70 pounds of food and fuel.

With light winds out of the south, as they always had been, I struck camp and headed east, perpendicular to the prevailing sastrugi. Immediately, I discovered this was going to be a truly challenging day, as the light and shadows played across the ice, making it impossible to see obstructions until I was on top of them. The lone sled still on skis still glided, but it snagged on sastrugi, constantly forcing me to stop, back track, and then drag the sled out of the hole and keep skiing. Since I only wanted to spend one day traversing east before turning back south, I picked up the pace as much as possible, making solid time. At the first break, the GPS showed me having traveled 1.6 miles in 75 minutes. I was excited, as this was rather impressive considering the conditions. Slipping and falling sideways into ice cracks made for a real ankle cranker all day. The quality of the snow changed during the day, too. It changed from powdery to granular, similar to popcorn.

I could not believe that the surface and snow changed that much in a mere 10 miles. There were no mountains or other major obstructions to change the snow. The popcorn snow iced up the skis on the sled, noticeably increasing drag.

At each break, I verified the course using the GPS. I did not want to waste any time heading anywhere but toward the cache. Within a half mile of the cache point, I pulled out the GPS and used it full time, scanning ahead in the sea of ice waves to guess where my cache point was. Soon, I approached the coordinates and scanned the area for what ALE said was a road or machine track.

There was absolutely nothing. No sign indicating the passage of anyone or anything. Pulling out the second GPS, I verified the coordinates. They were correct. Had I written them down incorrectly, even with reading back the written coordinates? No, it was unlikely. So, I set up camp and made water. I was wasted by the end of the day and my only relaxation was to wait for ice to melt. It was disheartening to lose 600 feet of elevation over the day. But the downhill travel made covering distance faster, so I told myself it was worth it.

During the scheduled call, ALE verified the coordinates I was at as correct, suggesting that the wind had likely blown sastrugi across the mechanized tracks from last year, so there may be nothing to see. They suggested I ski north or south to find remnants of the tracks. Chuckling, I declined. I was content that after checking the coordinates with every device I had, this had to be the spot. I was to mark each bag either "Cache 1" or "Cache 2", depending on what I wanted to stash in each place. Thanking them, I cut the satellite phone connection.

Staring at the pile of food inside the sled, I thought about sleeping right after eating dinner so I could rise early to prepare the cache. Then I realized all I would do all night was think about preparing the cache. Distracted by these thoughts, I ate the macaroni and cheese dinner too early and burned my tongue. Now there was no way I was going to sleep any time soon.

Since December 1, I had been calculating how many rations and fuel cans to drop to ensure there were enough supplies to last until I reached each cache, yet reduce the weight as much as possible. Once I had accepted that I was not able to make the round trip, the new logistics challenge was guessing what will happen in the future, based on current performance. Each night, thoughts of exactly what to do and how to do it filled my mind. Being in the Antarctic wilderness was the worst place to guess at expedition modifications. I was wrapped in the event rather than being an outside observer with no emotional connection. Yet, it was the perfect place to decide simply because my life depended on it. Should I make a supply calculation error, and poor weather hammered me, there was the chance I would run out of food and starve. As long as I could melt snow for water, I could nibble on crumbs and last a long time out here.

After endless rumination, I finished marking the four cache bags, along with two fuel cans, with how I wanted each placed. In addition to the markings, each contained a note where it was to be placed in the event the writing wore off for some reason. I did not expect this to happen, but Antarctica had taught me anything was possible.

Camp AC32
82°04.179'S 79°56.947'W
Distance: 9.5 nm, Time 10 hours
Distance to South Pole: 476 nm

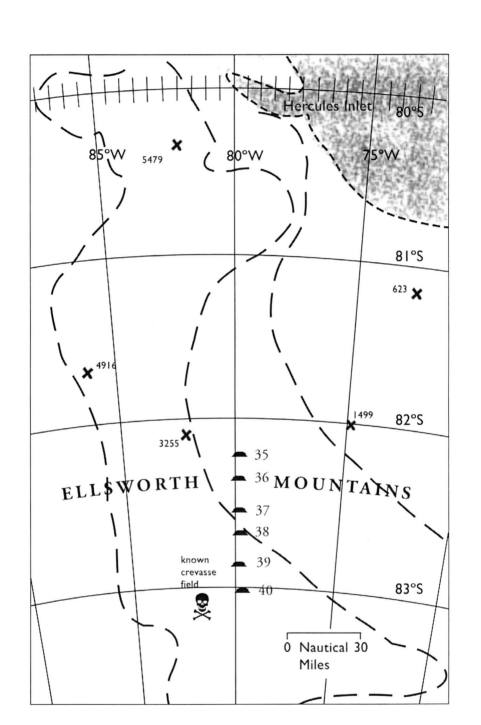

85°W 5479 80°W 75°W

Hercules Inlet 80°S

81°S

623

4916

1499 82°S

3255

35

ELLSWORTH 36 MOUNTAINS

37

38

known
crevasse 39
field

40 83°S

0 Nautical 30
Miles

14

Days 35-41

Wednesday, December 5, 2012 Day 35

EVEN THOUGH ALE REPORTED that there should be mech-anized tracks through the snow right where I was camping, there was absolutely nothing to suggest anything but wind had been through the area. To verify my position, I powered up both phones, the satellite beacon and both GPS units. My backup GPS failed to power up at all. At once, I grew alarmed. How had the GPS died? Other than checking it at Union Glacier, I had not turned it on since I left. Opening the back and taking the batteries out, I checked both lithium batteries with the little pocket multimeter I had brought along for this purpose. One of the batteries inexplicably had died down to 0.7V, as though it had been running the whole time, yet the other battery read as though it was new at 1.6V. Although I'd never had a lithium battery die on me before, I chalked it up to a random occurrence, marked it as dead, replaced it with a spare, and verified the cache position.

After using each GPS in concert to find the exact cache point ALE had given me, I spiked the spot with one of the bamboo poles I had been given at the start of my journey to mark caches. The spot was a hundred yards away from camp, so I shuttled the supplies over to the spot in a strong wind, which made preparing the cache point all the more entertaining. Roping the now empty sled to the bamboo pole spiked into the snow, it flipped and flailed around in the wind until I weighed it down with snow blocks. I had not traveled all this way only to chase a plastic sled across the plateau.

With strong winds also came hard ice right at the cache point, making hole digging with the broken shovel blade grueling. Blow after blow, the aluminum shovel blade vibrated in my hands. Only flakes of ice broke off. I wished for my old, heavy military folding steel shovel that would have made short work of the conditions. But that tool was on another continent. I realized the effort was futile at that spot, so I probed for a softer spot to set the cache. After fifteen minutes and widening the search circle by several yards, I finally found ice that broke under the aluminum blade. Quickly, I set to work, quarrying out bread loaf sized blocks of snow and piling them beside the hole. Although the snow was softer at this spot, this was only relative to hardened ice. To find larger blocks for building a mount on top of the hole, I had to quarry from several spots near the cache point. There were no soft spots that allowed for large chunks to be extracted, so much rooting around the sastrugi was necessary.

It took some time to chisel out a hole wide enough to support the four bags of food and two gallons of fuel. ALE had suggested burying the supplies at least two feet below the surface and burying the stash under a three-foot mound of snow blocks above the surface to protect the supplies from being blasted apart by storm winds. Had I planned to retrieve the cache on the return trip, I would have needed to build a six-foot snow block mountain. As ALE's snow tractor mechanized train was to be by in no more than two weeks, the cache only needed to be under three feet of blocks. Also, I was directed to fill in the holes between the blocks with loose snow, otherwise the wind would tear apart the blocks.

It took two and a half hours to the dig a hole and build a mound to cache the fuel, food and trash. Spiking the second bamboo pole and setting the black flags on them, I walked back over to camp.

Now skiing toward the pole, lighter and happier, I traveled swiftly. Now all I had to concentrate on was heading south for a degree, with no likely crevasses or anything else. I was stunned how rapidly the cache disappeared into the sea of sastrugi as I skied away. The sastrugi rapidly enveloped the flags and poles. How does one become bored in Antarctica? I was incessantly absorbed with travel, feeding, hydration, safety and the barrage of thoughts racing through my mind.

As Hannah had mentioned, the area was rippled by endless rolling hills. Even with the hours of climbing, I didn't recover yesterday's lost elevation. My legs were sore all day from yesterday's death march. Thoughts of mom's satellite message came back to me.

"Imagine that every time the wind blows, we are sending hugs to you," she said.

I cried for a minute after the cache completely vanished.

The headwind cooled me, but with the sleds so much lighter, I skied faster, generating more heat. So much so that no matter what I did, I wasn't able to stay cool in my heavy parka. During my mid-afternoon break, I switched over to the eVent jacket. I'd sweated out my boots, gloves and shirt. I hate changing clothing during the day in strong wind, so I hid inside of the parka while swapping clothing, using it as a shelter. In high wind, it was scary because it was easy to have an irreplaceable glove blow away.

The wind was a thief waiting for my first mistake.

Both pulks handled wonderfully today. I didn't have to hip-buck them over anything. Though now, because they're light, the sled with skis dragged the other into every pit I neared. Again, I debated if tracking was more consequential than drag. My ankles were sore today after smashing through 10 nautical miles of perpendicular sastrugi yesterday. I didn't mind pain because I moved so much faster.

Finally, after dropping 70 pounds out of the pulks, I finally made real speed. At this rate, it was now possible to ski upwards of 12 nm per day in the same conditions. It was a huge difference. Now I was forced to cover at least 10 miles per day, every day, to reach the Pole before both supplies and time run out.

After repairing my boot sole on December 1st, I had been vigilant about inspecting everything. I brushed off all the ice at night so the boots would dry and I did not have to put on frozen boots in the morning. Now, scrutinizing them, I saw that the nylon had shredded around the toe, both on the toe box and on the ski binding tongue. Did anything last in Antarctica? I did not want ice melting into water at night in the toes, so I smashed the nylon down as best as I could and applied a generous coating of glue. There was no glaring defect on the bindings to cause the damage, no obvious causative agent. The best I could do was build a hard glue outer shell on the toes and inspect them closely each day.

Camp AC33
82°11.191'S 79°57.097'W
Distance: 7 nm, Time: 5.5 hours
Distance to South Pole: 469 nm

THURSDAY, DECEMBER 6, 2012 DAY 36
After wearing bandages secured by duct tape on my hips for a full two weeks to prevent the chilblains from deteriorating, they finally fell off. Although the duct tape was strong, it would not stay attached to my unwashed skin indefinitely. They smelled rotten, inducing the sinking feeling that there was an infection. The bandages had protected my skin, but wearing them continuously did not allow the it to breathe. As I had no mirror, I used the digital camera, took pictures of my hips, and zoomed in to check for anything infected or falling apart. The camera zoom was far more effective at taking a close look than a mirror was. There was nothing apparent. The chilblain sores had dried up and were only tiny bumps.

Since I used only the shovel blade to dig out snow for water and tent protection, I knelt on the snow constantly. By this point, the skin on my knees was rather flaky and purple, indicating frostbite. Although knees were tough, I did not want to deal with a cold injury on such a critical and constantly flexing location. With the synthetic blanket stuffing I brought to protect the fuel cans, I fashioned knee pads on the polar thigh guards with some duct tape. Although they were crude, the relief was immediate. My knees did not burn any more when I knelt to shovel snow.

My body was starting to smell rather badly, as it had been 40 days since I'd taken a shower. Even though the wool underclothing retaining little odor, I still felt beyond grimy. Using a technique adapted from Dansercoer's *Polar Exploration*, I squeezed out the evening's tea bag and used it as a sponge to absorb the oily buildup my skin developed, masking my odor. Now, all at once, I found myself smelling like pleasant chamomile rather than a locker room.

By this time, I had taken to turning my sleeping bag inside out while I ate breakfast. I had noticed that the bag did not have the same fluffiness as it had when I first arrived. A combination of both sweat and body oils had been dampening the sleeping bag's loft. So, instead of immediately jamming it into the stuff sack on waking up, I flipped the bag inside out and piled it into the back corner of the tent. After doing that, I found it was more difficult to put the bag into the stuff sack, indicating that it had regained its loft in the short hour of airing it out. This added no time to the morning preparations, yet helped maintain the bag's warmth.

The strong winds last night had died down to a light breeze, leaving me nauseatingly hot in the tent as I ate breakfast. The thermometer showed +30°F inside the tent, which was incredibly uncomfortable. I was reduced to sitting in my thinnest wool shirt and underwear. I laughed out loud at the absurdity of the situation. Outside, the air was −10°F and yet here I was inside, as stripped down as possible.

The sastrugi grew to immense heights, over six feet, by noon. Though they were large, they were widely spaced, allowing me to maneuver around the monoliths. Had there been a wall of this, preventing southward motion, I would have had to unclip all my gear and hoist it up and over the whale-shaped ice, drop down and repeat. I had a blast finding my way around them and pondered how they could have grown to this size. Each sculpture stood by themselves, separated by 10 yards. To comprehend the landscape, my mind dreamt I was wandering through piles of ancient frozen giants.

Camp AC34
82°21.493'S 79°59.788'W
Distance: 10.5 nm, Time: 8 hours
Distance to cache 1: 159 nm
Distance to South Pole: 459 nm

FRIDAY, DECEMBER 7, 2012, DAY 37

Skiing over a huge ice dome today caused me significant eastward drift, over a half mile. Even though I used the compass to target sastrugi as far in the distance as was visible, the imperceptible slope to the east dragged me to the left, making each sighting about 10° off south. Even though it did not seem like I was inadvertently drifting off course, I did. After a GPS check at 2 p.m., seeing that I was wasting southward travel with eastward drift, I corrected the compass to 170°. At 4 p.m., I checked the GPS again and found the correction had worked. Even though I slipped eastward while skiing, my pointing slightly to the west had nullified the slope on the ice dome. I was becoming obsessive about any wasted effort traveling anywhere but south. To make up for the loss of southward distance, I made the last session 90 minutes rather than the usual 75. Even though it gained me another half mile, it cost me in seriously throbbing feet and puffy toe joints. As much as I wanted to put in the extra time to add miles, my body resisted the request to give more.

While making water from snow chunks this evening, I had the door open to let some of the heat out, as there was little wind to cool off the tent heating up from the solar radiation. Twice, I thought I glimpsed something in my peripheral vision moving out on the Antarctic plateau. Attributing it to fatigue and my brain playing tricks on me, I continued with preparing food and writing in my journal. Deciding to entertain myself with the delusions my brain served me, I sat facing out of the tent while writing. At 8:45 p.m., I saw real motion. Not out of the corner of my eye but dead straight on. Unbelieving, I sat up and strained my vision for all it was worth.

Yes, there was indeed an object moving on the far horizon.

Staring for what seemed an hour yet only a few actual moments, I wondered who or what was traveling out this late. Lacking binoculars, I opted for the digital camera with 20x zoom, which revealed black blobs marching across the landscape at a decent speed. They were not human shaped, but at this distance, it was difficult to tell. Taking a few stills and zooming in on them, I still was unable to identify the objects. Had I a larger computer screen instead of the dinky camera LCD, I could have been able to determine what was out there. All throughout the evening, I would glance at the horizon and see in the distance whatever-it-was moving until it finally winked out of sight over an ice dome, miles off. It was both disconcerting and exciting to imagine that there was something else out here. As I was on the bottom of the globe on a mostly unexplored continent, thoughts of crazy scenes raced through my mind, attempting to formulate a plausible scenario of what was out there. All I thought of was Carpenter's film *The Thing*, the only movie based in Antarctica that I could recall. Daydreaming about an alien attack out here, in the middle of true nowhere, made me laugh at myself.

Camp AC35
82°32.416'S 79°45.797'W
Distance 11 nm, Time 9 hours
Distance to South Pole: 448 nm
Rations remaining: 19 days

SATURDAY, DECEMBER 8, 2012 DAY 38

Now I grew excited, as I had covered a half degree in the past three days, far better than I had in the first few weeks of travel in Antarctica. The navigation journal made it easy to see that I was moving toward my goal, far more than what the passing landscape revealed. There was no way to see that I had moved anywhere on the ice, for as the sastrugi fields changed from day to day, they all seemed similar. I could have been walking in circles save for the shadows from the sun. The GPS data told me otherwise, though. I had not seen anything other than ice and snow since I last saw Three Sails and the Ellsworth Mountains, so it was impossible to be confident I had moved anywhere without navigational instruments. There were no birds, no trees, no mountains nor anything else, other than white snow and blue sky infiltrated by clouds, to indicate that I had moved any closer to my goal. Perceiving no forward progress taxed me mentally. Had I approached and then passed a mountain range, I would have felt better about what I had done so far.

Although I had avoided injury by using the face mask I had brought, the light breeze had been chilling my cheeks to the point of burning. Fearing frost damage, I chopped a piece of fleece off my reserve supply and fashioned an awning taped to the goggles to act as an additional wind screen. It still allowed air to circulate but did not cause overheating. Soon an icicle draped down from my chin, the lowest point of the fleece drape, to the middle of my chest. It looked as though I had a single, hazy white fang dangling from my mouth. I laughed about how absurd it was.

Dropping temperatures caused a problem with the buckles on my harness. To make changing my clothing easier, I had been wearing the harness over my wool shirt and then adding all the other clothing layers on top of that. Having the harness on the outer layer made it difficult to swap outer shells when I became too hot or cold and also reduced the insulation. The shoulder buckles were made of nylon and drew heat from my skin. As a consequence, there were red cold burn spots on my chest from the buckles. Placing bandages on those two spots on my chest this morning kept the pain at bay. I added bandages to my evening checklist of body maintenance. Taking care of each item on the list at night made the following day more pleasant.

Following the cache drop on December 5, the sleds had stopped floundering. As only one sled now had skis, it started dragging the other sled into holes and crashing it into sastrugi. To alleviate the problem, I placed the sled with skis in the lead. That seemed to help balance out the drag force. Using the ski-less sled like a drogue sea anchor improved sled tracking, making the long day of hauling more enjoyable.

ALE had asked how my weight was doing during the scheduled call this evening. The doctor was worried that I had been out here so long that I had lost too much fat and muscle mass. I reported that there did not appear to be any significant loss, as my 6,000 calorie load seemed to be keeping me both fueled and maintained up to this point.

Thoughts of Hawaii stirred in my mind. As much fun as I was having trekking across the Antarctic plateau, I eagerly anticipated a time when my biggest worry was what beach to lie on and what drink to have in hand. Had there been a way to bring dehydrated rum with me, I would have much enjoyed it this day.

Camp AC36
82°42.870'S 79°49.342'W
Distance: 10.5 nm, Time: 8 hours
Distance to South Pole: 437 nm

Sunday, December 9, 2012 Day 39

The 2010 French encore group Les Enfoirs song, "Si l'on s'aimait, si," played in my head all day. Being a fan of European internet dance radio stations, I was acquainted with this song prior to it appearing on American radio stations. Even though my high school French had deteriorated badly after years of neglect, the rhythm and sonorous blending of words I barely understood stuck in my mind today, keeping me occupied as clouds drew in and enveloped me in a ground whiteout.

During the whiteout, I started bobbing and weaving my head in an attempt to see the surface. It was a technique of super-stereo vision I learned that cats used. Keeping my eyes moving constantly allowed my brain to refresh the image in my head. The technique made it easier to see what I was headed for, even when there was nothing immediately apparent in the snow. At 4:15 p.m., it happened.

The bracket holding the skis to the second sled broke.

When I felt the alarming sensation of the sleds pulling completely sideways in a flat area, I turned and knew exactly what I was going to see. There, lying on its side, was the pulk with the ski grotesquely twisted off, the heavy aluminum bracket shattered. I was stunned that it had happened in a flat area, devoid of sastrugi. It had suffered one too many collisions and, like the sled before it, the bracket had broken in the exact same spot.

Days prior, I noticed the brackets had bent in the same place as on the other sled. Being careful while flipping the sled over to scrape ice off, I did my utmost to keep the brackets from breaking as long as possible. It was such an ignominious death for an otherwise neat idea.

Rapidly extracting my tools and camera from the lead sled, I documented what had happened and set to work removing the brackets and skis from the disabled pulk. In 30 minutes, the surgery was complete and I was off. There was no reason to linger. I turned away from the site and skied on.

In a fit of rage, I raced off skiing as hard as possible to flee the area. For a full hour, I pulled with all my strength, yanking at the sleds, making them go as fast as my body would allow. Smashing directly over sastrugi, barely following my compass, I tried to recoup the distance I had lost while disassembling my failed idea. Without the skis, the sleds now did not slide laterally, so I did not have to worry about them falling into holes or rolling off sastrugi. Several times I stumbled and fell. I ran blindly through patches of sastrugi. My dream of reaching the pole was slipping away in a swirl of snow. Each time I fell on my face, I swore. I screamed into the wind. I had, for that long hour, gone mad. There was no way I was going to give up. I tugged harder and harder. Checking my watch, I saw it was 6 p.m. Unclasping my skis, I collapsed and wailed for what seemed forever.

Once I calmed down, I pulled my goggles off and tore away the frozen tears that sealed my eyelashes shut. Although there was nothing but whiteout, I clearly saw my destination, over 420 miles away. At least so I thought. As I collected myself, I set to make camp while wiping away tears of frustration. I did not want my eyes to freeze shut.

The operator at Union Glacier said last year a French skier ditched out and caught a ride with a passing vehicle on a traverse to the South Pole. I can't say I blame him. Crossing Antarctica can be emotionally crushing. Understanding what he had gone through now, I could not blame him for quitting, even though he was uninjured and had not run out of food. While reporting the sled failure to ALE, they informed me that the specter I thought I saw on December 7th was the mechanized Thiel's traverse. It was exhilarating to think I saw them in the middle of nowhere, only because I happened to look out of the tent. I learned later that Roland Krueger, who was at 84° on his trek, had also seen the equipment traverse heading toward Thiel's Corner.

In bed, I listened to the hard snow coming down outside. With both sleds' skis broken, this promised to be a most challenging run for the pole. I wished I could figure out how Aleksander Gamme posted the miles he did (nearly 30 a day by the end). The best I've towed to this point was 11 nautical miles. One crazy Norwegian with massive experience had rolled me. Ha ha! Now, I was in the ultimate fight to reach the South Pole.

Camp AC37
82°52.302'S 79°52.958'W
Distance: 9.5 nm, Time: 8.5 hours
Distance to South Pole: 428 nm

Tuesday, December 10, 2012 Day 40

Brooding about my now disabled ski sled, I missed its company as much as a dear friend. Even though I held no particular regard for inanimate objects, this rig had been with me through my trip into Yellowstone last winter and, as such, was a trusted tool. Had I been able to effect the necessary repairs to bring the sled back to life, I would have been happy to undertake the work and again have everything as it was. Depressed, I knew that there was no way to fashion a repair without pliers, a vice and spare parts. Whatever was going to happen with my rig was now going to be the way it was.

It was a wildly unpredictable weather day which kept my mind off of how the expedition had gone sideways up to this point. For as much training and effort as I had put in, I was in a rough way, though I loved every minute of it. Wendy, my friend in Japan, sent me a satellite text message.

"Love the worst parts the best."

Although I knew she was right, it was difficult to embrace the worst. I recalled all the difficult times I had working through my undergraduate degree in engineering, where I would emerge from the computer lab at sunrise. I was bleary eyed, terribly tired, and yet incredibly satisfied that I had succeeded in slogging through the tough parts and made it happen. Antarctica bore a decent resemblance to those college years. The difference was that this challenge lasted infinitely longer than those single nights in the computer labs. Inside of my mind, I saw that as long as I kept my perspective at the day-to-day level, the cumulative effect of this physical, mental and emotional challenge did not add up to something beyond what I could handle. I was out here, having a wonderful time, and I wanted to live it up for all it was worth.

The first ski session progressed well, better than in several weeks. The threat of whatever was going to happen to my rigs was gone. It had happened. With the sword of Damocles gone, there could be no more major surprises with sled failures, so I thought.

Then, the unexpected happened.

I glimpsed east and saw the sun striking a snow berm and sastrugi rubble. What had caused blocks of snow to form out here, when everything else was perfectly aerodynamic? A vehicle had driven through here and torn up the surface recently. The sky was only clear for a short while, allowing sunlight to strike the berm for a short while. If these events hadn't coincided, I would have completely missed it. I rarely looked anywhere but straight, so it was chance I happened to glance east. At first I couldn't figure out how there was such a perfect and long line of rubble way out here. Then I remembered about the Thiel's traverse rig several days ago. My thought was, "No way, could that be the road?" I saw it meander south and thought I would eventually intersect it. But then the track was only a few hundred yards east and I would lose it in the whiteout, so I skied directly over to it.

As I neared the rubble, a full whiteout enveloped me again. Keeping my bearing, I continued forward.

I fell into the Thiel's track road. This must be the traverse! The surface was perfect. There were occasional dirt and grease globs on the pristine snow. Whatever drove by here was recent, as the wind and snow buried everything in short order. The rubble of broken ice hadn't even been wind-polished or covered with fresh powder.

At first, I was elated that I had found something man-made to keep me company and, possibly, help me along my journey to the South Pole. Then, just as quickly, I became depressed, because it meant that I faced an ethical dilemma. Here I was, making significant strides in chasing after my goal of being the second American to solo ski to the pole, and I had discovered tracks that would help me navigate the vast Antarctic plateau. But doing so compromise my unsupported status. It would change how I traveled. There was a chance this would lead to the first cache at 85°. I debated long and hard.

I started following the hard track but checked the compass constantly in case the road swerved in a non-southerly direction. It meandered a few hundred yards this way or that, but it tracked in a primarily southward direction. I felt guilty. Had I still been able to go on without dropping a cache on December 5th, I would have eschewed the road and kept on without it. I thought about telling no one what I had found. I suspected ALE would quickly figure it out based on the Thiokol's GPS coordinates that I followed their tracks. But, as I sat there, I told myself that would be dishonest. I had gone through so much already that this seemingly helpful track would not be any bigger help to me. Being an Antarctic rookie, the temptation to stay with it for now was too powerful. People talk about climbing mountains or traversing polar regions with style, not being a mess, and finishing strongly to put on the best show possible. With what I had already failed and succeeded in accomplishing, did the tracks deduct style points?

I was not sure.

Not having experienced polar travel before, I doubted myself and sat for a few moments to filter through my conscience. I was glad for the light breeze, for anything stronger would have distracted me from my introspection. Should I follow the tracks? Would I reveal that I had? Given my performance to this point, did it matter from the style perspective at all? And, the biggest question: would this track even help, given that it wandered and didn't allow for the sleds to track exactly behind me? There was the chance the incessant lateral pull would hurt my back.

I made my decision.

I would follow the track as long as it headed in the correct direction. Also, I chose not hide this discovery. Having to hide something forever, when people would eventually figure it out, would tear at my conscience. And then, there was the chance someone would expose me, ruining my reputation. There was little value in being dishonest, as I had read so many controversies over past explorers not being completely open that I didn't want to suffer their fate.

Following the track for the rest of the day was both a stress and a relief. It was fun to be with other humans in a virtual sense. Though no one accompanied me, there had been someone here not too long ago. Following mechanized grooves was also stressful. At any time, they could wander off in a useless direction, so I had to verify constantly they were headed south. Too, the sleds refused to stay in the same channel as I skied in, continually pulling me sideways.

I had the feeling the lateral pull would return to haunt me.

Camp AC38
83°03.235'S 79°55.023'W
Distance: 11 nm, Time: 8 hours
Distance to South Pole: 417 nm

(Main) *Repairing the torn off ski skin. I drilled holes into the ski base with my Swiss Army knife awl, then placed 5 more screws in addition to the existing 2 to hold the skin in place.*

(Below left) *The broken shovel was a major hindrance. I had to kneel and put my knees on the ice, freezing my skin, to shovel snow for protection and water.*

(Below right) *I took most of a travel day to add a double layer fleece to my Polar Thigh Guards for additional protection. Chilblains hurt and I didn't want to develop a serious case.*

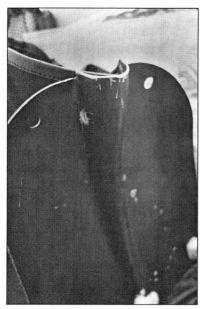

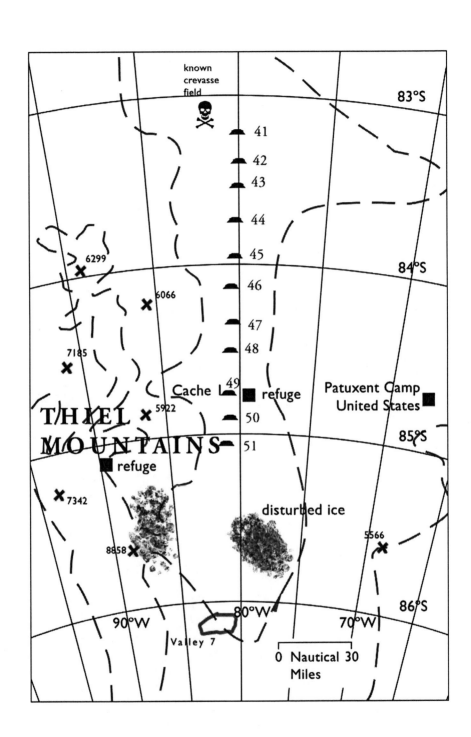

15

Days 41-51

Tuesday, December 11, 2012 Day 41

PEERING OUT OF THE TENT when I woke up, I laughed at the forecast. "Light winds in the forecast my butt. It's a breezy 15 knots." Any stronger and the wind would start shifting and picking up the snow. And worse—there was a total whiteout. Based on the sastrugi surrounding camp and the wind, I'll lose at least a mile of travel today, not to mention the frustration of blindness caused by the white out.

During the day, I suffered from physical and emotional turmoil. Having a hard packed track to follow made towing easier, but I fretted constantly about losing the track. In my mind, if I didn't take advantage of this find, I'd never reach the South Pole. The path wandered all over the place, so I knew it was inefficient and caused joint troubles, yet it provided solace after such a poor time in November. Ultimately, the hard track created rather than relieved stress.

The excitement of having tracks to follow induced me to go too fast for the first hour. As a consequence, I bonked and was fatigued from 10 a.m. until 3 p.m., making for a long slog until I recovered.

After 3 p.m., a full ground whiteout descended, making it impossible to keep a speedy pace anyway. In the whiteout, I constantly rammed omnipresent sastrugi patches. Each mound was not huge, but they were unrelenting, being packed together, though the skis and sleds bridged oblique east-west sastrugi easily. The challenge of traversing north-south orientated sastrugi was an adrenaline thrill, as skiing parallel to them left me on a perpetual icy knife edge. Each step was a potential ankle twister, a knee cranker. The sleds rolled repeatedly, yanking me to a halt. Treating the sleds like small children, I carefully righted them each time, speaking to them gently. This kept anger at bay, as it was pointless to be upset at inanimate objects. I had to be vigilant to prevent the sled bags from flopping out to prevent damaging the contents smashing my spare ski pole or, worse, tearing the tent.

At 5:30 p.m., I futilely peered a half mile ahead for any place to camp. The whiteout made it impossible. All I saw were vague, hazy white shapes with electric blue trolls lurking under the cake frosting-like forms. My only depth clues were slightly blue-tinted shadows. After several hours of incessant stumbling, my laughter turned to gritted teeth, as I fought not to be defeated by immobile ice sculptures. Hoping for the best, I kept on the rigid schedule, not stopping until after 5:45 p.m. Happily, one minute after my stop time, I skied into a clearing scantly larger than my tent.

"All stop!" I cheered, happy to find a clearing exactly when I needed one. Amundsen must have laughed in the face of whiteouts when he made his trek to the pole in 1912.

ALE reported the mechanized traverse was forced to camp 25 km away from Thiel's Corner at 85° due to bad weather last night. It was a consolation to learn that someone sitting 10 feet above the ice in a tank-tracked machine with a cabin, headlights and a heater had also been forced to stop. Being stymied by the same weather and only being on skis, I was comforted to know that a far better equipped snow tank was having the same issues. The equipment train was headed to drop my cache, drive out to the Thiel Mountains to drop off scientific supplies, and then return along the same path. I was excited at the chance that I would see them.

After bedding down at 10:30 p.m., I woke up sleeping on ice at 1 a.m. The air mattress had deflated during the night. Grimly chuckling, I opened and cleaned the deflation valve, hoping to alleviate the problem. As I re-inflated the mattress, I was shocked to discover an inch-long shard of steel in the tent's corner. A flash of panic set in. Had it punctured the mattress? Where had this cat claw piece of steel come from? Carefully checking the air mattress for punctures, I wracked my brain to recall the source of the errant piece of steel. Coming up with nothing plausible and finding no damage to the mattress, I continued refilling the mattress, calming my mind. At first, I thought to keep the shard as a memento of the troubles I'd experienced. Then, thinking better of it, I unzipped the door and pitched it northward, toward the barely discernible sled tracks. Had the fragment became lose again, it could put a hole in the mattress, or worse, myself. I foresaw regretting its companionship. Settling back down, my mind continued inventorying the possible source of the metal. These disturbing thoughts were a poor substitute for counting sheep, keeping me awake for some time.

Camp AC39
83°14.182'S 80°03.303'W
Distance: 11 nm, Time: 8.5 hours
Distance to South Pole: 406 nm

Wednesday, December 12, 2012 Day 42
Even though I cleaned both mattress valves last night, it was mostly flat when I woke up at 6 a.m. At first I shook my head, angry at another equipment failure. Then, I chortled. Had this not been part of what I had trekked to Antarctica to experience? My face turned from a sneer to a grin. One of the goals of going on this trip was to learn how to work through adversity in the worst possible conditions.

"If this is what it's going to be, then bring it on," I proclaimed.

While packing, light snow fell outside, draping a dusty blanket over the sled bags. Other than the subtle ticking of flakes pecking at the tent, there was no sound, leaving me to think about my Dad, his standing on his feet on concrete for 40 years, stacking innumerable tons of produce at grocery stores, and then the prostate cancer he endured. He survived it. My trip was going to last, at most, three months. He endured five years of wondering if the cancer would return. Thoughts of my parents filled my mind while I rammed the sleeping bag into its sack. I told myself to stop fixating on what might happen. Quit worrying about the weather conditions. It was beyond my power to change either of those issues. My mind kept spinning into the what-if land, which I knew was an unproductive waste of energy. Yes, my body was having a difficult time and all sorts of problems had occurred, but I was still out here. I had not given up. No matter how miserable I felt, how many whiteouts blinded me, and how many treacherous sastrugi-laden hills there were, I would not quit after coming this far. No way.

The first cache was only ten days away, halfway to the South Pole. Reaching it would be a huge morale booster. Achieving any goal, like when I traversed eastward and reached the cache drop-off point in a single day, showed me the power of short-term motivation. The little but distinguishable goals made this herculean effort possible. The huge goal of skiing 600 nautical miles was overwhelming. But, surely I could ski another 12 miles. It was doable. All I had to do was keep doing it.

The day started out agreeable enough, with the sun cutting through the clouds, improving visibility. It made travel decent in spite of 2 inches of fresh snow. However, clouds obscured the sun, creating a ground whiteout at 9:45 a.m. Undeterred, I dropped my gaze and waggled my head back and forth. My hope was to extract any information possible out of the surface, checking for subtle shadows and blue glow indicating a hole or tall sastrugi. By 10:30 a.m., the clouds covered the minuscule patches of blue in the sky, returning me to life inside a ping pong ball. Even though I had a grooved track to follow, I stumbled, losing my balance. The snake head maneuver helped find obstacles, though the inability to see the horizon was disorienting. Every fifteen minutes I paused and shook my head to regain my equilibrium. Once, a tiny blip of nausea hit me. Feeling this, I halted, turned and stared at my orange sleds to stabilize myself. There they were, hovering in whiteness. Keeping my eyes on a fixed, solid object cleared the sensation in a few moments and I pressed on.

After 2 p.m., the sun winked in and out of the soupy clouds, bringing the landscape into and out of focus, as though I was dunked and then removed from a tank of milk. Able to see again, I sped up.

With the utter lack of life out here, save for myself, my brain constantly scanned for patterns and uniqueness, looking for something beyond amorphous ice sculptures. While resting at 3 p.m., I glanced at the jacket sleeve where a smattering of snowflakes landed. What I saw astounded me. There, staring back at me, were several specimens of perfectly mirror polished snowflakes. At one angle, they caught and reflected the sky. Tilting my arm slightly, they then completely vanished, save for the six crystal spokes outlined on my jacket. Even though I've seen plenty of snow, never had I seen flakes as perfect as these. Even though new snow cut my speed, I enjoyed the sky's gifts. Dreaming of how these originated, I envisioned a laser cutter scoring the glass to form the shape. All the while, I dumbly grinned at the flakes on my arm.

ALE reported other teams ran into the same massive snowfall I experienced and not to expect any changes for several days, if not a week. Knowing what I faced in the coming days made me feel better. The unknown was the psychological enemy. There were plenty of novel problems yet to experience. Knowing the ground conditions ahead reduced my sense of foreboding. With only five minutes of rest time between making water, eating, grinding dead skin off my feet and preparing food for tomorrow, there was little time to ruminate on what would happen.

"Bring it on," I hissed.

Camp AC40
83°24.072'S 80°03.516'W
Distance: 10 nm, Time: 8 hours
Distance to South Pole: 396 nm

THURSDAY, DECEMBER 13, 2012 DAY 43

Even though I woke up tired from nightmares of the mystery metal shard of two nights ago, I was pleased to see it was sunny and the wind was dead. This meant I'd cook from the solar radiation, but that was preferable to stumbling blindly through a white out. Putting on my lightest wool shirt and long underwear, I prepared for the day. Cleaning the mattress valves paid off, as it stopped the overnight deflation.

At 10 a.m., I glanced east and was treated to seeing Kelvin-Helmholtz waves in the Antarctic clouds near the horizon. They are evenly spaced cartoon renditions of surf waves, but rounder. The seven white swirls marched in a perfect row, slowly building up above the horizon in the pale blue sky. Every minute, I glanced over my left shoulder, enjoying the morphing shapes. They formed and then closed out in half an hour, like a perfect wave in slow motion. If only real surf waves lasted that long. This was only the third time I have ever seen these formations in my life, the other two times being in southern California. To see these unique formations in Antarctica was a real treat.

As I sat on the lead sled for a break at 11:45 a.m., I faced the sun, examining the ashen-colored sastrugi dusted with snow. Adjusting my gaze off the sun by 30°, a rainbow of color specks jumped out at me, saturated as LED Christmas lights. Watching them sparkle reminded me of the coming Christmas.

"Yes," I thought, "I am out here by myself, living my decade old dream to trek across Antarctica." And then another thought said, "No, I don't expect to live long enough to do the funky chicken dance on my 75th wedding anniversary." Had I gone along my parents' path, my first kid would be 18 years old this year. While staring into an endless sea of white, thoughts like this coursed through my mind.

Even though I appreciated the lack of wind and whiteout-causing clouds, the sun cooked me. I was unable to keep cool, even with my shell jacket draped over my neck as a traveling cloak. Rolling up my sleeves to release heat only froze my skin from the -15°F air temperature. To be both hot to the point of sweating and having my skin freeze at the same time was a mind twister. I pondered the thermodynamic possibilities.

Putting in a full nine hours of travel today paid off with 11 nautical miles. At this pace, I'll make 84° in 2.5 days, then 85° in 5.5 days after that. With varying sastrugi conditions, sometimes incessant and other times completely gone, my speed varied widely. By noon, I zoomed along with virtually no sastrugi. Yet, by the end of the day, I crawled over thick heaps of it.

After charging up my satellite phone, I made my phone calls, one of them to my nephew to wish him a happy 7th birthday. Teasingly, I told him I have been a little cold for a few days and wondered what to do. Being a boy of few words, he replied that I should build an igloo for shelter with blocks of snow to stay warm. With an exasperated sigh, he handed off the phone to his dad, thinking I was a complete moron for not putting up an igloo every evening. My brother and I enjoyed a laugh out of it.

Camp AC41
83°35.384'S 80°04.816'W
Distance: 11.4 nm, Time: 9 hours
Distance to South Pole: 385 nm

Friday, December 14, 2012 Day 44

The silence this morning was absolute, with the only sounds coming from me rustling around in my nylon castle. While chowing down the same breakfast for the 44th time, I unzipped the door and entertained myself by testing Antarctica's acoustics. Under a sky that transitioned from faded blue jean color on the horizon to fully saturated Crayola blue directly overhead, with all the tints in between, I yelled in various pitches. There was no echo. No discernible response. Even a boat in the middle of a calmed ocean produces more sound. Water reflects voices, providing reverberation. It felt like I had noise-canceling headphones on. The snow-covered sastrugi absorbed all sound, reflecting nothing. As the synthetic clothing I wore made a constant zish-zish sound, I had to stay perfectly still to enjoy the rare experience of hearing nothing but the blood rushing in my ears.

I had woken up with my throat parched, as yesterday's windless day took it out of me. Drooling while eating salt-covered almonds, I knew my salt levels were low. I needed to kick up the hydration a notch, adding another 0.5L of water to today's schedule. As I skied through the day, my muscles tightened to the point that at 1 p.m. my abductors cramped. Knowing this to be the weakest leg muscle, I massaged them every ten minutes to keep them from completely failing, hurting my knees from the imbalance their cramping caused. Even though I took magnesium to maintain my electrolytes, I did not anticipate needing so many salt pills to deal with the radiation-induced overheating. Chalk one more up to unique Antarctic experiences.

Even though the day's travel with low wind and cloud cover was pleasant for visibility, the soft snow was brutal for sled drag. Ironically, I needed 20+ knot winds to pack the snow down to reduce sled drag. Yet those same winds cost me a mile of travel each day. With the stable weather, the surface would not change for the foreseeable future. Having soft snow also cushioned my feet, reducing their aches. It was both a blessing and a curse on the hard track.

Too, the middle joint of both big toes became swollen and puffy this week. They didn't hurt as severely today, but when I flexed my feet upward, they hurt. I needed two or three days of rest to recover. At this point, unless a major storm arose and trapped me in the tent, I would not stop. I was conservative with my anti-inflammatory medication, as I didn't want to exhaust my supplies with still over a month of travel remaining. Using and maintaining consumables was a tough balancing act. I needed to manage the pain to keep up miles and prevent further injury. Yet, I needed to verify there were enough for the remainder of the trip. Each evening, for the past couple of weeks, I counted the number of pills to double check there were enough. I derived pleasure from the counts because they kept my mind occupied, off my troubles. Knowing the count was still correct boosted my confidence in knowing that, if I kept pace and managed everything well, I would reach the South Pole with time to spare.

Camp AC42
83°46.096'S 80°06.101'W
Distance: 11 nm, Time: 9 hours
Distance to South Pole: 374 nm

Saturday, December 15, 2012 Day 45

The breeze was variable today, shifting from completely dead up to 10 knots. As this area looked flat, with easy rolling hills, I decided to enjoy my iPod. Knowing that music became dull after but an hour of listening, I had brought several audio books. These were as much to educate as keep me entertained for the long days on the ice. It was a logical plan. That was, until the iPod announced the battery was low and unceremoniously shut off. And that was that. Considering the now dead device, I pressed it to my forehead and laughed at the comedy of the situation. All the effort to prepare audio books prior to departure was now wasted by basic battery chemistry.

I recalled Hannah McKeand noting in an interview that she uses her iPhone for music, as its larger battery lasts four days. This was a perfect time and place to recall that quote. As I pulled off the ear buds, I listened to the subtle puffs of air, the synthetic fabric sounds of the parka, and the crunch of snow under my skis. Realizing that my time to enjoy this peculiar Antarctic symphony was short, I stowed the iPod and ear buds away, happy not to have electronic noises. Dansercoer's Polar Exploration admonished readers to turn off the music to allow for hearing the subtle shifts in the sound of snow, allowing for adjustments to achieve the best possible efficiency. Once the iPod died, I knew that I was better off without it. The random memories were far more enjoyable. I was happy to be away from the distractions of emails, text messages and phone calls.

By 3 p.m., I watched a low, hazy wall of clouds slowly rise on the horizon. The mass was formless, almost ghostly, as it approached from the east. My hopes that it was not fog were dashed after I set up camp and commenced making water. Ice fog overtook camp at 8 p.m., the temperature plummeting for want of sun. As I watched, frost smothered everything in a strange, computer graphic-like motion.

As the fog obscured the sun, I did not even bother connecting the solar panels to recharge the incapacitated iPod or the satellite phones. Going through the effort only risked damaging the electronics. And, it impacted my sleep time. ALE's weather forecast called for fog patches and increasing winds. As I could easily observe the weather outside and I had no choice but to travel, regardless of conditions, I questioned myself as to why I even bothered asking for forecasts. It made no difference. Coming from perpetually mild San Diego, I never cared about a forecast. So now I thought about Antarctica the same way. Whatever was to happen was out of my control, so enjoy the challenges and live every minute of it.

While grinding the dead skin off my feet outside the tent, I had to balance against resting my foot on the snow and preventing my bare leg from contacting the tent. In these temperatures, the cold-soaking effect made nylon feel like frozen steel. Each night, I enjoyed the satisfaction of knowing that I took stock of and managed my body issues to prevent minor problems from devolving into crippling, bloody nightmares. The ALE doctors told me of how other explorers suffered snow blindness, polar thigh and horrid foot blisters tearing half the skin off their feet. At least avoiding those problems was under my control.

Camp AC43
83°57.141'S 80°07.388'W
Distance: 11 nm, Time: 9 hours
Distance to cache 1: 63 nm
Distance to South Pole: 363 nm

SUNDAY, DECEMBER 16, 2012 DAY 46

Waking up at 5:30 a.m., I was astonished at how cold the air was and how frosty the tent had become. Normally, keeping the vents open prevented icing over from my breath, but the fog that rolled in last night brought ice through the open vents. That, combined with the warmth of my body, caused the fog to melt and refreeze on contact with the tent wall. I needed a defroster! To clear out the slightly moist frost, I opted to open the door, cool the tent air way down, then use the brush to swish the frost off every surface and out of the door.

While skiing at 11:30 a.m., I suffered my first navigation snafu. The track I'd been enjoying forked at 84°00'. One track heading dead west and the other 330°, both useless to me. Having become psychological-ly dependent on the track, I was crestfallen. Though being on a hard surface made both feet and hips hurt, and the track wiggled all over the place, wasting valuable travel time, it had been the only sign of humans since I had left Union Glacier. Digging out the GPS, I gazed into the vast emptiness where I was now headed. Departing the fork and heading directly south, I looked back forlornly. The soft snow slowed me down, but traveling in a straight line balanced out extra drag from the soft snow. It wasn't that the track helped my speed (it didn't), but rather it kept me company. Monster, my stuffed compan-ion, was agreeable company, as he was handmade by my aunt Nancy Takeda. But he was safely ensconced in the sled bags during the day, out of sight. This track was the only visible human companionship. It was, for better or worse, something I was a part of. While pondering these thoughts after leaving the hard path, fog enveloped me.

Perfect, another white out.

Two hours south of the fork, a black shape appeared in my right peripheral vision, barely visible, flitting in and out of view in the fog. What was that? At first, I was frightened. What could possibly be out here? And, then, I saw it stir. My eyes widened as realization sparked my weary brain.

Way in the distance was the Thiel's traverse rig, moving north. Panic, elation and fear all grabbed me at once. I was sure they were coming back from Thiel's Corner, where my cache was. I longed to ask the driver where he'd driven from. Was it Thiel's Corner? There was no real value in asking and yet my mind swirled with the desire, overwhelming rational thought. I became obsessed with one ques-tion: where did you come from?

They appeared to be far off but not moving quickly, at least at this distance. I picked a bearing that I thought would intercept them and skied hard towards them. At first, my intercept plan appeared to work.

As I slowly closed in over half an hour of mad skiing, I drew only marginally closer. I traveled west rather than south, away from where I needed to go. Yet I didn't care. Crashing into and over sastrugi, the sleds overturned several times.

Going all out was a huge mistake. Unzipping and stripping off as much clothing as possible, I desperately bowled over sastrugi. As I closed the distance, the machines appeared to gain speed. And then I realized how far away they were. The snow tractor was still barely visible on a flat plain, meaning it was a mile or more away. I realized I'd have to turn north to catch them—a total waste of effort. Again, it appeared to gain even more speed. I stopped.

My arms went noodle limp.

Catching them was impossible. I broke down. It was nothing less than hideous, a worse moment than when the skis on the first sled broke. I should have filmed myself so I could slap myself silly later. It was ugly. Now I knew how castaways felt when they see potential rescue boats pass by, fleetingly close and yet impossibly far. I was crushed. Scooting over to my rig after accepting defeat, I sat and stared, waiting for my mind and emotions to clear. To comfort myself, I ate some spare cookies. Allowing several minutes to pass, I resolved to return to my original plan and schedule. Being dehydrated from the haste, I chugged water. Once I calmed down, the adrenaline cleared and I was happy to have enjoyed the rush. Watching the snow tractor roll north of me, it abruptly turned east. It must have been tracking one of the forks I left hours ago. No matter, I was back in the sastrugi. A calmness descended on me, and soon, after an hour of skiing amongst them, I felt more at home than with the track. They were what I yearned to see, not a machine that made tracks on the ice.

I skied until 6 p.m., keeping to the schedule, and made camp. From the effort of chasing the snow tractor, I fogged my goggles and breathed so hard as to freeze the neoprene mask to my bearded face. It was solid ice. After some effort, I tore away chunks of beard. The pain was awful, yet I was giddy knowing I survived another test. Once I slipped off my boots, I saw my right large toe was bruised on the underside. The kartankers were wet inside and covered by frost on the outside. Not having frostbite from wet footwear was a minor victory. I thrust my arms into the sky with the universal sign of triumph. To dry out the socks and kartankers, I put hot water bottles in them to thaw them out. Too, I boiled the sweat-soaked sock liners to take the heat-robbing moisture out of them. Smiling while doing this, I was satisfied in experiencing something few ever have, seeing a passing ship in the night, being unable to do anything about it, and accepting that I was never to catch it.

Camp AC44
84°06.938'S 80°11.646'W
Distance: 10 nm, Time: 9 hours
Distance to South Pole: 354 nm
Distance to cache 1: 53 nm
Rations remaining: 9 days

Monday, December 17, 2012 Day 47
Waking up, I felt more refreshed than I had been in weeks. Yesterday's emotional chaos helped eliminate some of the junk from my head. The ground whiteout still persisted. But it didn't bother me. I knew my mileage would be poor today, at least so I thought, when I woke up to gray skies. In fact, I covered a satisfying 12 miles, as the whiteout dissipated at noon and gave way to sun, with a medium breeze, to keep me cool. If I keep making 12 mile days with the cache 46 miles to the south, I estimated reaching it in four days.

The pulks still were not tracking, pulling to the right. After inspecting the harness traces, nothing appeared overtly wrong. I even adjusted the lead trace in hopes of clearing up the side pull. It did not help. Not wanting to waste more travel time, I chose to accept the problem until I could find a cause for it. As I peaked over an ice dome, a massive empty space appeared before me. It was at least five miles to the horizon. This was the first time during this entire expedition that I had been able to see this far. The vast, empty expanse frightened me. It was the first time I had been able to see the incredible distance I had yet to cover. While being awestruck at this incredible view, a crack split open on my right heel, sending needles of pain shooting through my foot. It helped distract me from the work yet to go. At this point, I laughed at the pain. What was one more ache?

The liner and alpine gloves were cold all day, likely from yesterday's sweat. So, when I made camp and finished making water, I stewed the liner gloves to clean them. The water turned greasy brown from 47 straight days of use. The alpine gloves had no removable liner, so the grease in them was unremovable, reducing their warmth. Since the old liner gloves were now wet, I put on the reserve pair. I was startled how warm they were in comparison. To keep the new ones as clean as possible, I planned to use the old ones once I stopped at night.

My spare collection of uneaten rations had grown to a full day's meal. To extend my stock of food, I ate all the spare rations. Eating these brought back happy memories of mom's cooking and how I loved the leftovers. There was something comforting about them, some vestige of my childhood memories.

Camp AC45
84°19.177'S 80°17.511'W
Distance: 12.3 nm, Time: 9 hours
Distance to South Pole: 341 nm
Distance to cache 1: 41 nm
Rations remaining: 8 days

TUESDAY, DECEMBER 18, 2012 DAY 48

Dreams of finding my cache, with life-sustaining food and fuel, snapped me awake. I did not want to fail and be picked up simply because I did not manage my resources well. Even though I had plenty of rations to cover the next 40 miles, I imagined being stuck in 60 knot blizzards, like the ones that doomed Scott's team in 1912. They were only 11 miles from their massive cache, a One-Ton Depot, when they perished by starvation and cold. These prominent explorers were with me in spirit. They had to make do with primitive, heavy equipment and tasteless foodstuffs, but had an enduring desire to succeed. I felt the same aspiration.

There was no way I was going to give up until absolutely forced to. Knowing that there was a bailout option, by making a phone call, was something those polar greats did not have. The huge storm of six days ago left me with sled-impeding soft snow, increasing my fatigue. The additional drag caused my primitive mind to give me reasons every hour of why it was okay to quit. Though it was easier to quash the negative thoughts since my mileage increased, they were still persistent. Yelling out like a warrior running into battle, I forced the thoughts away and rose out of bed, wide eyed and ready to ski miles. As I threw my sleeping bag off, Killaflaw's "Set Me On Fire" played in my mind. It repeated over and over, all day. It was invigorating motivation.

Over the day, the landscape changed from relatively flat to being made of huge ice domes, so grand that I was not aware of being on them. That was, until the sleds chased me down the north face of the valley. Descending these mountains affected navigation, too. As I lost elevation, the bubbles in my compass disappeared. For the past several days, an altitude-induced bubble had developed in the compass housing, a common problem. This air pocket prevents the compass needle from moving properly, making orienteering difficult. I rocked the compass back and forth to shift the bubble out of the way, all while not tilting the base to jam the needle, to navigate.

Checking my compass direction against the GPS indicated that my compass declination was not correct. The online calculator from the National Oceanic and Atmospheric Administration (NOAA) showed the declination error at the Hercules Inlet to be a whopping 39°. At this position, it was 43°. Due to my slow progress in previous weeks, a 4° error was insignificant. Now, over a 12 mile day, I wasted a half mile in lateral travel. I was glad to finally be traveling where tiny errors added up to significant distance. Using the trusty little steel screw, looped through the red compass lanyard, I corrected the declination. Had I forgotten about this correction, I would have drifted farther off course each day. By the time I was near the South Pole, my bearing would be off a full 10°, causing me to be miles off target.

While dragging gear into the tent that night, I felt a change in my perspective. Unexpectedly, the tent felt like home rather than only a tent. This little nylon hovel, in the middle of Antarctica, had a place for everything. It was comfortable. To me, it was essential that everything stayed in its place, so I wasted no time searching for items. Being in the tent felt comfortable and normal, as though it were some place I had lived for a long time. I laughed out loud at myself, pleased at the mental shift.

Camp AC46
84°30.797'S 80°23.363'W
Distance: 11.7 nm, Time: 9 nm, Elevation 4,400'
Distance to cache 1: 34.4 nm
Rations remaining: 8 days

WEDNESDAY, DECEMBER 19, 2012, DAY 49

The snow trench formed by digging blocks out had completely blown over. The sleds had a contrail of packed drift snow, as though they had been in a wind tunnel all night. Even though it meant work to dig the tent out, this meant the wind was strong enough to pack the snow, firming the surface. Travel would be easier today. Up to this point, there had been three inches of loose snow, adding constant drag to the sleds. I was elated. And, the best part, I had slept right through the wind, being dead to the world last night.

The wind also knocked the snow off the sastrugi, eliminating the ashen shade of everything. For a week, everything appeared as though it was covered by volcanic ash. Too, yesterday I noticed a peculiarity about the wind in this area. More than four times, the snow on the sastrugi changed from perfectly settled to completely windblown within a span of 50 feet. There was no obvious reason why snow drifts appeared or disappeared. There were no obvious hills to shape the snow drifts. I wondered if anyone had studied this. The surface change was so subtle, it was astounding to see such variation and wind transition zones. Drifts on the hard surface appeared all at once, in a few feet, then disappeared as quickly. At 1 p.m., I blundered across the tracks from the mechanized traverse again, much to my dismay. So many times, the snowcat tracks ended up being a curse rather than a blessing.

One of the optical illusions sastrugi-covered ice caused was the effect of seeing slopes and hills when there were none. Facing in the direction of the sun, where the sastrugi facing me was in the shade, made that direction look uphill, regardless of the true topography. The reverse was true: sastrugi facing me, lit by the sun, always looked downhill. Near the end of the day, when I was fatigued, I had a perpetual sense that the landscape to my right was uphill because that's where the sun always was. And, after 5 p.m., everything ahead of me looked uphill, regardless of the reality. Fatigue made hills appear in front of me, even though the ice was flat. Between the morning and the afternoon, when the sun traversed to the other half of the sky, the landscape appeared to see-saw from left to right. What was uphill when I made camp was now downhill and vice versa. The power of psychological optical illusions was incredibly strong in Antarctica.

Seven weeks of eating the same, repetitive diet was beginning to take its toll. I had become a reluctant connoisseur of butter. At first all the butter tasted to be the same. Peter McDowell at ALE recommended purchasing Kerry Gold butter for its lower water content. I had also purchased some less expensive Chilean butter. Never having studied the qualities of butter, I was now receiving an honorary degree in the subject. The Chilean butter was of poor quality compared to the Irish butter. The Chilean butter crumbled, rather than having a creamy consistency, and the paper wrapper stuck to it. Handling the Chilean butter required care to avoid contaminating my gloves. As such, I was compelled to ingest paper scraps. And, too, there were ice crystals inside the Chilean butter, meaning it had a higher water content. There was a real difference. Imagine my surprise when biting through the Chilean butter and crunching into ice crystals. The bargain butter was not a deal.

I increased my water intake by another liter today to stave off dehydration. As a consequence, my bladder ached from the pressure of the towing harness. The feeling was like a combination of having an uncomfortably full bladder while riding in a car while someone purposefully and randomly stomped on the brakes. While training in Jackson Hole, I suffered from this problem, unable to relieve myself out on the public pathways. I learned to run somewhat dehydrated, knowing it was easy to recover upon returning home. This was not possible out here, as there was no recovery time for rehydration. I reveled in the constant vigilance required to maintain my body.

As I continued my process of randomly pulling food packs, I'd not had spaghetti with meat sauce in over two weeks, so I was overjoyed to find it for dinner tonight. I mused what the chances of not picking out the spaghetti for two weeks was. With nine hours of nothing to contemplate but towing, I welcomed the mathematical distraction.

During the scheduled call, ALE noted that the supply traverse had left after I requested a replacement shovel and tent stakes. Thus, they'll need to air drop my cache tomorrow. All at once thoughts of poor weather preventing the cache drop weighed on me. I was happy for the distraction of freeze-dried spaghetti probability calculations.

Camp AC47
84°42.454'S 80°31.290'W
Distance: 11.7 nm, Time: 9 hours
Distance to South Pole: 322 nm
Distance to cache: 22 nm
Rations remaining: 7

December 20, 2012, Day 50
What a mega hill I ascended today! It didn't appear large or steep, yet it took three hours to ski up it. I didn't even realize I was heading uphill until I felt weak and wondered why I was bonking. Then, staring north during a break, I saw how far up the escarpment I was, skiing up mountainous foothills.

With the breeze in the morning, I was able to tow rapidly. But when the wind died at 2 p.m., near the hill top, so did I. The sun's radiation cooked me. Though I was in a hard track, with the best possible weather conditions, I only covered 12 miles up this hill without overheating. Others have reported skiing 12 to 15 miles. Did they keep ice cubes in their pockets to keep them cool?

On cresting the hill, the Thiel Mountains came into view, thrilling me to no end. At first, I thought the gray-orange mounds were a distant scientific base, based on their blocky shape with a checkerboard of light and dark that were window shaped. As those shapes rose from the horizon, I realized my mind was playing tricks. I was not used to seeing anything but ice in the distance, so my mind conjured up the foolish notion of manmade structures. It was dumb to think I'd see a base that huge, way out here. Distances were deceiving. What I thought I saw up close was days away. I wondered how far away the biggest mountains to the west were. What about the four peaks to the southwest? Had anyone ever climbed them? These questions rolled through my mind as I realized how massive the peaks must be. A local map would answer these questions, but it was as much fun to wonder about them. At least I had finally traversed from west to east Antarctica, through one of the longest mountain ranges on Earth.

ALE confirmed what my continent-scale map showed. These were the Transantarctic Mountains. They also reported other teams have passed me, one already at 85°81'S. Another team was coming up on me at 84°80'S but was far east of me, so I'd never see them. To my dismay, Alice McDowell, the ALE operator, remarked the weather at the cache was poor for a drop off today, so it hadn't happened. It was only 10 miles south of me, yet the horizon was clear. Did the mountains obscure weather over the horizon?

Based on my calculations, if I was able to maintain 10-plus mile days for the next 32 days, my arrival at the pole would be on January 22. This was uncomfortably close to the last day I could be in Antarctica. My mind kept imagining worst-case scenarios; I wished the iPod was alive to drown out these thoughts. To add to my troubled thoughts, sun dogs flanked the 24-hour sun as I bedded down, meaning snow was on its way, confirming ALE's report of poor weather.

In the last two days, I started gagging while eating food again. Not since mid-November had this happened. I deduced this was from my anxious mental state, due to worrying about the upcoming cache drop. One of the satellite messages I received from Nancy Takeda was simply this, "Left Right Left—one foot in front of the other." That was all I needed to focus on, irrespective of the mind junk I fought with.

Camp AC48
84°54.140'S 80°39.364'W
Distance: 11.7 nm, Time: 9 hours, Elevation: 4,554'
Distance to South Pole: 306 nm
Distance to cache: 10.9 nm at 184°

December 21, 2012, Day 51

Waking up to my first Austral Summer solstice, I was excited to find my first cache today. Even the six inches of fresh, soft snow did not bother me. The powder had all but wiped out the hard track, so my speed would not change tomorrow when I left it. As the tracks wandered this way and that, I was excited to be free of their company.

My right ski's epoxy coating chipped off, exposing the wood, from me stumbling over sastrugi today. This was extremely bad. If the wood became damp, the water would wick into the middle of the ski and, when it froze, the ski would explode. For whatever physiological reason, the left ski chipped on the right, not the other way around. Was one leg longer than the other? Once I saw the exposed wood today, I wished I'd preemptively put on epoxy when I first saw deep scratches on the skis last night. The epoxy would have prevented further damage. Now that it was overcast and cold, I'd have to wait until sun reappeared after the storm passed.

While ruminating how to deal with the ski damage, I saw something flittering on the southern horizon. Like with the mountains, I was not sure what I saw. After another fifteen minutes of skiing and staring at the flickering object, my brain snapped recognition.

I had found the cache at Thiel's Corner in a ground whiteout! My exuberant cheer was carried away in the breeze. After 45 minutes of hard skiing, I reached the cache at 3:45 p.m. Screaming, I whooped at the top of my lungs. Everything was in my cache. I jumped up and down, flapped my arms and had a generally enjoyable time celebrating. Everything was there, including the new shovel and replacement tent stakes. I wandered around the site, inspecting the groomed runway, fuel barrels and footprints. As I would not return here, this was

my one chance to look around. Taking the scenery in when it presented itself was essential. Packing the food, fuel and gear into my sleds,
I bolted southward, using the burst of energy to cover an additional
mile in half an hour in soft snow. Never had I done this before.

Sorting the new supplies while making water and dinner, snow
fell, pecking at the tent in otherwise silent conditions. Last night's
sun dogs were delightful, but they heralded today's snow. A hundred
nautical miles south of here, near 87°, was a large crevasse field, compelling me to adjust my bearing to 190°. Making this minor adjustment now saved miles of extra skiing. I did not want to hit crevasses
at all, especially in a whiteout. I had not skied this far to disappear
into the ice.

Camp AC49
85°05.948'S 80°51.064'W
Distance: 11.9 nm, Time: 9 hours, Elevation: 4,425'
Distance to South Pole: 295 nm
Distance to cache 2: 134 nm
Rations remaining: 19 day, fuel 5.7L

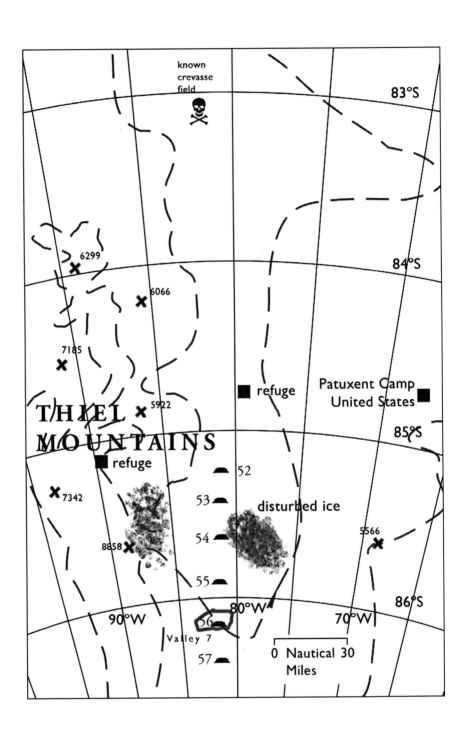

16

Days 52-57

December 22, 2013, Day 52

Today I skied in the flattest place I've ever been on the Earth. The 85th parallel was so perfectly flat that I had trouble navigating. The sun was out, but there was nothing to use as a navigational reference point. The ALE crew who had traveled through this region told me how they had difficulty navigating because there was nothing to focus on. There were minor, occasional hubcap-shaped lumps of ice, as thick as a hand and the diameter of a pickup tire. Even though these bumps were thin, they stood in relief to the rest of the ice surface which had, at best, the surface variation of office carpet. The edge of the horizon was completely devoid of sastrugi, making a perfect edge against the sky. Except for the Thiel Mountains barely visible behind me, there was truly nothing to see.

Without distant sastrugi to use as waypoints, I referred to my compass frequently. Moving efficiently through here required extreme concentration. My pacing had to be controlled, balancing between wearing myself out by skiing too fast and making sure to cover enough distance during the day.

With an additional two inches of powdery snow on the ice surface, I had expected the mileage to drop. I stared through slitted eyes at the GPS as it powered up.

"Come on, give me miles," I whispered. The distance took forever to appear on the display. The day's travel distance winked onto the diminutive display. My eyes bugged out, both hands clutched the GPS and thrust it upward in triumph, striking the tent's ceiling.

"Yes!" I roared. Not only had I kept up the distance in the soft snow, camp was only a tenth of a mile off the ALE-suggested route. With mouth agape, I laughed heartily in jubilation. After wandering the absolute nothingness, I had made solid distance and stayed right on course.

The damage to the ski's top coating grew frighteningly, exposing more of the wood core. With the clouds overhead at night, the tent was not hot enough to cure the epoxy by tomorrow morning. I debated making the repair. But, I knew that if it did not solidify, the glue would spread all over everything, causing even more trouble. Deciding to wait one more day in hopes of a sunny, wind-free evening, I skipped the repair. Instead, I enjoyed my last day of being 38 years old in Antarctica by performing the ritual of melting snow and rehydrating spaghetti.

The new shovel worked wonders. It reduced tent pitching time by 10 minutes. Even though the replacement shovel weighed two more ounces than the broken one, the enhancement in digging speed, coupled with no longer having to shovel on my hands and knees, more than made up for the added weight. The replacement tent stakes cut stress off, too. Able to relax for a moment, I charged the iPod, after weeks of disuse, and played Maxwell's *Put Your Dream to the Test*, absorbing the author's wisdom in my nylon mobile home. Finally, the weight the iPod cost me was justified. With the Thiel Mountains making a backdrop to the west, I felt far more confident than I have in a long time that it was possible to reach the South Pole.

Camp AC50
85°17.948'S 81°22.156'W

Distance: 11.5 nm, Time: 8.75 hours, Elevation: 4,603'
Distance to South Pole: 282 nm
Distance to cache 2: 123 nm
Rations remaining: 18 days

Sunday, December 23, 2012 Day 53

And now here I was, in my 39th year of life, enjoying a dream I've entertained for ten years, out on the Antarctic plateau, preparing for the day. Though I treated myself to sleeping in an extra fifteen minutes, I still needed to put in nine hours of travel. There was no respite from daily polar travel.

With a 20 knot headwind, the long, rolling hills here seemed even steeper. Though the headwind cut a mile off my day's distance, it was a boon. The sun does not harden the snow in the interior of Antarctica like it does in warmer climates because the air temperature never rises high enough to melt the snow. Only air motion packs the ultra-dry flakes. I was happy to face wind for a full day.

At the end of the day, it took a half hour of searching to find an area flat enough to pitch my tent. On the windward side of a sastrugi patch, I made my birthday camp.

For dinner, I enjoyed freeze-dried chicken noodle stroganoff for the ninth time. I learned early in the expedition that the stroganoff required the food thermos to be sanitized with boiling water. On previous mornings after this meal, a nasty odor wafted from the thermos. No other food caused this problem.

This was the first sunny night in several since I discovered the ski damage. As the weather was stable, the tent was warm enough to cure the epoxy. I had to use a disposable mixing stick or anything I didn't mind coated in steel-hard glue. Casting about, I grinned. My eyes settled on the bike gear cleaning tool for brushing snow. Its handle was perfect. The top of the ski served as a mixing surface. Having more epoxy on the ski top wouldn't hurt. As the glue was gummy at this temperature, it created tar-like strands. These coated both my shell pants and the air mattress. With some gentle scraping, the errant glue left only discoloration and thankfully didn't harden. I spent extra time making sure the epoxy was thoroughly mixed, because I only had one shot to do it right.

To let the epoxy set, the ski needed to remain inside the tent to stay warm. After seeing what a mess the epoxy made, I knew the ski had to be kept away from everything. This was not an easy task inside a 6' x 4' tent filled with gear. I settled on hanging the ski by tying some spare line to the tent's apex, fashioning loops in each, and ever so carefully dangling the ski. Though it was risky to have a glue-covered ski hovering precariously over my head the whole night, inches from my sleeping bag, it was the only option. It made sleeping, eating and managing toilet activities extra challenging, as I had to do it all lying down.

My dad had edited together a birthday song from all of my closest friends and played them over the satellite phone when we talked tonight. Wendy Davis created the lyrics.

That was so neat! A bunch of the closest people in my life sang happy birthday and also added individual messages. It was, by far, the most cherished birthday present I've ever received. Along with the cards from mom and Kelly, this was the coolest birthday ever. Hearing this, over satellite phone, on the far side of the Earth, touched me and renewed my vigor and resolve.

Camp AC51
85°27.483'S 81°50.032'W
Distance: 10.6 nm, Time: 8.75 hours, Elevation: 5,044'
Distance to South Pole: 273 nm
Distance to cache 2: 113 nm

MONDAY, DECEMBER 24, 2012 DAY 54

After talking with my parents until 11:30 p.m. last night, I woke up tired this morning. Having been able to share the experience of being down here with them was worth the fatigue. The epoxy did not completely harden after nine hours due to the extreme cold, but it felt stiff enough. I hoped the repair would survive the day's beating. Inspecting the tent, there were no globs of epoxy on anything, so I was happy my setup worked. The biggest risk of handling this epoxy was coating the ski bottom or the steel edges. I was happy not to have the ski smash my head at 3 a.m. That would not have been the best way to wake up to Christmas Eve.

At 9 a.m., I began climbing several hills, each successive one leading to a plateau, which shortly left me with another hill to climb. On approach, the hills were imperceptible. The surface was so flat that every direction looked like up. Only when I stared back during a break did I realize I was on a grade. It was steep enough to make me feel weak, as though I had little energy. Only by seeing I was not on flat ground was I able to allay my fear the fatigue was from the incline and not a lack of energy.

After 1 p.m., I crested one rolling hill and found myself in a zone of utter flatness at 85°33'S 81°53'W. I thought the surface on the 22nd was flat. The minor egg-yoke-shaped lumps of the days before were gone and only the tiniest pock marks in the ice were visible, flat as a parking lot. I recalled an article in the now defunct *National Geographic Adventure* magazine describing a dead zone in the Sahara, encompassing one-third of Chad and much of southern Libya. The author said he sped up his motorcycle, put his hands out and closed his eyes without fear of hitting anything. There was nothing out there to hit. Here was a place steeped in ice instead of sand, but otherwise the same. I closed my eyes and skied, with no fear of falling over anything, for 30 seconds at a time. Longer than that and my balance failed me. When I opened my eyes, it took some time to refocus. There was nothing on the surface to see but blazing white snow. It was as though my eyes failed to work. It was thrilling to be in such a flat place on Earth. There was nothing to distract me from concentrating on moving forward, all while enjoying the completely random thoughts coursing through my mind.

At noon, while I passed through this *Flat Earth* zone, the temperature plummeted for no obvious reason, forcing me to stop and rapidly don the fleece jacket skirt to protect my stomach skin from freezing. The temperature had dropped 15 degrees in mere moments. Once adjusted, I skied on, relatively unhampered. Then, at 4:30 p.m., the temperature warmed like I'd walked in front of a fire on a cold winter day. I immediately overheated. Ripping off the stomach skirt and stowing it in the lead sled, I forged on. It was as though the air conspired to distract me from the absolutely featureless landscape. Thus far, Antarctica had proven to be anything but a boring place.

At 5:15 p.m., a sastrugi field rose up on the horizon, tearing the razor-edged delineation between white and blue. The sastrugi appeared to approached me rather than I it. There were no visual cues around me to impart the sensation of motion. Inside the sastrugi patch, I pitched the tent and prepared for the evening. The epoxy coating on the skis held up well, considering my drunken stumble through the sastrugi patch. I melted snow and made water to rehydrate a Christmas Eve meal of macaroni and cheese.

Sitting, listening to the white gas stove roar, I was absorbed in writing my journal at 7 p.m. and capturing the experience of being here when the unbelievable occurred. I heard my name called out. Once. Twice. Fearing that my mind had finally come unhooked, I peered out of my window. Were my senses playing with me?

"Aaron, is that you in there?" shouted a disembodied female voice. Peering out the north facing window again, I saw legs attached to skis only five yards away.

Vilborg Arna Gissurardóttir, a female solo skier from Iceland, had found me in the middle of Antarctica.

She saw my tent an hour before and used it as a target to ski toward. At first, Vilborg thought the tent was some weird sastrugi. Then, realizing it was a tent, she immediately knew it was me, as I was the first out in the field, departing a month before any other teams. One-way ski teams usually depart Union Glacier for the South Pole in late November, depending on weather. Having skied across Greenland's ice cap, she had far more experience than I and was able to travel much faster. My visitor said she was attempting a completely solo trip, without resupply, caches or any other support. Planning to ski to the pole in 50 days, she was far behind her schedule, though not as badly as I. Slogging through the same massive snow dump I had encountered had hampered her speed. Still at 280 miles from the pole, she had been in the field for 35 days and estimated it would take her another 20 days to reach the pole. But, she only had 15 days of rations remaining.

Standing at barely over five feet, Vilborg sported a patchwork of sponsor logos, covering her red fur trimmed parka, black pants and smartly coordinated teal-colored ski boots. She looked sharp, save for the duct tape dangling from her skis. Her sled setup was the same as mine, save for the navy blue nylon sacks filling them and the short yellow cord with bungee shock protection looped in. Her smile was warm and genuine. Her eyes hid behind protective glasses, which she repeatedly nudged with her red gauntlet-sized mitten gloves while talking, like a diminutive blonde Clark Kent. There was a minute sore on her nose. The sun and wind had been rough on her. How she stood to wear glasses instead of goggles surprised me, as the sub-freezing wind constantly bit at my face, compelling me to wear fog-trapping goggles rather than breathable glasses. I was only able to wear glasses a few times during no wind days.

"I was not sure if I should approach you, as some people can become angry at the intrusion into their wilderness experience," she said.

"No, no, meeting you out here is a welcome shock. I'm not mad at all," I quipped.

"I had planned to be out here fifty days but I think it will take me at least five additional days to make it."

"Oh, that's not good. What are you going to do?" I asked.

"With my rations short, I have not decided what I'm going to do."

"Have you spoken with ALE about it?"

"Yes, and we are discussing it. I want to do this trip solo unsupported and unaided. So the food is a big problem."

"Yes, that it is. I had to give up my unaided status, too. This year has been difficult."

"It has. But it is my second expedition this year, so it's no surprise."

"Really? Where did you go before this?"

"I crossed Greenland in the spring."

I was stunned. She was adept at being out here, moving quickly and appearing to have no particular troubles. Although Vilborg said she was having a thrilling time out here, the concern of what to do about the food situation seemed to weigh on her. She said she planned to discuss her options with ALE. I felt bad for her to have such hard luck with food in this difficult Antarctic year. Mentioning how her kartankers had developed large holes in them, I showed her my duct tape kartanker armor wrap trick. One of the ALE staff told me to secure the kartankers with duct tape; otherwise the matted wool would shred apart. I was happy and proud that I could, after proving to be the slowest person ever, share and help someone more experienced. We took a few photographs of each other to email once we both returned to civilization.

Vilborg shared how she had left her job as manager of Iceland's Eyjafjallajökull park. She was there when the park's volcano exploded in 2011, grounding European flights. She seemed to have an adventurous life. Declining my offer to share a modest Christmas Eve meal of macaroni and cheese, she skied south, continuing her journey. I bid her farewell and watched her go.

As she disappeared into the distance, I sat there laughing out loud. I wondered if she thought I was crazy for the jocular laughter, as she increased the distance between us. What was the chance of someone running into me in the literal middle of nowhere? Everyone who arrived after me at Union Glacier knew who I was, as there was a large map of Antarctica with team positions dotted across it. ALE's staff kept close tabs on what was happening with expeditions in the field, as that was one of their primary purposes for being in Antarctica. I wondered who else was out here.

Camp AC52
85°39.100'S 81°59.357'W
Distance: 11.7 nm, Time: 9 hours, Elevation: 5,382'
Distance to South Pole: 261 nm
Rations remaining: 17 days

TUESDAY, DECEMBER 25, 2012 DAY 55

Merry Christmas! And what a white Christmas it was. The sun, in spite of the light breeze, felt warmer than yesterday. Eating my morning ration, I kept laughing about the unlikely chance encounter with Vilborg yesterday. The thought of someone finding me out on this lonely plateau seemed all but impossible. Though there was absolutely no place to hide, as the sastrugi provides no cover, finding another person out here was as likely as the moon smashing into the Earth. And yet, it had happened.

During the day, I learned Antarctic travel techniques that had eluded me to this point. With Vilborg visible in the distance over a mile off, I saw her tracks in the ice and learned why, in part, she traveled so much faster. Simply put, she skied in an absolutely straight line, regardless of the obstacle. Only twice did she go around sastrugi, immediately reconnecting with her previous bearing. All this time, I dodged sastrugi, pits and their ilk to prevent crashing or snagging the sleds. As the sleds' skis had failed some time ago, my sleds were now tracking like hers. This was a new and welcome approach.

While passing over rolling hills, I learned from Vilborg's tracks all day. I had trained myself to dodge everything, increasing the total distance I traveled while reducing effective southward travel. Crashing over hundreds of sastrugi I previously circumvented, I learned from this petite woman from Iceland. She barreled over everything. The previous approach of dodging was like swerving back and forth across a street while driving somewhere quickly. The odometer would show 120 miles traveled, but only 100 map miles were covered. I took mental measurements of the sastrugi patches I had formerly gone around and was shocked. A 30-foot diversion here, 50 feet there. Repeatedly, all day, every day. Calculating it out, I had wasted at least a mile each day by avoiding minor impediments. When the skis were attached to the sleds, dodging everything was the only safe way to travel, as the sleds repeatedly slid into pits and snagged on sastrugi. Now I saw, with late clarity, why Aleksander Gamme ditched his sled skis the previous year. At first I thought it was because he broke them. Now I see that they were impeding his progress, too.

There were other items I noticed. Vilborg's two sleds were extremely close together. All throughout this trip, I'd struggled, pulling the sleds up an ice face twice, as my sleds were spaced far enough apart so the skis did not crash into each other. As a consequence, I constantly fought having the sled rig strike each sastrugi twice. Seeing her rig with the two sleds nearly touching, I realized that having the sleds far apart without skis was dumb. While I geared up in the morning, I adjusted the traces between the sleds, reducing their separation to three inches apart. Upon hitting the first few sastrugi, I learned what a difference a single sled face to strike the ice walls made. It was incredible. The forward sled lifted up the trailing one, preventing the second from hitting the sastrugi. They now glided over each obstacle. No more being slammed for each sastrugi, repeated hundreds of times a day. This alone was a back saver if nothing else.

Also, Vilborg wore her compass free-hanging while mine was constantly mounted on my chest harness. Having it dangle instead forced me to check a sighting once and stick with it, rather than constantly stopping to recheck. This change easily saved 10 minutes, or one-third of a mile, per day. Over 80 days that would have been a whopping additional 26.6 miles. Two days saved.

She must also carry her food in her pack because I never saw tracks returning to the sled. That must save 10 minutes, again improving mileage. Her backpack had sled trace mounts. She had polar travel down. Each minute saved over her 50 days added up to miles gained and travel days cut! Clearly, there was much I didn't know about travel down here. Her ski pole stride was shorter than mine, yet she traveled farther every day.

These subtle little adjustments, improving my efficiency, paid off immediately.

I covered over 13 miles. Farther than I had ever gone in Antarctica in a single day. I could grow used to this! While skiing, I enjoyed seeing another human in scale, over a mile ahead of me, peaking above and then disappearing below the next hill crest. Now I knew what my imagined telephoto helicopter view of me looked like. This was the only day I saw anyone, as Vilborg quickly left me in her dust.

I passed Vilborg's camp at 9:30 a.m. and learned another efficiency improving tactic. Where her sleds stopped was where they stayed until morning. I always staked the tent to the sled while pitching it, then dragged my sleds back to the entrance for unloading. The snow revealed her superior technique. I thought little about how much time and energy I spent dragging them around the tent after using them as ballast. This maneuvering cost 5 minutes per day. That added up to a mile wasted over 80 days. Now when I stopped, I pitched the tent in front of the sleds and then pull them up to the door, never again dragging them backward.

I felt guilty about not offering to share some of my rations with Vilborg. She lacked food and I had a few rations to spare. Not offering the food bugged me over the next several days. That was, until Steve Jones at ALE confirmed that Vilborg was attempting this as a solo trip, without aid or support. So, she could not have accepted supplies even if I had offered them. And, too, it was fortunate that I didn't step out of the tent to shake her hand. According to the rules of exploration, human contact could have ruined her solo status. I did not want to hurt someone who inadvertently helped me out.

While on my phone call with James Hayes at Union Glacier, he wanted to know how I was doing.

"Have you cashed in on Vilborg's Christmas gift?" he asked.

"Heck yes. I never thought to travel directly over everything. I have been going around things, wasting so much time," I said with glee.

"Great, then we expect you will pick up the pace."

"Yes, now that I understand the travel method down here."

What a huge Christmas present her tracks turned out to be. I've gone farther and faster than I ever have. The onus of having to incessantly dodge everything was lifted from me. At this rate, the Pole felt closer than ever. It was still over 280 nm, but it now did not seem as far. At the end of the day, my speed improved by 15 percent. With some of the pressure relieved, my brain relaxed, sticking the remixed song of "To the Moon and Back" by Discotronic vs Tevin into my mind.

At 9 p.m., in the bright daylight of the 24-hour Antarctic sun, I celebrated Christmas by opening the cards mom and Kelly sent with me, the only two Christmas presents I packed. They meant so much more to me out here, by myself. And, I enjoyed an unexpected gift from a heretofore stranger all day. This present had given me enough speed that I will touch the South Pole before running out of time at the end of January.

Camp AC53
85°52.274'S 82°02.575'W
Distance: 13.2 nm, Time: 9 hours, Elevation: 5,600'
Distance to cache 2: 87 nm
Distance to South Pole: 248 nm

WEDNESDAY, DECEMBER 26, 2012 DAY 56

Upon waking, my mind spun out of control with thoughts of how much retraining I had to do in a short amount of time. Taking a completely straight line, skiing over everything sounds easy. It was not. The inclination to skirt obstructions hampered me the entire time I've been here, cutting southward mileage covered by a surprising amount.

I made short work of breakfast and toilet activities, as I was excited to mount up the skis and move as rapidly as possible. With light wind and sun, conditions were ripe for me to recover so many miles that my inexperience had stolen from me. With Vilborg's tracks occasionally visible, I saw she continued directly over sastrugi I still thought to skirt. Now, I forced myself to keep my path as perfectly straight as possible. The sleds, now close together, worked as a single unit, tracking perfectly, making it possible to cut close to deep pits, staying tight around tall sastrugi, which was impossible with ski-mounted sleds. Only once did the sleds slide into a pit. The time and energy savings were immediate. I no longer felt the dead fatigue of the previous days. Tracking did matter and was and equally important a factor as sled drag.

I was stunned how strong was the urge to avoid sastrugi. When I thought a sastrugi was too tall to ski over, I steeled myself, tossing one ski-laden foot on the sastrugi, then the second, confident the ski skins would hold. Only twice, over the whole day, did the skin-clad skis slip backward. With the mass of steel on the skins, I worried little about them being torn off. The sleds were now running smoothly enough that I had little fighting to do and, with the unified action of both, I was having a much better time of it. With pleasant weather, for Antarctica, this was the perfect opportunity to make fantastic mileage.

After breaking camp, it took three hours to cross the first valley, with the opposite side a total dead zone, devoid of any sastrugi. The landscape was now even more riveting with my renewed spirit.

Beyond the valley, I crossed three ice domes and stopped on a fourth rise at 6 p.m. It was still a long way to 9,000 feet from my current 5,900 foot elevation. Laughing, I recalled how I used to think Antarctica was a flat place, devoid of undulations. The Thiel Mountains were only visible from here because they wore lenticular clouds. Dark clouds hovered on the horizon to the south. I hoped they would not bring a white out to cut my speed.

As I lay down, after eating a late lasagna dinner at 10 p.m., I listened to more of the *Put Your Dreams to the Test*, all while scraping the dried cheese off my titanium spork with my teeth. The book made a brilliant point. It noted the phrase "You can do anything you set your mind to" was rubbish. If you're a 5 (out of 10) at something, the best you can do is ratchet it up one or two points. But you'll never be a 10. I felt that, though being a polar 10 was far from my current skill level, with experience I would achieve an impressive feat.

Camp AC54
86°06.045'S 82°03.268'W
Distance: 13.8 nm, Time: 9 hours, Elevation: 5,900'
Distance to South Pole: 234 nm
Distance to cache 2: 73 nm
Rations remaining: 13 days

Thursday, December 27, 2012 Day 57
Burying the tent valences last night paid off this morning. A strong 20+ knot wind built up at 3 a.m., burying the tent with drifting snow. Had I not sealed in the tent, the space between the fly and tent would

have filled with snow, burying me and increasing the time it took to break camp. When I woke to the sound of the wind, I saw the barometer had dropped a half-inch of mercury from last night. Not good.

Strong wind, a ground white out and snow greeted me as I slid out of my feathery cocoon at 6 a.m. So much for the agreeable weather of the past week.

Both Vilborg's tracks and mine disappeared in the morning's whiteout. Putting on the always accessible chest compass mount, I took a bearing on a cloud on the horizon and skied toward it. The lack of sun or landmarks impacted my energy levels, too. My mind had become used to docile conditions and revolted at the glum sky by making me feel sluggish.

Fighting my way up a hill, blinded from the whiteout, I stumbled along until 3 p.m. In sastrugi, I shortened the harness traces to improve stability at the expense of my hips. The stubby traces pulled downward on my back, exacerbating the pain. My right hip burned constantly, ever since I departed the hard track. Not figuring out how to prevent the sleds from pulling to the right for 60 miles was a huge mistake! All errors and problems here come back to bite. The pain in my left big toe was increasing, too.

Only when I traveled through the long, sastrugi-free zones did I hurt, especially when there was fresh snow dragging the pulks. When I straightened up to ski with proper posture, which was difficult to do while towing 260 pounds, my toes felt better. Subtle technique errors and fatigue caught up with me. The left toe problem started on the road, too. It took longer each day to dial the harness position in. It was distracting and time consuming to fiddle with it. Having perfect harness alignment was key. Yanking the sled traces to the left and right helped reduce the hip and toe pain, but only a little. The flat sections should have been easy, but they caused the most problems. Body management was a full time activity down here.

While pitching the tent, I scrutinized the ice fog hanging on the horizon. I hoped it wouldn't envelop me. Otherwise, the vaporous ice would melt into dew on everything in the tent, making for a cold, frosty morning. Also, if the fog hung around through tomorrow, the landscape would be invisible. Efficient navigation would be impossible. I would have to use the chest harness compass and refer to it constantly, slowing my progress.

It was worth taking time to weave a new bungie cord into the sled traces while making water tonight. My back was hurting from the constant sled impacts against the sastrugi. The old bungie was worn out. While eating chili mac for dinner, I also unpacked the new kartankers. I realized two months late that I had not pre-molded them in the boots. They were not ready to wear. If kartankers were not broken in and duct taped, they disintegrate. My hope was to swap the well-worn kartankers out tonight to increase the padding for my painful toes. Angry at myself, I prepared the new ones by entombing them in duct tape, covering them with women's nylons, and then using my feet to mash them into the boots. It will take a few nights of sitting with the boots on to form the kartankers. I cursed myself for not pre-forming them. The now worn out ones were ready to go upon arriving in Antarctica. I had my spares; they weren't ready to wear at a moment's notice. I felt so foolish for not preparing them. Then again, I felt foolish for not anticipating all the problems.

Camp AC55
86°19.152'S 82°07.836'W
Distance 13.2 nm, Time: 9 hours, Elevation: 6,116'
Distance to South Pole: 222 nm
Distance to cache 2: 60 nm
Rations remaining: 12 days

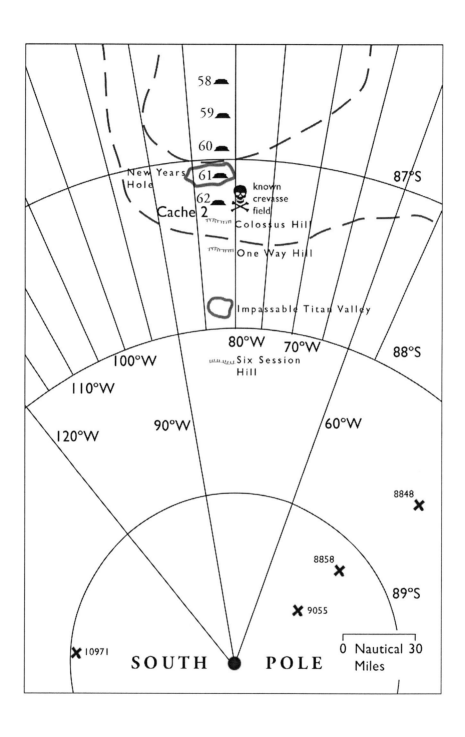

17

Days 58-62

S NOW BLINDNESS NEVER afflicted me. The sand-in-the-eyes itchiness and blurred vision were simple enough to avoid. I knew not to go without eye protection. Ever. As I had already had ultraviolet damage to my eyes as a child from not wearing eye protection in the mountains, I was extra conscious of the dangers.

I flirted with this blindness a few times while filming during the expedition. But, as a rule, I treated the sun glaring off the snow as Medusa. Several people warned me that snow blindness occurred easily here and was miserable to endure. Learning from other people's mistakes was key to avoiding problems in Antarctica. In my rare moments of being outside with neither goggles nor glasses, I used my arms or hands to protect my eyes.

By now, I sported a crescent tan line on my forehead, making a perfect outline between my goggles and balaclava. It looked absurd. Even though I thought the mask was abutted right against the foam of the goggles, it was not. Avoiding a sunburn was vital, as it was impossible to treat. I had no aloe vera gel, cooling sprays or anything. They were too heavy and it was better to avoid the problem.

Antarctica is peculiar in that a sunburn and frostbite can both happen at the same time in the same conditions: sunny yet windy. Katabatic [gravity driven] winds pour down from the highlands of Antarctica, creating a near-perpetual and constant headwind. Over the whole expedition, the wind shifted from southwest to southeast, in my face the whole time.

The worst days were when the wind rose above 20 knots or, alternately, completely died. Above 20 knots, I lost a mile per day. And, there was the constant danger of losing clothing. On the rare days of no wind, my body broiled. Yet, when I pulled my shirt sleeves up to cool off, my skin instantly began freezing. The solar radiation is stronger in Antarctica than at the equator. It was like being in space.

North of the 87th parallel, the surface conditions shifted from relatively bland to interesting. That word suggests something positive, but that was not the case in Antarctica. Interesting means, "How can these conditions become worse?" They did, and how.

Every explorer I contacted prior to the expedition had warned me about the 87° area. For everyone, this region of Antarctica was notorious for large sastrugi. ALE noted that expeditions usually slow down to ten miles per day in this latitude. Afterward, they tended to speed up again. The change was so dramatic that nearly every expedition talked about it.

I had read online, prior to coming down, comments like, "The sastrugi at the 87 degree—wow. It's bad." ALE also relayed that Hannah McKeand, who started in early December at the 100 mile shorter Messner Start, ran into tough conditions, far worse than she's seen in her decade-long guiding career.

The transition at 86° was a peculiar place, as it switched from flat to areas of rubble so large they look like a mirage. After six days of travel through the most featureless, flattest place I have ever experienced on the planet, anything larger than a few inches tall garnered my attention. Focusing on objects in the distance made navigation easier. Sastrugi were visible from far away, making tracking easy and resulting in little time wasted navigating.

As the large sastrugi loomed on the horizon, it looked threatening, causing my mind to reel with visceral fear. The massive sastrugi in this place I named *The Pit* was shaped like a looming army of frozen yeti. How quickly I became accustomed to the easy, flat travel in past weeks. The transformation was jarring, rude and upending. There was no choice but to accept the new conditions, so I told myself to get over it and keep skiing. Antarctica presented nothing but change, so I needed to remain malleable in my thinking and adapt as quickly as possible.

Adapting to change back home was easier, as I had a support system. Friends and family provided an emotional safety net while losing a job, relationship or loved one. Antarctica was different. Changes here required an inordinate amount of energy to deal with and demanded an immediate response. It was impossible to ignore problems without dire consequences. In San Diego, I was able to disregard troubles for a long time, even though I had to deal with them eventually. There was never a time where ignored decisions routinely ended in total failure or even death. Conversely, there was no place to hide from the environment to collect oneself here. Withdrawing into my mind by summoning deep memories was the only way to hide emotionally. The little red tent I called my home provided the only solace.

Once the tent was up and I was inside at the day's end, my problems did not seem so serious. The wind wasn't driving into me, searing my skin with scalpel precision and baseball bat brutality. The mental break of the familiar, relative safety of the tent was comforting. It became my mental safety after a difficult day.

Each time I hopped into the tent, I took a moment to collect myself, especially when the wind was severe. The sides of the tent thundered from strong wind, louder than any overly loud club music in Tijuana, Mexico. The comfort of having a nylon sheet, a mere plastic shield, between myself and the ravages of Antarctica was enough to calm me.

In an interview on Explorersweb.com, Hannah McKeand reported that, after making a few traverses, she was able to concentrate on what was happening outside rather than inside of her mind. As this was my first foray into a multi-month venture into the polar hinterlands, I had not figured out how to control my mind yet.

In fact, later, hiding in my mind became my perfect refuge from the tyrannical punishment of wind and whiteouts. For whatever reason, I was blessed with a deep, accessible memory of past events. I had an old reliable computer system of a mind. Upon making a request, the machine slowly spun to life and presented whatever I desired.

Why was this so valuable, having the ability to disappear into my mind, to keep going? After two months out in the field, I had become emotionally wrapped around the axle. My slow caravan was that. Too slow.

I figured out part of what ate me up. It was the constant stress to make miles rather than having fun. This was the ultimate time of my life and all I needed to do was calm down my mind. I was less than 200 miles away from the South Pole. I needed to distract myself by taking photographs.

Fighting psychosomatic mind junk consumed too much energy.

December 28, 2013, Day 58

Finally enjoying some decent sleep last night, I woke up yawning, more like I was on a weekend camping trip and less like I was on the biggest expedition of my life. The awakening was the type that made me feel ready for the day, rather than having been tossed around all night, robbed of restful slumber.

The sun was out. Thin, light clouds abounded. All the landscape was visible. It was breezy, with 15 knot winds from the southeast. These were perfect conditions for towing. Landmarks were visible far ahead, making navigation efficient. And, with the consistent breeze, keeping cool was relatively easy.

Now, finally, the wind blew from the southeast, after being a dead headwind for so long. I wondered if the British Antarctic Survey possessed a general wind model to explain this.

With the 15-knot winds and the extremely flat conditions, my tracks disappeared behind me. I watched the glittering diamond dust fill in sled runner grooves, obliterating my tracks. Had I dropped my GPS or other valuable item here, finding it would be virtually impossible.

My feet felt cold all day. The kartankers were covered in frost. Still,

I was too hot. My left toe hurt all afternoon. The perfect flatness of the area was perfect for speedy travel but little else. Flat surfaces induced repetitive motion injuries. Sastrugi, for all of its beauty and irritation, kept my foot and joint problems at bay.

Crossing the valley in the morning took three hours. There was only small sastrugi in it, enough to take the edge off the foot ache. Once on top of the far, southern edge of the valley, a massive flat plateau appeared ahead of me. I traveled on it for the rest of the day with no end in sight. All the way to the horizon, even with the 20x zoom on my camera, there was no variation. Pure white land and a horizon. Friendly clouds hovered motionless in the sky.

During my early afternoon, two ibuprofen helped to suppress my foot pain. The problem was the pain intensified daily. That considered, I was having a sensational time. I was able to close my eyes for a time and ski, using only the wind for navigation. Only doing this for half a minute at a time, I enjoyed being completely inside my mind. Though it was fun to do, it took a while for my eyes to refocus, as there was nothing to focus on. After I skied with closed eyes four times, I realized that disorientation was not safe out here, so I refrained from doing it again. I refocused on the serious business of singular-minded skiing.

And then, I stumbled.

On nothing.

Planting my right ski pole across my body, too close to the left ski and catching the tip in the snow, I fell over. I felt the familiar sickening bending of metal as I stumbled. Why was I bending the right ski pole while falling left? I collapsed in slow motion, as though it took seconds to happen.

Instantly, during this slow motion, I entertained a nightmare scenario: being impaled by a broken ski pole in the middle of nothingness. While falling, I was able to pull up the ski pole and throw it away from me so neither the tip nor the possibly broken aluminum tube would stab me.

There I lay, laughing. How could I have stumbled and snagged a ski edge on an imperceptible bump of snow? I wasn't sure, but it sure was funny. How could I, the now not-so-great polar explorer, have fallen down only a handful of times this entire trip, in the craziest of sastrugi, and now taken a tumble in what amounted to the biggest parking lot of flat ice I've ever seen? Easily apparently. A wandering mind was dangerous down here. Regaining my wits after the laughter subsided, I examined what was left of my ski pole.

Sure enough, it now sported a bend, right in the middle. Luckily the metal had not creased. Had I brought graphite poles, it would have snapped. The basket and tip had jammed on the snow, forcing me to place it too close during the fall, rendering it a danger rather than help. Normally, I placed my poles far out to arrest a fall and keep the pole stressed along its length rather than flexing it, preventing bending. Normally, I was vigilant about putting the pole tip far out to regain my balance. Not this time.

Was it salvageable? I only had one spare pole and I didn't want to use it until I was absolutely forced to. Todd Carmichael, the only other American to solo this trip, mentioned in his blog spending some time attempting to repair his broken ski pole. Had he not brought a spare in attempting to cut down weight for his speed record attempt?

I was already impossibly far behind and didn't want to waste more time fixing more broken equipment. But, the pole was not broken, only bent. Tapping the reserve equipment was only for emergencies. And this was not.

Setting about to repair the bent pole, I flexed it to assess the damage. Even the paint coating had not crinkled, so I knew I had a chance of repairing it. After spending ten minutes gently straightening the pole, it was still bent but was far better.

As I continued skiing along in the limitless flatness, I stopped and made more minor adjustments to the pole during each break, rendering the damage nearly imperceptible. Happy with the repair and laughing at myself for being so stupid for stumbling on nothing, I continued on.

That evening, ALE relayed that the second cache was located at 87°17'S and that Eric Larsen's cache was co-placed with mine. While still far ahead of Larsen, with his fat-tire bike, I thought he would eventually pass me as Vilborg did, in the middle of nowhere. Feeling like a lumbering elephant being passed by everyone was not enjoyable. For the moment, I stowed the thought in my subconscious to stew over, as I had more fundamental issues to think about. Keeping myself healthy and preventing anything else from breaking were constantly on my mind.

Steve Jones communicated to me their worry about Vilborg being so close to me, thus ruining her solo status. I related that I'd not seen her since she outpaced me on December 25th and her tracks disappeared on the 27th, after losing them in a whiteout. So, as far as seeing another human, there was no one but me.

"You've been out for a long time and not giving up is impressive," Steve Jones said during our conversation.

"Thank you. There is no way I am going to quit until forced to," I said.

"Well, keep it up. It's not everyone who keeps up after all that has happened."

"Thank you, Steve."

At this, I was elated. I took it as a compliment.

While chowing down on dinner, I thought about what Steve said. Did people expect that I would pitch all my effort and quit? My body had suffered no real damage, nothing lasting. There was still plenty of time. Would another person quit? That bothered me. I kept my mantra going. "Don't quit. Never give up. Keep going." I knew others had quit, had caught a ride and gone home. I couldn't. Why would I? Quitting was never an option.

I learned Eric Larsen was unable to cover the mileage he needed on his bike, so he headed back to Hercules Inlet. His cache was now available to me if I wanted or needed it. All I thought was about him on his bike. Out in these huge flat areas, a bike would be perfect. But elsewhere, I couldn't see how biking was possible. Every sastrugi needed to be dodged. Perhaps the massive speed advantage nullified that issue. As I now know, skiing around obstacles adds huge mileage to a trip, so the thought of doing anything but blasting straight over all obstacles was now total anathema to me.

I was sad for Larsen, as I learned his project had been a long time in the making. Balancing that, I was glad he was happy to return home and enjoy his newborn son. It was a reminder that family trumped everything. It was strange to sense a swirl of emotion for a person I had only exchanged emails with. I hoped some day he had the chance to return and try again.

Antarctica will still be here.

Camp AC56
86°32.032'S 82°05.401'W
Distance: 13 nm, Time: 9.25 hours, Elevation: 6,775'
Distance to South Pole: 208 nm
Distance to cache 2: 47 nm
Rations remaining: 11 days

DECEMBER 29, 2013, DAY 59

Last night, I slept on rather than in my sleeping bag because the sun kept the tent plenty warm. The wind died completely as I bedded down, raising the air temperature to 30°F inside the tent. Even sitting in the thinnest wool shirt and sleeping shorts was still uncomfortable, considering the air temperature outside was -15°F.

Upon waking up, I found the big toe pads of both feet were inflamed. The last extra fifteen minutes I spent scooting to cover 13 miles last night was not worth the foot tenderness I now reveled in. Sighing, I asked myself, out loud, why I hadn't learned my lesson from last time. Every time I thought I could power beyond the day's end, for no other reason other than to tack on a few hundred yards, my body failed me.

The thought occurred that I needed to take more photos while resting. Thinking about it, I had only taken 100 shots thus far. How was I going to share the experience with everyone when I returned home? There have been so many compelling landscapes to photograph and video thus far. I was too obsessed with making progress. Slowing progress to photograph all day was tempting. Now, suddenly, capturing the variety of landscape and sastrugi was foremost on my mind.

Because my feet hurt, I sat for breaks again. I have been standing for breaks for the last five days to save time, but today I needed to sit down. It was enjoyable to take the load off my feet for a moment!

During the day, I crossed over two huge but otherwise uneventful ice domes. As I initiated my last towing session, I topped a hill and started rolling down. At first the slope was tolerable. But it eventually steepened, so much so that the sleds glided on their own accord, chasing me. The slope was extraordinarily steep. Had I unhooked the sleds, I could have ridden them down the hill. What surprised me more was how oversized the sastrugi were at the bottom of the valley, too. They were huge. Each was easily six feet tall with two to three foot deep moats surrounding them. The size of the individual sastrugi was beyond comprehension. As this place was a hole in the valley filled with monster-shaped sastrugi, I named it *"The Pit"*. [This hill is referred to by other explorers as *"The Ski Hill"*]

The sastrugi were beautiful and I wished to photograph them, but then I realized why the sculptures were so towering here. The winds started picking up in the bottom of the valley and on the north facing slope. The ground here was covered in rubble with a streaked surface, making camping impossible. The east wall was even steeper, offering no relief. The immensity of the slope made *Doom Valley* seem tame.

As I had already consumed the day's rations and I was already down to my minimum one liter of water, I forged on, consuming nothing. Worry, the most useless emotion, clouded my mind. Would I ever find a campsite before my scheduled time with ALE? Keeping my call window was paramount.

I should have suffered through the night on the badly sloping and uneven ground, but I needed a solid night's sleep. Based on the steepness of the hill, I knew finding a campsite was impossible until I crested the valley lip. Feeling like a wuss for wanting to be out of the windy valley to have a relaxing night's sleep bothered me. Why was I not tough enough to chisel out a hundred square feet of space to sleep in? Why was I worried about the wind-built sastrugi when I had already survived the Patriot Hills *Killing Zone*? This was nothing. And yet, in my mind, it was. Instead of spending the time creating a camp, it made more sense to use that time and energy skiing southward.

Once I found a campsite, on the south side of the valley, barely adequate for my tent, I stopped. I was lightheaded from ingesting neither food nor water. It was risky to have pushed on so far. But, in my mind, I had to leave the valley and it was growing late. I named this place *Valley 7* because it took me into a seventh towing session to escape it.

[*Valley 7*: 86°43'S 81°59'W]

The tiny square of relatively flat snow forced me to align the tent differently than in past nights. The steep edge of the tiny shelf made it impossible to place the sleds near the door. This was important because in terrible weather I preferred to bring the sleds inside for loading, preventing lost and blown away gear. Plus, it was less taxing to handle gear in the shelter of the tent. Normally, I aligned the tent northeast to southwest. This kept the tent warm both at night and in the morning. The sun striking the tent's broadside made charging with the solar panels inside the tent possible, too.

It was disturbing to have the tent aligned differently after 56 straight days of a particular tent orientation. Instead of a broadside light, the sun percolated in either end of the tent, making everything gloomy and cold. It felt like the tent was placed in a narrow, dark tunnel rather than in a vast expanse of snow and ice. Even on whiteout days, the inside felt different.

The mildew inside the top of the tent tarp had returned. I had closed the door vent prior to breaking camp this morning. That must be a causative agent. Although there was no one out here to see this, the embarrassment of having this problem was palpable. I felt foolish to be dealing with mildew in the middle of Antarctica. I took pride in maintaining my gear. As a response to having a primitive organism plague me, I placed my face into my hands, pushed my shaggy, oily hair back and heaved a sigh.

Camp AC57
86°44.994'S 81°59.288'W
Distance: 13 nm, Time: 10 hours, Elevation: 7201'

Distance to cache 2: 34 nm
Distance to South Pole: 195 nm

Sunday, December 30, 2012, Day 60

For what seemed the first time in weeks, I slept soundly. The late start to ski out of *Valley 7* was worth it, as the wind was calmer up on the ridge than in *The Pit*. Right now the sun was out with nary a cloud in the sky. Looking back at *Valley 7* from the southern ridge, it doesn't look like any of the other valleys I'd crossed, save for the ogre-size sastrugi in *The Pit*. Yet I knew the view was deceiving. Though the incline was visible, it didn't look as steep as it felt last night. It must have been a combination of both the lighting and my fatigue level. The steepness also was due to the optical illusion of shadows in the sastrugi. The darkened side always looked more uphill.

During the day, clouds drew in and marched overhead, obscuring and then revealing the landscape. For being thousands of feet above me, it was incredible how clouds directly impacted my perception of the landscape. It was as though a white veil was pulled over my eyes every time a singular cloud overshadowed the ice.

I stopped at 6:30 p.m. instead of 6 p.m, as I didn't want to be stuck in a massive sastrugi patch in case a storm moved in and blinded me. The sastrugi was both prodigious and dense. It was like navigating through a furniture show room with tightly spaced, solid-ice coffee tables, all while dragging a love seat. Though it was easy to bridge the east-west oriented sastrugi with my skis, they took the most effort to traverse, as the sleds slammed into every icy knife edge, yanking me back.

It was fortunate I asked about the cache during the evening scheduled call. It was two miles away from the initial coordinates. I would have completely missed it and been forced to backtrack! This meant I needed to add some distance by detouring to it. As I was hungry and needed supplies, there was no choice. Even though any deviation was costly, the speed I had gained by dropping the cache in the first place made up for the diversion. I'd never have made it this far without having caches.

Camp AC58
86°56.376'S 82°04.930'W
Distance 11.5 nm, Time: 9 hours, Elevation: 7,600'
Distance to South Pole: 183 nm
Distance to cache 2: 20 nm
Rations remaining: 10 days, Fuel: 5 L

MONDAY, DECEMBER 31, 2012 DAY 61

It was the last day of 2012 and the Earth was still here. All of the world's ancient calendars terminated at the end of 2012, and there was a big scare that the Earth would terminate, too. I laughed. Was the end of the world on Greenwich Meridian time or Santiago time? Would Antarctica be spared, a safe place to hide from the end of the world?

Weather conditions varied wildly over the night and through the morning. When I fell asleep, it was cloudy and cold. Then, I woke up sweating at 3 a.m., as the clouds had passed by and the wind stopped, turning the tent into an oven from solar radiation. By 6 a.m., the air was still, but the clouds returned, sending temperatures plummeting again. During the morning's preparations, a 15 knot wind rose from the southeast. While packing, I prayed the clouds would stay away. I did not want to wander through sastrugi-filled valleys blind.

The sastrugi field at 87°S was several miles wide. Individual formations were desk sized, packed together in patches up to 20 feet wide, with no more than a few yards between patches. It took five hours to traverse the field. I crested the far side of the valley at 2 p.m., then, as immediately, I dropped back down another steeper hill into a crater-like area, a place I called *New Years Hole*. As it was the end of the day when I reached the bottom, I decided not to push on reduce the risk of foot pain. The wind was stronger here, 20 knots. Surrounded by sastrugi, it was not an ideal place to spend New Year's Eve, as I only had tough conditions to look forward to in the morning.

[*New Years Hole*: 87°06.056'S 82°11.087'W]

Today's sastrugi patch ate me alive, cutting travel down to 10 miles. It will be an all-day effort to hit the cache tomorrow night. I had hoped to reach it earlier to gain an hour of rest. If there were no more sizable sastrugi patches, I would be okay. I was motivated to find that cache rather than camp only a mile away from it.

Union Glacier reported the sastrugi ends at 88°10'S, according to Hannah McKeand. The worst, she said, was at 88°0'S. It was worse than in any of the years she's been here. And she's been doing this for a decade. If Hannah said it was bad, I knew I'd have a hard time of it.

ALE also reported her cache was moved to 88°S, so mine was not co-located any more, as one of her team was forced to drop out. They had to carry extra supplies, changing their cache positioning. They started the Messner route on December 2 and passed me several days ago. They were moving so fast that they were a degree ahead of me.

Everyone who was out here had dusted me, so I thought. Knowing this had made the whole activity humorous at this point. With so many mishaps, I was lucky to still be out here. My sad, pathetic march toward the pole was going to win the record for taking the longest ever. It wasn't the most noble record, but I earned points for persistence.

Camp AC59
87°06.056'S 82°11.087'W
Distance: 9.7 nm, Time: 9 hours, Elevation: 7,800'
Distance to South Pole: 173 nm
Distance to cache 2: 11.5 nm

TUESDAY, JANUARY 1, 2013 DAY 62
Happy New Year in Antarctica! Although it was a new year on the calendar, the day felt no different to me. Down here, trekking every single day, the only calendar date I was haunted by was the final pick-up day by ALE. Days of the week had completely lost their meaning. Not being in the five-day a week work grind, I found myself far less stressed by thinking about the weekend or what Monday would be like. Here, losing track of days was a wonderful experience.

Sastrugi had achieved insanity level in the trough and on the north facing slopes of the valleys here. Sticking to what I learned from Vilborg, I kept my line unless absolutely forced to dodge an ice wall, then

I immediately returned to the path to reduce navigation time. ALE related that Hannah McKeand covered 12 miles a day, and Roland Krueger skied 10 miles a day in the 87°S sastrugi area. Incredible. Hannah made her mileage no matter what. I was glad to have received her advice. It saved me from total failure.

It was colder at this latitude, causing another problem: the water bottles started icing over in the lead sled. I kept two bottles there to reduce time spent digging out bottles from the sleeping bag. Now they'd have to stay in the sleeping bag until I was ready to drink, as I didn't want to fight with iced up bottles any more than I had to.

Cache pickup day was exciting. I kept straining my eyes to see anything besides ice on the horizon, scanning for flittering black flags in the distance. I had trouble managing the negative thoughts building in my head, worrying that I had written down the coordinates incorrectly. Had I entered them into the GPS correctly? No matter how many times I rechecked the data the night prior, the worry was uncontrollable. Failing to find the cache out here was a show-stopper, for without it I cannot go on.

At 3 p.m., I had my first hallucination. It struck my mind with stunning force. My vision was replaced by what my mind made up. Instead of ice, I saw a perfect image of St. James church in Imperial Beach, California, full of people at Christmas. The image was so strong, it completely blinded me to the world and, before I had realized it, I stood motionless on the Antarctic plateau. The image of the standing room only, warmly lit church, with children dressed up to play out the timeless Christmas story, was all I saw. It was the strangest sensation ever, as I've never had the experience before. It was as though I'd momentarily left my body and instantaneously traveled in time and space.

I've read others having this happen, where they depart themselves and see their body skiing through the sastrugi. One of the ALE staff said this might occur. Sure enough, it did. As my vision cleared, there was a black flag flittering on the horizon, in the distance.

The cache appeared.

"Yah!" I cried out into the wind. I was saved, my cache was there, and in a short while I would have the supplies necessary to arrive at the pole.

There the flags were, on the top of a hill. I knew that it would take another half hour before I reached the cache. Distances were deceiving here. The air was perfectly clear, when snow wasn't flying, so I saw much farther than I was used to. When I saw them, I guessed the Thiel Mountains were several days away, no matter how close they looked. That was how far away objects were and how distorted distance perception becomes in Antarctica.

As I skied up to the cache, I saw two wind-whipped flags for both my and Eric Larsen's caches. And then, to my shock, I saw the bags and fuel cans were unburied.

What happened? The cache at Thiel's Corner was buried and protected. Yet here, both bags were only partially covered in snow. Were the protective snow blocks being ablated away by the winds? As I lifted the orange sack, the top tore right off, as though it had been in the sun for months. Yet, it had only been here for a short time. Had the Antarctic sun destroyed the nylon that quickly?

As I attempted to make camp, I discovered why the caches were not buried. The snow on this lofty ridge was hard packed, virtually solid ice. I'd never been on this much hard ice for the entire expedition. Careful to protect my new shovel, I gingerly probed until I found an area, 50 feet from the cache, where the snow was softer, so I could dig up snow blocks for water and tent protection. Where the aircrew landed, the ice was hard enough to require pick axes. Had they buried the cache under the ice, it would have taken an hour to break through the icy tomb.

Because Eric Larsen's cache was to be picked up by ALE, I was able to deploy trash and drop a few more pounds. I carefully transferred the stove fuel from the metal cans to plastic water bottles. I took extreme care while making the fuel transfer far away from the tent. I did not want the gas to contaminate the snow meant for water and poison myself by carelessness.

The staff at ALE was so thoughtful! They included Christmas food in the cache: Latvian cookies, breadfruit cake from Maria and a bag of pizza. However, I saw that everything was wet from overheating during calm air, so all I could do was smell the treats and enjoyed the thought of eating them. I felt guilty for not eating them, but if they were spoiled, I would become sick, possibly ending my trip. They had also packed hand-drawn pictures of me arriving at the pole. ALE's staff knew how to encourage a lone explorer, way out in the true middle of nowhere.

Being the holiday season, the song "Little Drummer Boy" played in my head most of the day. It was not the classic choir version but rather a modernized, semi-rock edition. By this point, I've learned that if my mind wanted to grace me with a song for five hours straight, it was best to enjoy the entertainment. Fighting it only made me mad and wasted energy.

There were only five days of punishing sastrugi left at 10 nautical miles per day.

"This is no time to get soft and fall off the nine-hour-a-day schedule," I told myself. I've been keeping it up for 20 days straight, without a rest day. I needed three more weeks.

Camp AC60
87°17.404'S 82°39.525'W
Distance: 11.5 nm, Time: 10 hours, Elevation: 8,000'
Distance to South Pole: 162 nm
Rations remaining: 23 days, Fuel: 7 L

(Upper left) *Camping conditions in the Trans-Antarctic Mountains were perfect. The mountains look close but were days away.*

(Upper right) *Cache preparation and location notes. I had to ensure I had everything correct, otherwise my food and fuel would be lost.*

(Left) *The 70 pounds of food and fuel that I left cached, buried in the true middle of nowhere with the hopes that ALE would find it and later deliver to 85° and 87°30'.*

(Below) *One of the massive sastrugi fields at 87° on New Years Day, 2013. I skied over many of these three foot tall ice chunks. There is a storm on the horizon.*

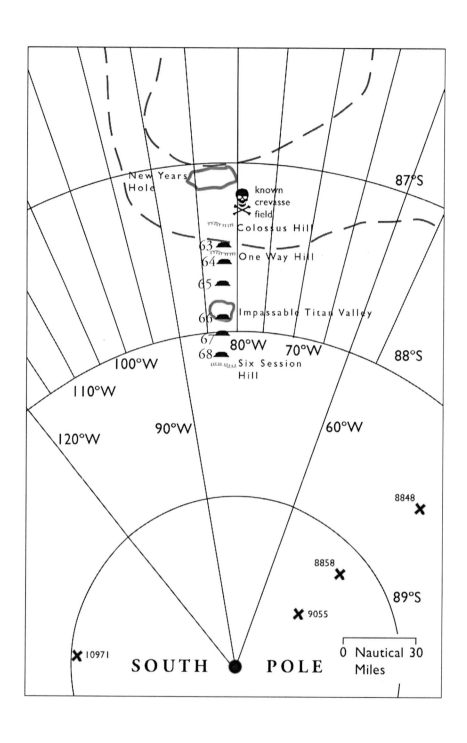

18

Days 63-68

Wednesday, January 2, 2012 Day 63

TODAY I TREKKED down a place I named *Colossus Hill*, after its stupendous sastrugi formations. They looked like a mêlée of massive buffalo had congregated, milled around and been flash frozen into place. Each of them was piled onto the other, obliterating any smooth ground. Too, the shapes did not have the common sharp edges but rather were massive and lumpy. As I gawked down the hill, envisioning returning via this route was difficult, had I been able to attempt the return journey. My first concern was how I was going to descend the hill in the first place.

[*Colossus Hill*: 87°21'S 82°35'W]

This was not regular sastrugi that I could ski over, but rather each formation had to be circumvented. Had I even tried to go over a single lump, the sleds would have slid sideways and yanked me into a confused pile of sleds, nylon and towing traces. This looked more like the pressure ice I had seen in photographs taken by explorers skiing to the North Pole. The only difference was the ice in the Arctic was sharp and blocky while these were smooth and relatively rounded. It seemed the farther south I skied, the steeper the hills became, and consequently the more dramatic the sastrugi were. Wind in the area was incredibly cold and severe, no doubt the source of the sastrugi. Since wind formed sastrugi, it only made sense that the steep inclines of the hills in the 87°S area generated massive sculptures.

ALE let me know that Roland Krueger was at 88°01'S and Vilborg was at 87°28'S this morning, so I wasn't terribly far behind them. Hannah reported that the sastrugi cleared up at 88°10'S, so I still anticipated three days of crushingly slow travel. I hoped my speed would increase once I was out of the area. I had been skiing so slow for the past couple of days that the thought of faster travel was a dream.

"Was every hill going to be this steep with this many obstructions?" I thought.

After three days of experiencing these particularly difficult ground conditions, I felt as though this was what the journey was going to be like from this point forward. Even though I did my best to think positively, knowing that the conditions would gradually improve over the next 40 miles, the size of the sastrugi intimidated me. Thoughts of them overwhelmed me, stymieing my mental game. My imagination spun out of control. I kept imagining ludicrous scenarios of running into massive crevasse fields or completely impassable sastrugi.

Camp AC61
87°26.301'S 82°35.456'W
Distance: 9 nm, Time: 9 hours, Elevation: 8,225'
Distance to South Pole: 154 nm
Rations remaining: 23 days

THURSDAY, JANUARY 3, 2012 DAY 64

While crossing the opposite side of the valley from *Colossus Hill*, my right hip throbbed, as though I had fallen on it badly. Looking back, I saw nothing amiss with the alignment of the rope traces from my harness to the lead sled. Inspecting the sled tracks, they appeared to be pulling slightly to the right of the ski tracks, so I knew something was wrong. Finally, thinking to check the connection between the front and rear sleds, I discovered a minor misalignment, an inch if that. Since I became desperate to eliminate the source of the pain, I stopped and loosened the clove hitch around the carabiner holding the sleds together, then shifted the knot. The change was minor, but I made it anyway.

Oh, what a difference it made. In a mere 100 yards of towing, the burning in my hip subsided and my lower back felt much better. I was relieved. I had checked everything over the past couple of days and hadn't found anything obviously amiss in the lead sled. That's where I guessed the problem would be. I was wrong. The trailing sled pulled to the right, causing the pain. Even though each sled had five, half-inch-deep runners to make them track, being one inch off center between the sleds was more than enough to induce serious pain. This made me wish again that I had a single light-weight sled to carry the complete round-trip load. I contemplated what changes it made in my travel. Visions of myself already making the Pole and attempting the round trip filled my head, driving me mad. The anger was wasted energy. I knew that having been ill cost me the round trip attempt. Plus, the two critical travel tips from Hannah and Vilborg came far too late. Having a fancier sled would not have changed my being sick nor my inefficiency.

At 3 p.m., I descended another steep hill. At first it had the same characteristics as *Colossus Hill*, so much so that I thought my naming had been premature. That was, until I skied to the first hulking sastrugi. This one ended with sheer six-foot drop-offs. Skiing off them was too dangerous. Even if I were not towing sleds or on skis, I would not have jumped down onto the ice, for it was a serious drop that had a sloped landing. There was no way I was able to lower the sleds down these faces, so I shortened the traces to five feet, as short as I could tolerate, and looked for a way around. If the fuel-bearing sled fell off one of these hills, one of the cans could be crushed by the impact, spilling white gas all over everything. I needed to be extra careful. If the sleds took off or rolled over, they would pull me with them, leading to potentially serious injury.

Time after time, I encountered more sheer drops, up to eight vertical feet. Looking down, I was aghast. There the drop-offs were, impeding progress. When I tried to photograph the drop-off, there was no point of reference, so it looked insignificant. This was where having a teammate would have been handy. After descending halfway down the hill, I looked back and saw only a wall of ice, certainly impassible if I were headed north. This gave me the idea for the name of this place: *One Way Hill*. Had I been able to ski the round trip, both this and *Colossus Hill* would have proven formidable barriers for the return north. With the constant diversions and slowness, my mileage dropped to below one mile per hour, a rate I hadn't been below in weeks.

[*One Way Hill*: 87°29'S 82°24'W]

"Don't give up, you'll be past it all in a few days," said James Hayes over the satellite phone.

"I'm not going to give up, it's quite a tough one to get through," I replied.

"You can do it. If you made it this far, you can do the rest."

At least I wasn't in Vilborg's boots, waiting to starve. On Dec 24th, she had 15 rations and now should have about seven rations remaining for the rest of her journey. She's only 13 miles ahead of me, so she had far more than seven days to go. If she reverts to the half-ration approach to maintain her unsupported and unassisted, she'll be starving for at least 10 days. Even though she could not have accepted food assistance to retain her expedition style, I still felt guilty about not having offered after two weeks. It seems no one expected to encounter these conditions, even those with far greater experience.

I didn't call Kelly tonight, as I had massively blown out my satellite phone budget. Even though I was on the bottom of the planet, I still needed to ensure I did not end in financial disaster upon returning home. At least the text message satellite unit had unlimited messages. One of the satellite messages I received from Wendy Davis was, "Enjoy the rough and bad parts of this." Though it was easy for her to write from 7,000 miles away, I knew that after this was all done, her admonition was truth. I have always reveled in figuring my way out of tough situations. It was a thrilling challenge to keep my head in the game and stave off anything else from falling apart in this last push to the South Pole.

Camp AC62
87°34.755'S 82°24.761'W
Distance: 8.5 nm, Time: 9 hours, Elevation 8,400'
Distance to South Pole: 145 nm

FRIDAY, JANUARY 4, 2012 DAY 65

The breeze intensified from light to full-on windy overnight. I put in ear plugs for the first time in weeks. Even though they dampened the roar, I was unable to fall back to sleep. Using a technique from yoga classes I'd taken, I concentrated on nothing other than breathing deeply, falling into a state of not worrying about being tired from the lack of sleep. It took 15 minutes of concentrated effort, but I experienced the sensation of falling asleep. I became so excited that it was working that I woke myself up.

"Crud!" I exclaimed, pulling myself out of potential slumber.

Yoda's immortal words sounded out in my mind, "Control, control, you must learn control!" This immediately made me laugh, breaking my concentration even worse, though easing my nerves and making me feel better. I resumed the exercise. This time, after 20 minutes of focused effort, I fell asleep.

I suffered through a rushed bowel movement this morning, as though I had eaten at a lousy Chinese buffet. There was nothing original in my diet, so I wasn't sure what caused it. It was as though I had consumed far too much butter like I did when coming out of *Doom Valley*. But I knew I hadn't. In fact, I did not finish yesterday's block of butter at all.

During the day, I noticed that I became sniffly an hour after eating one of the fruit bars in the rations. Though I knew I had no food allergies, I wondered if an antigen was building up in my system and bothering me. There was no way to perform a scientific experiment to figure out what was bothering me, at least in East Antarctica. As I had no choice but to eat what I brought with me, I had to live with it. As I was skilled at using snow as a nose tissue, it was a manageable issue.

Another nuisance that slammed my stomach today was a combination of chocolate, anti-inflammatories and salt all eaten at once. In concert, they were a full-on gut punch. I needed to take the drugs and salt on scheduled breaks. I could not allow myself unplanned stops. Timing the dosage for the best effect was the real difficulty. The ibuprofen had to be taken at 2 p.m. to provide pain relief for my aching hip and toes. This meant I took the salt tablets at 3:45 p.m. to help prevent late-day cramps. Even though I took the salt tablets later than I would have liked, being hit with a severe stomach ache was far worse than light cramps.

A half a mile west of ALE's suggested South Pole route, I was surprised I had not found any other sled tracks yet. The wind had continued from last night unabated, so I suspected that the tracks ahead of me were being obliterated. As the wind was even erasing my tracks right behind me, I doubted I would ever see tracks left days prior. Throughout the day, I crossed through perpetual sastrugi laced with finger wide crevasses. There was a known, dangerous crevasse area 10 miles east of my position. For all the miniature crevasses I saw, I could only imagine what the prominent fields looked like. The danger area was even marked with a skull and crossbones on the GPS.

The 25 knot headwind caused me to lose a mile of travel, placing constant backwards pressure on both me and the sleds. The partial ground whiteout did not improve travel, either. I had not had this low a mileage day since way back on November 28th. It was depressing to make such sizable strides in the past few weeks, only to be slowed down again, two and a half degrees from the pole.

Though the conditions were difficult, my clothing choices ended up being comfortable today. I wore the vest unzipped, inside the parka, and had another fleece jacket around my stomach to protect it. This balance made me happy and not miserably cold at the end of each break. It was the first time in weeks that I had been relatively comfortable towing, neither too hot nor cold. The strong wind caused the pogies to flap, requiring adjustment every three steps, making them more of a nuisance than a help. I started brainstorming of how to travel without them. If my core was slightly warmer, they weren't necessary. But, this required meticulous tuning I rarely achieved. I heard my Mom's voice in my head, asking if I wanted to attach Velcro

to the pogies and parka to prevent this problem. Not wanting to damage the waterproof shell, I had refused her suggestion. Now, months
later, I regretted it. I knew that, though the Velcro would have solved
one problem, putting holes in the shell ruined the waterproofing.

I saw the moon today, for the first time since early December. It
was dead north of me and visible when the clouds cleared. At night,
as I pitched the tent, it was barely visible to the south, having fully
circled me during the day. I took several photographs of the moon
and sastrugi, hoping that one would turn out. It was impossible to
see anything on the camera's LCD, as the sun reflecting off the ice
blinded me.

When Steve Jones came on the satellite phone tonight, I tensed up.
We only seemed to talk when problems arose. After chatting, though,
he assured me there were no pressing issues. I was relieved.

"The 87° area is a self-induced purgatory, a punishment of pushing
a boulder up a hill," Steve said.

Laughing, I heartily agreed with him. "That's about right."

"Your mileage is actually okay and you are on schedule to make the
pole based on our projections."

"Good, my calculations show the same, though it's difficult not to
worry about it."

"The hills ahead are more gentle, so you should start picking up
speed again," he comforted. "There is only a little more climbing to go."

"Great, thanks. It's been a heck of an experience," I replied.

Based on his data, there were four more days to muddle through,
and then I would break free.

Camp AC63
87°42.198'S 82°36.470'W
Distance: 7.5 nm, Time: 9 hours, Elevation: 8,947'
Distance to South Pole: 138 nm
Rations remaining: 21 days

SATURDAY, JANUARY 5, 2013 DAY 66

Determined to salvage lost mileage from the previous days, I found a marvelously long stretch of clear ground. I sped up as much as possible. Being able to break above a turtle-like pace was exciting since moving south of the 87th Parallel. Everything was going superbly and, though I suspected there were more challenges yet to come, I felt better about travel than I had in some time. The breeze was light. I felt confident. A quick look at the GPS showed I was covering miles. The best part was I was having a thrilling time. Even after being out here for over two months, this was fun.

"Wooo!" I yelled, laughing diabolically.

While heading along the ALE-provided GPS route, I found several sled tracks converging all at once! There had been many people by here recently. And, no surprise, they all seemed headed to the South Pole. Though the tracks were unidentifiable, all followed a southward bearing. Reaching out for human contact, I stooped over and touched the different tracks. One set resembled the tracks from mine. Then there were two other sets of grooves: one from a sled with wide ski-like runners and the other from a slightly narrower rig. Being the last person out here, it was comforting to know others had gone through similar difficulties. And, it was fun to have company, so it didn't matter that I was the last person out here. Even though the tracks ran southward, I still used my compass and navigated my own course. My hard-won experience told me not to trust anything out here but myself. If the tracks suddenly veered away from my course, I knew I needed to keep my line and depart the nascent company.

It did not take long before I had to decide to stay with them or not.

While heading down a gentle slope at 3 p.m., I passed over an ice ridge and encountered a scene that dumbfounded me. The hill dropped steeply and into the biggest mass of sastrugi I had ever happened upon. This valley was not particularly wide. I could have easily crossed it by the end of the day. That was, had it been smooth. It seemed impossible to cross this morass. It looked like some giant hand had taken the sastrugi from both *Colossus* and *One Way Hills*, mashed them on top of each other, with the number of sastrugi multiplied by ten-fold. There were sastrugi on the sastrugi.

My jaw fell slack.

Apparently, this was what other trekkers who had gone before me had talked about. Their reactions, based on the sled tracks diverging at this point, told me everyone chose their own path. I couldn't believe what I saw. Overwhelming fear rose up inside of me. How in the world would I cross this valley? The pits were humongous. If I fell in, climbing out would have been a chore. Crampons and climbing boots seemed to be a better choice for hiking through this region. As I came upon this sight at a break time, I sat down, grabbed a handful of cookies, and pondered what to do.

Standing next to the existing tracks, it appeared as though everyone arrived at the same conclusion and diverted west, maintaining a constant contour along the edge of the valley. Now, after being with these other tracks for a short time, I needed to decide whether to crash through an impassible valley or follow their lead and dodge the valley. Going around seemed like a huge waste of time. Yet after seeing the sled-eating holes beside the 10-foot-tall sastrugi, I seriously doubted I could even ski through this morass. There was part of me that wanted to valiantly battle my way through what others had avoided. Then the more logical part of me said it would be stupid to simply ski straight through. It was like skiing through a mile-wide boulder heap. Eventually I would fall and break something or myself. I named the place *Impassible Titan Valley*.

[*Impassible Titan Valley*: 87°50'S 82°37'W]

Though Robert Frost's poem "The Road Not Taken" had inspired me to travel to Antarctica, I suspect he would have thought twice about taking a less-traveled path at this moment. Even though the western edge of this valley kept me out of the worst sastrugi, I still struggled. The sleds repeatedly rolled over and crashed. I was glad to have packed the tent completely again today. So many times I thought my skis were going to snap, or the bindings break, as I bridged the six-foot-deep pits. The sleds simply crashed into the holes. Even though progress was halting, I edged along the valley ridge.

Never before had my sleds flipped and hit so hard.

After I made camp, a Twin Otter flew by at 7:10 p.m. The low clouds force it to fly low, making it easy to hear the engines over the ear-numbing roar of my stove. I immediately poked my head out of the tent and waved. Though I doubted the crew saw me, I could not help waving. It was comforting to see a passing aircraft, as I knew I was on the right track. I worried they would take my wave as a call for distress, if they saw me. But, I was sure they knew my position and had received no report of problems. All at once, they were gone over the horizon. I ducked back into the tent, out of the skin-burning air.

ALE warned me during the scheduled call to be exceedingly careful about following tracks out here, as there was no way to know exactly where they were traveling. Some tracks may lead to a cache far from where I needed to be. Or, the person I chose to follow wandered about, searching for another path, wasting my dwindling travel time. I acknowledged that and related the story of the snow tractor track fooling me at 84°.

My hallucinations increased in intensity today. Now, I saw vividly colored oval blobs in the sastrugi: electric blue, brick red and Popsicle green. Also, what I thought was a raven appeared in my upper-right peripheral vision. Was I going nuts? Or was it that my body and mind were beyond fatigue, with my brain hallucinating, substituting for a lack of color stimulation? Was the total silence wearing on me? When I yelled "Hello!", there was not so much as a whisper of an echo. I can see how people go nuts out here. I embraced the experience and enjoyed the tricks my mind played.

Camp AC64
87°51.938'S 82°38.198'W
Distance: 9.76 nm, Time: 9 hours, Elevation 8,900'
Distance to South Pole: 128 nm

Sunday, January 6, 2013 Day 67

At this point in the expedition, I disliked chocolate. So many people I told about the expedition said they would love to eat a bar of chocolate a day. After two months straight, it lost its appeal. As I had several food bars based on chocolate, in addition to drinking hot chocolate every morning, it amounted to an absolute overload. In fact, I came to despise chocolate. It was something I needed to put out of my mind, otherwise eating it would have been even more difficult. It wasn't that I disliked the taste, or that it made me gag, but rather it was too much chocolate. No other food bothered me up to this point. As I had never eaten this much of the same food day after day, it was my first expedition food disappointment I've experienced.

While towing through the rough sastrugi today, I was forced to shorten the sled traces as much as I could to prevent the sleds from veering off course. Thank goodness the skis had broken off, otherwise travel would have been impossible here. The huge sastrugi either caused the sleds to roll over or pulled the sleds into the pits beside them. Although shorter traces gave me more control, shortening them inflamed the pain in my hips. It was difficult to balance keeping the pain at bay and still not having the sleds roll out of control every minute.

To make the sled traces adjustable, I had tied butterfly hitches into them at one-yard spacing, with a total of five yards of possible trace length. The idea was that when towing on smooth ground, I used the farthest away knot from the sled to improve efficiency. The theory was that the longer the trace line, the lower the angle between it and the ground. That converted more of my effort into pulling rather than lifting the sleds. Other than moments of yanking the sleds over sastrugi, lifting force was a total waste of energy. Only pulling was useful in Antarctica. This initially led me to suppose that having a long line was best. This was true, up to a point. Once the trace line exceeded five yards, though, the line oscillated from its own weight. This motion in the traces yanked me back and forth, straining my lower back. The constant adjustments to maintain my efficiency kept my engineering mind occupied and off the overall stress of the trip.

The celestial show was absolutely stunning today! With the sun flitting in and out of the clouds, I skied through a partial whiteout. Then, at 3 p.m., something breathtaking happened. At first, a 22° sunbow developed. I always liked looking at them, even if they portended snow. After 15 minutes, a pair of sundogs appeared, bejeweling the sunbow, making for a prettier display. But, as the upper atmosphere changed and the ice crystals thickened, I was treated to a whole new surprise. In a half hour, a 46° double sunbow developed. That made me stop for a minute to marvel.

Then, by chance, I happened to glance straight up and saw a mirror reflection of the double sunbow dead overhead, a circumzenithal arc. The sight was stunning, as I'd never seen one before. As soon as I pulled the camera out to take a few shots, a full, 360° parhelic circle developed around me, completely ringing the sky with a white line. And, then, to top it off, there were 120° parhelia dangling in the sky. It was utterly spectacular. I stopped and enjoyed this display. Filming it was difficult but I did my best, as I did not expect to see this sight again. I figured this was a once in a lifetime shot. It was worth the time to stop and film this.

Camp AC65
88°00.457'S 83°07.141'W
Distance: 8.6 nm, Time: 9 hours, Elevation 9,257'
Distance to South Pole: 120 nm

MONDAY, JANUARY 7, 2013, DAY 68

The hill I started up and camped on this evening was immense. It started subtly, so much so that I did not realize I was even climbing. As the ice was inconceivably flat here and there were no obstructions blocking the horizon, everything appeared to be uphill, as though I stood in the middle of a round valley. Now that I had been through several of these areas, I recognized the difference. A line in the distant sastrugi with a subtle change in hue indicates a hill. When standing in a single spot and looking 360° around me, if there was no color shift, there was no slope. Because this hill was so immense, it took an hour to discern I was even heading up a slope.

This hill kept ascending, far longer than the hill near Thiel Mountains. That hill had only taken 4.5 hours to ascend. I had already spent more than half the day climbing and there was no end to it. I guessed that it would take a day to ascend it, so I named it *Six Session Hill,* meaning that it took six 75-minute sessions to ascend it. Although this name was not as romantic as those I had given other locations, it did match my experience.

The changes in weather were becoming more dramatic. Yesterday was windy after the storm that passed through. Although the wind made for difficult skiing, it packed the soft snow, making travel tolerable. Had the snow remained loose, climbing the continuous masses of sastrugi would have been arduous. Even though the sculptures were not individually as large as those of *Impassable Titan Valley,* they mottled the landscape and eliminated flat spots. This made finding a campsite exceedingly difficult. Even though I set about hunting for a campsite at 5:45 p.m., it took until 7 p.m. to find a spot. There were no suitable locations. I did not want to camp on the edge of an ice platform and fall off accidentally. For all the open space here, it was virtually impossible to find a puny 100 square foot space to pitch a tent.

Alice McDowell at ALE said the reports were that the sastrugi thinned out south of my location. I hoped so. There was going to be nothing left of my right hip and left toe. As I had been struggling to keep my harness stable, I had begun to tighten the belt on my shell pants. Consequently, the harness slipped more and hurt worse than if the belt were loose. It made no sense. Usually, tighter pants made the harness more comfortable. But, not in this case.

Satellite phone #1 started malfunctioning after operating perfectly for a month. The unit began self-resetting, reporting the message, "Please wait, initializing handset." It seemed the battery was not charging. With a quick check of the multimeter, I found the solar panel voltage to be stable and the battery was charged. But, this was one night when I hadn't warmed up the phone to 80°F and that likely was the reason it malfunctioned. I had been diligent about warming the phone up with hot water prior to using it. But, with the extra-long day, I did not have enough time to warm it up prior to the scheduled call. I chalked this up as an anomaly and hoped it was that: a random occurrence.

Camp AC66
88°10.476'S 082°18.508'W
Distance: 10.2 nm, Time: 10 hours, Elevation 9,453'
Distance to South Pole: 109 nm
Rations remaining: 18 days

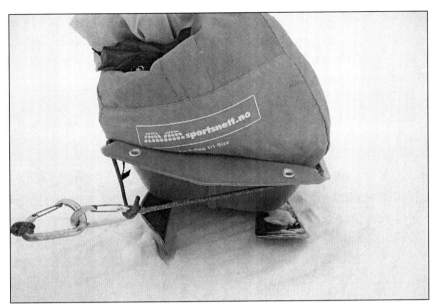

(Above) *The second broken sled ski. This happened in a completely flat area in a whiteout. I knew it was going to happen, so I did not become upset. I was back skiing in 30 minutes.*

(Left) *After having frostbite on my cheek, I kept an ample supply of bandages on my face. Although they did not stick properly on my crazy beard, they held well enough to prevent further injury. Notice my head is steaming.*

(Below left) *In addition to the one stick of butter mashed into my mug, I ate cereal, whole milk, sugar, and hot chocolate for each 1,400 calorie breakfast.*

(Below right) *The zipper on my shell pants tore in the middle from its base. The teeth were still connected together. I sewed a repair with heavy thread and duct tape.*

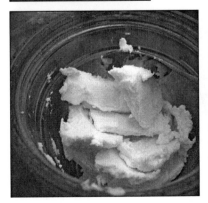

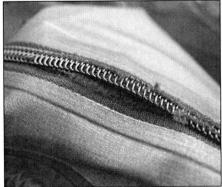

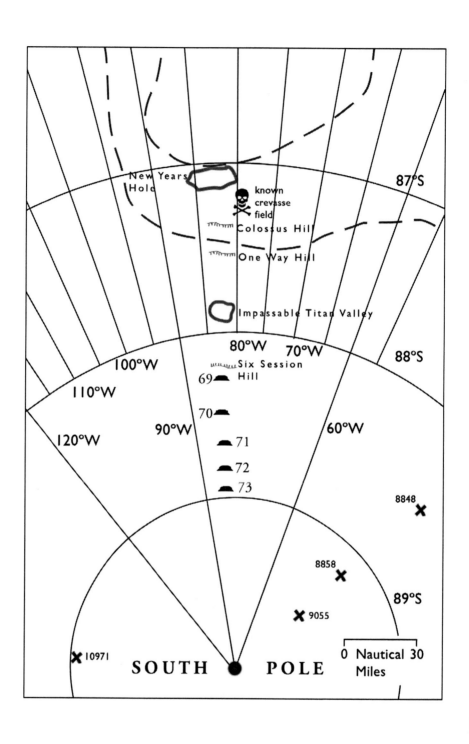

New Years Hole

known crevasse field

Colossus Hill

One Way Hill

Impassable Titan Valley

87°S

88°S

89°S

80°W 70°W

100°W

110°W

120°W

90°W

60°W

Six Session
69 — Hill
70 —
— 71
— 72
— 73

8848 ✕

8858 ✕

✕ 9055

✕ 10971

SOUTH   ● POLE

0 Nautical 30
Miles

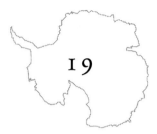

19

Days 69-73

Tuesday, January 8, 2013 Day 69

IT WAS WONDERFUL to only need to pack the tent fully one last time. The absurdly tall sastrugi should end today, giving way to conditions that did not flip the sleds over. All I could think when packing and unpacking the tent was that I was wasting travel time. Having to re-insert the poles each time made setup troublesome and dangerous in stormy conditions. Normally, the poles were already stuffed into the sleeves of the tent, reducing risk and saving 15 minutes each day. The stronger the wind, the more care was required, as other explorers have had their goggles smashed by flailing poles. I had rolled the tent like a burrito on the sled for the entire trip, making for quick set up. Thoughts of improved efficiency thrilled me. Regardless of how long it took me to deal with the tent, I had to put in my six travel sessions of 75 minutes each.

The sastrugi was east-west oriented in this area, making for punishing travel all day, cutting one-fifth off my normal distance. The conditions thrashed my body. With the sleds incessantly striking ice, it felt as though I kept hitting a curb, cutting my forward momentum, constantly making me stop and restart. It was akin to dragging a large desk over an endless series of sidewalk curbs. My back absorbed the constant stops and starts. Even though the in-line heavy bungee helped reduce the impact force, many times I was yanked backward. It was as though the land turned diabolical. Although it was painful and difficult, it was still rewarding to know that I was now less than two degrees away from the South Pole.

Though I had learned that it was possible for a random stranger to stop by, I did not expect to see anything else until I reached the Pole. The map showed no bases along the Hercules Inlet route. That was, until I saw a black blob on the horizon. At first I thought it was my raven hallucination again, but this object did not disappear when I stared at it. Since the mystery object was close to my bearing, I diverted toward it. For an hour, I pushed over sastrugi, excited at what was in all these miles of nothingness. As my excitement built, I could not contain myself. Towing faster and harder, I felt like a sled dog rushing back home. Finally, I reached it.

The "it" was a pile of trash bags full of snow.

What the? As I looked around, I quickly deduced what this was. A Twin Otter appeared to have landed here prior to the last snow storm, as the skid tracks had partially filled in. There were a couple of dug-up holes, so I guessed this was a cache point. The large pile of snow-filled black garbage bags acted as beacon of sorts. If an aircraft tried to land in whiteout conditions, the bags served as an altitude marker. Or the bags were used in lieu of flags for the team retrieving their cache. This area appeared to have been groomed by a Thiokol snowcat some time ago. As ALE had told me they had sent no traverse vehicles to the South Pole this year, I can only assume the grooming was from last season. For the lack of ruts I saw at my cache drop point, I was surprised to see the grooming had survived the Antarctic winter.

Let down, I laughed at being excited over garbage bags. After a short break, I moved on. More than once I glanced back to watch the makeshift landing beacon fade into the distance. It seemed to take an eternity before it disappeared over the horizon. While leaving the landing strip, I chanced upon two different trekkers' tracks. Seeing these made me laugh out loud, as I can only guess that others were as interested in trash bags as I. I felt foolish to be excited over ultimately nothing.

I started to notice the altitude. According to the GPS, I was at 9,600 feet. This didn't make sense, as that was 300 feet higher than the Pole. Personal GPS units are notorious for inaccurate elevation data. As my watch altimeter was out of calibration, I had no tool to accurately measure the elevation. All I knew was that I felt lethargic and breathed harder, even though my sleds were much lighter. Whatever the altitude was, I started to feel it.

Camp AC67
88°18.773'S 82°36.407'W
Distance: 8.3 nm, Time: 9 hours, Elevation: 9635'
Distance to South Pole: 101 nm

WEDNESDAY, JANUARY 9, 2013, DAY 70

The heavy alpine gloves were now dead. Although I had swapped out the liner gloves to keep these clean, the oil buildup overwhelmed the insulation and had permeated the gloves. The grime sucked heat out of my hands, making them feel as though I had put my hands into a vat of super-freezing lotion. As the pogies had been driving me nuts for some time, I was happy that the whole system didn't work anymore. I pulled out the heaviest mittens as my last defense against the wind. For most of the trip, they'd have been too warm, making my hands sweat. Although they were toasty, I had to remove them and face downwind to deal with everything.

The lateral sastrugi continued unbroken, all on another super-long hill. As I drew closer to the Pole, these challenges seemed to punish my body more. Yet my spirit held. Ever since I was forced to forego the round-trip expedition, I had been languishing under a dark cloud. I worked on thinking positive thoughts about my performance. Now with clothing problems, I did not have to think about maintaining happiness. Having a distraction to keep my mind occupied kept me from feeling like a failure at what I started out to do. The pain in my big toes helped distract, too. The bottoms had turned a bruised purple. But these annoyances didn't matter to me. Only making the Pole did. A steady diet of anti-inflammatories kept the aches to a manageable level.

Then, inexplicably, my goggles iced over today. I've not had that trouble since mid-November. The fleece face mask drove fog inside them now that the wind had shifted. When the wind was dead ahead as it was now, the mask did not ventilate, meaning the ice on my goggles blinded me. I debated whether the goggles were a hindrance or a help. It had been a long time since I had traveled blind, so I dredged up the courage to accept the new circumstances. On breaks, I faced toward the sun and thawed out the goggles. This did help for a while, but when I turned upwind, the goggles fogged, then iced over. My shoulders drooped with resignation. I skied on. There was no reason to become emotional about it. Instead, I mounted the chest harness for the compass, faced down and skied on blindly.

At night, Kelly read me some of the inspirational messages people had sent me. These meant a great deal and uplifted my fog-quashed spirits.

My high-school buddy Mark Lagamayo reminded me, "You are doing something most anyone else just dreams about."

Stephanie Cronin, a friend and one of my sponsors, said, "You're such an inspiration to all of us. The hardest part is always the end."

Wendy Davis said, "Relish in the difficult."

It seemed crazy, yet I knew that they were right and the final push was going to test me to the end. I was shocked, as I had no idea so many people were inspired by what I was doing. Feeling self-conscious, I concentrated to keep my act together and put on a brave face, even when I wanted to fall apart. One bright piece of news for me was that Hannah made it to the Pole today. Her success bolstered my confidence, knowing someone made it through this difficult environment. Even though I was struggling, it helped knowing someone had conquered the exact same conditions.

Camp AC68
88°27.740'S 82°22.818'W

Distance: 9 nm, Time: 9 hours, Elevation: 9,431'
Distance to South Pole: 92 nm

Thursday, January 10, 2013 Day 71

Using the mittens for a whole day was a pleasure. It was the first time in over a week that my hands were not freezing. Now I used the dead alpine gloves to strike camp, as it was easier to work with fingered gloves and suffer the cold. As soon as the tent was packed and the sleds secured, I switched to mittens and rewarmed my hands. By the time I made the change, my pinky fingers were on fire. Though the alpine gloves provided speed, they were only useful for a few moments.

Switching to mittens today was fortuitous, as I learned how cold it could become. The wind increased and clouds rolled in, making the temperature plummet. This was completely normal and not unexpected, as clouds had been hovering on the horizon all day. As shadows crept over me, the temperature dropped, forcing me to don an extra fleece jacket. Near 3 p.m., the wind rose to 30 knots. While drinking water during a break, I fumbled the water bottle. Though I recovered it, water had spilt on the sled bags and my pants. As both were waterproof, I did not worry too much. I was astonished at what happened next. The water on the sled bag froze and rolled off right before my eyes. I was in disbelief. Had this happened? Inspecting my shell pants and boots, I saw the water was frozen on them, too. Pulling back the parka, I exposed my watch to time this event. I poured water on the bag and watched. Again, the water flash-froze in 10 seconds. Now I knew how cold Antarctica was in the summer.

The kartankers I had been using have also ceased to keep my feet warm. I extricated the new kartankers and applied a full five yards of duct tape to the heel. The lighter weight tape ALE provided did not stick as well as my tape, but I wanted to save the heavier in case anything broke in these last 84 miles. At this point, I was confident that something else had to go wrong to keep the expedition entertaining. I was cautious with everything, as I didn't want to suffer another major equipment failure this close to the Pole.

I hollered in excitement as I left the southern edge of the massive sastrugi fields of 87°. ALE was right about where the sastrugi dissipated, freeing me for the final run to the Pole. I still was bewildered at how slight undulations in a wide-open landscape, with no apparent obstructions, changed the wind patterns. It was enough to build sastrugi to the size of cars. The area north of 85° was littered with sastrugi, but were neither concentrated nor of the size like those at the 87th Parallel.

Camp AC69
88°36.297'S 082°06.294'W
Distance: 8.6 nm, Time 9 hours, Elevation: 9,414'
Distance to South Pole: 84 nm
Rations remaining: 15 days

FRIDAY, JANUARY 11, 2013 DAY 72

At 3 a.m., I snapped awake, unable to breathe. Thrashing, I unlocked the cord holding the sleeping bag hood, unzipped the side and sat up. I sucked in air, then yelled, as though I had dove under 30 feet of water. Once I regained myself, I lay back down and stared at the tent ceiling, wide eyed. This had happened only once before in my life while camping in the Sierras. It felt as though the bag had constricted my neck, making it impossible to breathe. Feeling foolish for strangling myself, I was glad no one was with me. It took a while to calm my breathing down and even longer to fall back asleep.

As soon as I was free of the seemingly endless sastrugi field, it felt as though I had entered Dante's 9th Level. Moving from over 100 miles of endless sastrugi to an ashen landscape of indistinct lumps was shocking. All at once, I missed the sastrugi. Now I felt as though I'd entered the final bastion of Antarctica. I survived all the challenges: the unbelievable sastrugi, crazy hills and deep valleys. Now, there was only the specter of severely cold winds and deteriorating weather to deal with. Without definite objects to stare at, it felt as though I was going nowhere. There was nothing to pass by. I pulled out the GPS and checked it on breaks to reassure myself I was moving. It was surreal to feel as though I was on a treadmill. It felt lonely without the sastrugi to keep my mind occupied. For as much as I wanted to be free of the ridges of ice, they comforted me and kept my mind busy. I never expected to miss them. Inanimate objects soon became company out here, in a place devoid of humans.

At noon, I started having trouble breathing as I skied into the emptiness at 88°41'S. The wind shifted slightly so it blew dead into my face. As usual, the goggles fogged up half way, leaving me with a dime-sized window to squint through. But the air felt colder than usual, so I pulled down the hood on my parka to fend off the cold. With the sun playing hide and seek in the clouds, the temperature dropped, chilling me, even though I worked hard in the soft surface snow. Unable to stand the cold creeping through my outer layer, I started shivering. And then I could barely breathe, as though I sucked air through a coffee straw. Tugging on my face mask to realign it, my hands found ice rather than silicone rubber. The bottom of the mask had completely frozen over, obstructing the breathing hole.

It took a full minute of breathing hard into the mask to warm up the ice. My face, beard and mustache were fully frozen to it. My face was completely covered in ice. A rude chunk of hair pulled out, and tears streaked out of my eyes at the pain. After my vision cleared, I went to work on the mask, crunching off the ice. It was easy to break ice off the mask. It was another matter to pick the ice off my face. Since I knew it would build up again, I didn't completely remove the ice. I regretted this later.

While in the tent at the end of the day, I rubbed my face in fatigue. Thereupon I felt a large, wet scab on the right corner of my mouth. I'd never felt this before. After fiddling for a few moments with it, I needed to see what was going on. I grabbed the camera and took a close-up photo of my face. Zooming in on the picture, I was shocked to find frostbite. There had been lots of ice on my facial hair on prior days, but today the right combination of elements conspired to freeze my skin. At first I was shocked and embarrassed, as I took pride in keeping injury at bay. Once I quashed my ego, I set to work at repairing the damage and preventing more. Not wanting to develop anything more sinister, I proceeded to place tape and bandages all over my face, on every possible spot. There was no way I was going to arrive at the South Pole torn to shreds.

During tonight's scheduled call, I chatted with Hannah about her trip. Back in Union Glacier, she planned to depart on the 15th, so we would not meet. Gauging by how far I still needed to ski, I suspected there would only be a skeleton staff remaining at Union Glacier anyway. Hannah suggested trying to keep cool to prevent the goggles from fogging up. Warm air wafted from the mask each time I removed it. The upper vents were not keeping up now that I've worn them for over two months. It was a race against time with my gear and body rapidly deteriorating.

James also said I had become somewhat of a legend at camp as people watched and plotted my progress. There was a pin map in the main mess tent where people could stop by and see how other expeditions were doing, including the climbing trips to Mt. Vinson. I imagined my icon was a snail, sadly finishing out the long march to the Pole. I thanked James for his encouragement and laughed at the thought of why I was a legend. The only reason I could think of was because I had not given up, considering how poorly I had done. The thought of my map pin being placed on the Pole boosted my spirits.

Camp AC70
88°44.608'S 81°54.712'W
Distance: 8.3 nm, Time: 9 hours, Elevation: 9,011'
Distance to South Pole: 75 nm

SATURDAY, JANUARY 12, 2013 DAY 73

For as much as yesterday froze my skin, today I was on fire. Using the parka as a sun shield, I was again down to my wool shirt for travel. I was still nauseatingly hot, even though the air was -25°F. Each breath in felt revitalizing as it cooled me. As I exhaled, I felt my core temperature shoot up. The cycle was relentless. To cool down even more, I rolled up my sleeves. Within seconds, my arms were burning from the cold, as though I had lain down on a frozen block of steel.

I fantasized of ways to construct an umbrella out of tent poles to keep the sun off me. I now appreciated the effort put into designing astronaut suits.

Beyond the thermal overload, my body was holding up. The refreshed kartankers made a world of difference. They were warm and, though there was frost on them at day's end, I knew my toes would not end up purple by 6 p.m. Knowing this thrilled me to no end. For as much as I looked forward to the challenge of stark cold temperatures, the primitive human inside of me needed comfort. Otherwise, negative thoughts surfaced and flooded my head. A steady stream of dumb arguments I'd had in the past churned in my mind, all for nothing. I knew that when these thoughts emerged, I had to make an adjustment. I slowed down, sped up or made whatever adjustment necessary to quash the discomfort. As soon as the discomfort ebbed, the negative thoughts disappeared. As much as I loved pushing myself, my mind fought to stay stable, so I backed off until all was quiet.

Camp AC71
88°52.861'S 81°21.244'W
Distance: 8.3 nm, Time: 9 hours, Elevation: 9,043'
Distance to South Pole: 67 nm
Rations remaining: 13 days

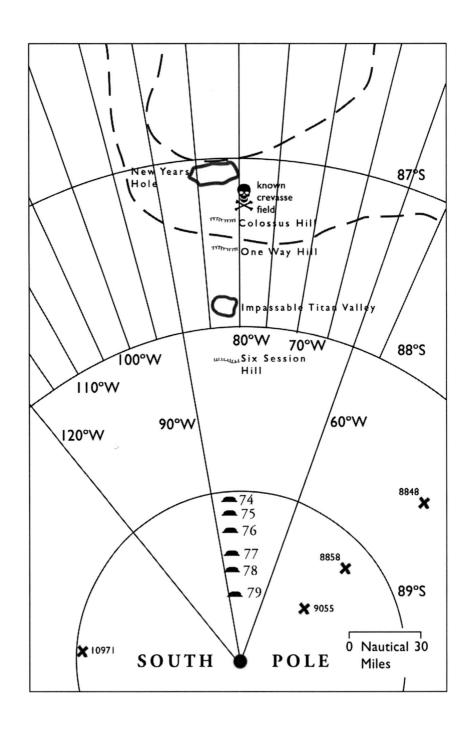

New Years
Hole

known
crevasse
field

Colossus Hill

One Way Hill

87°S

Impassable Titan Valley

80°W   70°W

88°S

Six Session
Hill

100°W

110°W

90°W   60°W

120°W

8848 ✕

74
75
76
77
78
79

8858 ✕

✕ 9055

89°S

✕ 10971

SOUTH   POLE

0 Nautical 30
      Miles

20

Days 74-79

Sunday, January 13, 2013 Day 74

THIS MORNING'S BREAKFAST unsettled my stomach. The cereal, milk, sugar and butter mixture tasted slightly stale, as though I'd left the cereal open for weeks. It made me feel like when I had first started out, as though I was eating far too much food. By now, my body had adjusted and craved every calorie I threw at it, yet today the cereal and butter made me nauseous. I slowed down and took little spoon-sized bites as I prepared to go out and do battle with the elements. There was the chance I had not cleaned the hot food thermos adequately enough from last night's meal, so I took a ciprofloxacin as a preventative measure. Dysentery and food poisoning was the last setback I wished to fight so near my goal. To compensate for the lack of energy from breakfast, I added an additional cookie to each break meal. Doing this maintained my energy, preventing me from bonking.

The sour stomach in the morning allowed a real rush of negative thoughts to fill my mind even before I stepped out of the tent. I felt as though, so near to the end of the expedition, there was the potential for disaster. I grew scared. After two months and so close to the Pole,

I feared something would go wrong at the last second. I could fix any mechanical problem, but now I fought a biological one. A sense of foreboding overtook me. How could I be this close and all of a sudden fall ill again? I felt overwhelmed. It was a new and unwelcome emotion.

New kartankers, though comfortable and soft, meant I had to deal with overheated feet for several days until they broke in. This irked me, as I should have easily broken them in before coming to Antarctica. It was embarrassing to have missed this detail. I laughed at the thought of telling my buddies over drinks that I'd not thought to smash and test these clown-sized booties. While working as an engineer, I was paid to anticipate every possible scenario. Though I did not always succeed, I had a consistent track record. Now, on my maiden voyage into polar exploration, I worked through all the same failures and mistakes that every rookie makes.

As a consequence of being too warm, my feet sweated. As soon as I felt the hot flash pass up my legs, I knew the kartankers were already moist. And, once wet, they caused my feet to be cold much of the day. To attempt to compensate for that and the persistent goggle fogging, I drove myself into mild hypothermia. By the end of the breaks, I shivered violently and needed to start skiing to warm up. My thought was that if I were cold, at least the goggles would not fog. If nothing else, being cold motivated me to keep making miles. It was a serious test of my mental fortitude. Would I be able to drive myself to be terribly cold in order to keep my feet dry and my goggles cleared?

By the end of the day, frost coated the outside of the kartankers, something I'd not seen in a while. This was easy enough to deal with at night, as I had been putting everything that needed to be dried out inside the sleeping bag every night. Even though it made for a lumpy sleeping surface, having warm, dry boot liners, gloves and socks every morning more than made up for it.

Camp AC72
89°01.162'S 81°14.948'W
Distance: 8.32 nm, Time: 9 hours, Elevation: 9,625'
Distance to South Pole: 59 nm

MONDAY, JANUARY 14, 2013 DAY 75

Today's breakfast was worse than yesterday's, even more stale. It took longer to eat, pushing back my day's starting time. I became concerned, as I thought that there was something gravely wrong with me. I knew that I didn't have far to go and I would be able to tough it out if need be, but I wanted to finish with some style. I did not want to stumble into the Pole, vomiting and unable to eat. This made no sense to me. I had woken up hungry every day for two months, so my body needed the food. Slogging through the meal, I dressed and buckled the towing harness. As I stepped out of the tent, the wind started howling.

To prepare my body for the final push, I slipped a fleece jacket under the waist harness to reduce the pain and chafing I had been fighting for two weeks. It had reached the point that a harness adjustment of one-inch up or down made the difference between pain and mild discomfort. If it was too low, it restricted leg motion, causing the rapid onset of leg fatigue. But too high and it strained my lower back, making breathing difficult. Since my pants now kept falling down, I was constantly trying to find the sweet spot for belt tension. Adjusting the harness on top of the pants, while maintaining a balance between too cool and too warm, required full-time attention. Even the slightest misalignment now plagued me. For all the annoyance and agony, I still reveled in what I was doing. The challenge made me giddy. After working as an engineer for over 15 years, I felt right at home having problems to work through.

Some deep part of me hoped for perfect sunny conditions and light winds to carry me into the Pole. I considered the South Pole as my island after being lost at sea for months. Though I had a vague memory of what the pole station looked like from photographs, I had no idea what my emotions would be when I finally saw it. As it had been so long since I had seen anything other than ice and snow, I was not sure what to expect. It felt as though I had been marooned on an island for years and was now within a few days of escaping. In some ways, though, I did not want to escape. This was the first time in my entire life that I was free of distraction and had clarity of purpose. There was no one nor anything restricting my creative problem solving. It was only me and one singular goal. The thousand distractions of home life were far, far away. No arbitrary rules dictated how I managed what I did out here. Only necessity for survival and motion dictated what I did. It was simply me and what I could do with what I had.

On the satellite phone tonight, ALE operator James Hayes, had fun at my expense, breaking the tension.

"I have to let you know that the Union Glacier camp is enjoying tiramisu for dessert tonight. What are you having for dessert?" he prodded with his South African accent.

"Well, exactly the same thing as I've had for seventy-five days straight, a freeze-dried dinner with no dessert," I said with a smile.

"I'm sorry to be such a bastard. I just thought you should know that."

Unapologetically laughing loudly into the satellite phone, I quipped, "I really appreciate that James. It's nice to know someone is eating good food."

We both seemed to know that I would happily eat anything, including an Italian dessert. With the jocularity aside, I asked, "When do you think I will see something as I get close to the Pole?"

"You won't likely see anything until your approach day," he said.

"I have to tell you, I've been hallucinating that I see an arrow blinking on the horizon, showing me the way," I said. "But each time I try to focus on the arrow, it disappears."

"Sorry, I'm afraid that feature has been disabled," he countered. "It's best to keep using your current navigation tools."

He also said that I, Vilborg and a team of South Africans were still out here, making the final push. I was amazed at the mileage the South Africans were achieving, a whopping 11 nm per day. I consoled myself with knowing they were fresh and that their supplies were distributed among team members. And, too, I knew that after being out here so long, my body ran on fumes alone. I was glad I could not detect the fumes emanating from me, as the cold inhibited much of my sense of smell.

I learned Roland Kruger had arrived at the Pole on January 12th.

"Are you kidding me?" I asked incredulously. "I thought he was planning to cross the continent."

"Yes he was," said James. "Even though he did the Messner Start, conditions were so bad that he had to give up at the Pole."

"I can't believe that I'm not that far behind him."

"He had far less miles to cover than you, but things were no easier for him."

I sat slack-jawed. Even someone with so much experience was overwhelmed this season, not even coming close to his goal. This season seemed to be the year of crushed plans.

Camp AC73
89°09.138'S 81°02.217'W
Distance: 8 nm, Time: 9 hours, Elevation: 9,059'
Distance to South Pole: 51 nm
Rations remaining: 11 days

Tuesday, January 15, 2013 Day 76

This day I had it with the stomach churning breakfasts. The mix of cereal, milk, sugar and butter had finally nauseated me. Barely able to stomach it, I grew mad.

"What the heck? Why does my cereal taste like it's been sitting around for five years?" I screamed out into the void.

I hungered to eat anything else. But, there was the only one breakfast I had to eat. After forcing down half a cup, I nearly vomited.

"Screw it," I growled.

Cereal flew out of the cup and onto the ice. Sitting there, I mashed my hands to my face and groaned.

"I have backpacked farther in a long weekend than I am from the Pole now," I cried. "Even if I have to starve and not eat breakfast, I will make it."

After three heaving sighs, I packed my gear and readied myself. There were enough spare rations that I knew I would not starve. They were not a normal breakfast but rather cookies, leftover bars and such. Nausea had shoved me over the edge. It was so obnoxious that I again chased the slop with an intestinal antibiotic. I was not going to become debilitatingly ill less than 50 miles from my goal.

As I skied through the morning, I felt better. The deteriorating weather kept my mind off the hunger gnawing at my stomach. My energy was low. Moral had sunk. I was fighting a bitter headwind. But I had not vomited, so I cheered the minor achievement. By the afternoon, I felt better, so I chowed down a food bar, chased by butter.

On taking my first bite of butter of the day, I gagged and spat it out. "Blech!" I blurted.

The butter tasted horrid.

In a flash, I realized what was wrong. Somehow my remaining stash of butter had rotted. After sitting and thinking it through, I realized that the butter I now ate was from the sun-exposed cache back at 87°30'. Sometime during windless days at the cache, the food had spoiled inside the nylon bag, even though the air temperature never rose above -20°F. My food had roasted at the same time as I did. With my sense of smell paralyzed from the cold, it was impossible for me to detect rotten food. There had been a light odor coming from the sled bags, but I guessed it was the mass of crumbs and soiled clothes. Now I knew. Hoping that my sense of taste had gone awry, I stuffed the brick of butter right under my nose and sniffed as hard as I could. Nothing. Then, I gently licked the butter.

"Yuck! What the heck?" I cried out as I scraped the rancid butter off my tongue with the back of my mittens. No wonder breakfast had been killing me for so long. During the day, I only ate bite-sized chunks of butter, so it never hit me. But at breakfast, I ate a whole stick.

I had been ingesting rotten food for over a week.

This explained a great many issues: why my energy had collapsed, why I felt horrid during the mornings and why I was having so many negative thoughts. While my rations were bland, they kept me going and thus happy. But with the food slowly poisoning me, I was deteriorating into an unhealthy mental state. Slinging the brick of butter as far as I could, I realized why I was having such a miserable time. With that butter now staring at me from several yards away, I felt better. Even though my stomach was queasy from the last bite of rancid butter, I was happy knowing I had found out what was wrong. Of all my problems, this one had a simple fix: don't eat the spoiled butter.

Today I learned the South African team was going to reach the Pole tomorrow, Vilborg was three days out, and there was another skier way back at 87°11'S. My voice pitch rose over the wind noise on the satellite phone.

"What?!" I blurted out. "How could anyone possibly be behind me this late in the season that far back?"

"His name is Richard Parks. He had a rough go at it," said the operator.

When I heard this, I was in utter shock. How was someone not only behind me but all the way at the beginning of the 87° degree sastrugi field? Apparently, he had trouble with his supplies arriving on time, and then had been injured on his way across the continent. Those two problems conspired against him and he was now insanely behind. I felt terrible for him. Yet, though I was guilty for having the emotion, I was happy that I was not the last person out here.

Camp AC74
89°17.420'S 80°20.831'W
Distance: 8.3 nm, Time: 9 hours, Elevation: 9,112'
Distance to South Pole: 42 nm

Wednesday, January 16, 2013, Day 77

Based on my calculations, I should see the South Pole station rise above the horizon on Sunday. My excitement was growing, causing sleeping difficulties. It was as though I was a horse banging into the starting gate, yearning to ski the final sprint as fast as possible. As much as I wanted to, covering more than eight miles seemed impossible at this point.

"It's okay," I told myself. "There were still plenty of rations, fuel and time to make it to the station even if the distance collapsed to six miles per day."

Not that I wanted that! The only impediment that would slow me down that badly would be insane sastrugi or winds. As other teams had reported that the surface was flat but sticky, I was not too concerned. But the winds were another matter. On January 10th, the weather deteriorated: the winds increased and snow buried the sleds. This had not happened in over a month. I was in a race against the calendar as Scott had been over a century ago. After a certain date, conditions deteriorated and made reaching the Pole a desperate dash. Now I understood why the season was cut off at the end of January. At the rate the weather was worsening, I suspected that it would be like the November conditions: brutal. The trekking season was remarkably short here.

While skiing, I discovered a set of sled tracks heading 30° to the west of where I was headed. With strong winds, I was surprised that there were any tracks out here at all. Stooping over, I touched the tracks. Though I had no idea who they were from, I imagined what struggles and triumphs this person experienced. Since I adjusted my course two days ago toward the VLF (very low frequency) antenna marker and not the Pole, I expected not to see any tracks at all. As I was 35 miles away from my target, my course was off the recommended route. But, this approach saved me an extra half-day of skiing, traveling along the hypotenuse of the route rather than reaching a corner and making a dog-leg turn east. Correcting at this distance saved me four extra miles of travel at the Pole.

ALE notified me that they had closed down their base at the Pole and flown everything out this morning. That explained the air traffic I had heard but hadn't seen. My original hope was to reach the Pole and use the ALE charging stations for my phones to call sponsors and supporters. That was no longer possible. Now, I needed to be extremely mindful of the satellite phone battery levels. There had been no useful sun in several days. I promised a phone call to all the people backing me. I had to make these calls, even if I had to activate my backup phone.

As I was short on rations, I asked ALE if it was possible to leave food in case I was stuck at the Pole. And, if it were possible, to air-drop cookies as they flew by. I knew it was crazy, but I asked anyway. With the loss of the butter rations, I was hungry at the end of each 75-minute towing session. As the cache was not buried, I felt miffed at having food issues when I shouldn't have. For all that I had fought through, anything short of hurricane force winds was not going to stop me.

A century ago, Scott and his team were pinned down by such a storm for 10 days when they perished. I was half that time away from the Pole, yet I feared some unknown disaster wiping me out at the last minute. As my mind had gone haywire by this point, one of the nutty scenarios it produced was born of Hollywood material. I dreamt that the requested air dropped cookies smashed into my tent and severely damaged it. Then, I was beset by thoughts of a massive network of mile-deep crevasses opening up around my tent.

At this point I knew my mind hallucinated wildly, doing anything it could to prevent me from going outside. Because these thoughts were so laughable, they were easier to ignore. To help remind me these thoughts were only imaginary, I formulated a mantra.

"Space aliens. Space aliens are going to prevent you from reaching the Pole," I kept telling myself out loud.

Saying this helped separate myself from the schizophrenia churning inside of my head. This must have been apparent in my audio blog because Kelly sent me the following satellite text message:

"Leave the cracking to the ice."

Upon reading this, I laughed out loud so hard that I gave myself a headache. My mind fought off thoughts of space aliens attacking me, a flying box of cookies destroying my tent and falling into a crevasse while skiing through a whiteout. It was best to keep these crazy thoughts to myself.

Camp AC75
89°25.722'S 79°10.252'W
Distance: 8.35 nm, Time: 9 hours, Elevation: 9,101'
Rations remaining: 9 days

Thursday, January 17, 2013 Day 78

Excitement made for fitful sleep. Normally, sleep was never a problem for me, as I was wasted by the end of the day. Now, I had been sleeping five hours a night for the past few days, and my throat was becoming sore. Sucking on lozenges, I desperately wanted to stay healthy for the final push. There was no one to catch a cold or lung infection from out here, so the threat of catching a cold was nil. But, fatigue of my mind and body could make me sick anyway. While awake when I should have been sleeping, I laid there and practiced breathing to rest. I kept my eyes covered to prevent the 24-hour sun from fully waking me up. It took massive effort to stay down and rest. Resisting the urge to rise and start moving took more energy than getting up.

Today my mind devised a new doomsday scenario to forestall progress. What if all of my GPS units had been wrong the whole time and I was completely lost on the eastern Antarctic plateau? Of course, I knew this was impossible. Five different GPS devices indicated I was right on course. But what if the Cold War GPS scrambling had been reactivated, slowly causing me to drift into east Antarctica? No, ALE would have warned me. And, if this did happen, my position would have dramatically shifted. I would know something was wrong. Nothing of the sort had happened. My mind was digging deep to drive me mad. If nothing else, I would be reduced to compass navigation all the rest of the way in. Without landmarks to provide some guidance, I would need a clear day, otherwise my imperfect alignment between the magnetic and geographic pole would shoot me off into nowhere, too. After entertaining this laughable scenario, I regained control of my mind and refocused on preparing for the day.

This morning, I pulled my fourth and final roll of toilet paper out from deep inside sled.

"Woo! A whole new roll of toilet paper! I still have toilet paper," I declared into the wind. I was thrilled to have calculated exactly how much I required for three months, with this spare in reserve. As I had stopped eating butter, my digestion had improved and everything worked better in this respect. It was such a pleasant change from the past two weeks. The excitement of toilet paper made thoughts of GPS errors dissolve from my mind.

The day turned out to be pleasant, with an extremely rare 3-5 knot tail wind. It was the perfect speed because it allowed me to strip off everything but the shell jacket and the fleece jacket around my waist, protecting my hips from the harness. This wind also allowed me to use glasses instead of goggles, as my face wouldn't freeze from a tail wind. I saw without obstruction for the first time in over a week. The mental unburdening provided by proper vision was a relief. Instantly, my attitude improved and I was having an exhilarating time, even with pain in my hips and feet. Even when the clouds threatened to plunge me into a ground whiteout, I didn't care. I was not completely blind. I could deal with a whiteout. As long as my lenses were free of ice, I didn't care.

In the afternoon, I discovered the shortbread cookies from the second cache had gone rancid, too. They were made of butter and thus susceptible to overheating. 30 miles out, my rations were rapidly falling apart. The cookies even smelled rancid. They had to be rotten if I could smell them. Inspecting them closely, I saw they had even partially melted in their plastic wrap. Picking through the remaining rations, I found some pouches of cookies that were still edible. With the cookies rotten, my stomach grumbled constantly. My body now felt thinner.

Camp AC76
89°33.835'S 75°53.430'W
Distance: 8.3 nm, Time: 9 hours, Elevation 9,158'
Distance to South Pole: 26 nm

Friday, January 18, 2013 Day 79
For as pleasant as yesterday was, today was exactly the opposite. A 20-knot head wind kicked up out of the southeast and shoved me backwards. With the partial ground whiteout, travel was again difficult. With icy goggles, I was blind. It felt as though the continent conspired against me. Combined with the now incessant hunger plaguing me, travel was slow. And yet, it was satisfying. As difficult as the weather had turned, I was only a marathon's distance from the pole. Since these winds cut one mile off my day's travel distance, I would have to push to arrive at the pole on the 21st.

The kartankers had packed down well and now were comfortable, even if they were too warm. The pain in my toes slowed me down, too. Again, I did not care. I adjusted my stride and continued the course of anti-inflammatories. There were so many parts of me that were aching, tired and generally worn out that the pain became another background noise. With this all going on and the wind pushing against me, I escaped into my mind and explored old memories. Thoughts of sixth grade reoccurred to me. I remembered learning to square dance, then miraculously ended up in the front row to show off my mediocre dancing skills in the school musical New York, New York.

I let ALE know the coordinates to *Impassable Titan Valley*, to warn Richard Parks about it, since he was at 87°47'S. As I wasn't sure what his longitude was. He could miss the valley altogether or stumble into it during a whiteout. With him being so far behind, I hoped to share some hard-won knowledge to help him reach the Pole. So many people helped me on this trip that anything I could do to help another made me feel valuable.

The wind blew snow into the air, making distant objects disappear, impeding navigation. Though the sun was in the sky, the heavy cloud cover cast the landscape into a dusky twilight. I could not look at the chest mounted compass very long because the wind kept knocking me off balance. Also, the compass refused to settle due to the increasingly weak magnetic field. It took five seconds to take a stable reading, cutting my speed even more. I kept wandering off my bearing. The combination of the wind and hidden sastrugi from the ground blizzard channeled me in the wrong direction relentlessly.

After doing some quick calculations, I figured out I was losing even more mileage skiing blind in whiteouts. I was off course by as much as 30° in as little as 60 seconds. But, I did not want to stop incessantly to take readings, otherwise I would lose even another mile. The headwind would already cost me one. I made up a game to both keep me on course and keep my head out of the whiteout and mean weather.

The objective of the game was to keep on course and make positive headway without ever stopping to take a compass sighting. Since I knew that each step took one second, I started counting each ski kick. Each 60th step, I checked the compass momentarily to realign myself without stopping. In addition, I counted how many times I checked the compass. As each check happened every minute, I was able to time how long I had been skiing without checking my watch. On the 80th compass check, it was time to stop for a break. In order not to lose count of the checks, I shoved other distracting thoughts out of my mind. It took absolute concentration to ski, be efficient, ignore 25 knot icy head winds, ignore pain in my feet and legs, take accurate compass readings and keep two running numbers in my mind. This all helped to pass the day quickly and methodically.

Camp AC77
89°40.962'S 72°01.818'W
Distance: 7.3 nm, Time: 9 hours, Elevation: 9,126'
Distance to South Pole: 19 nm
Rations remaining: 7 days

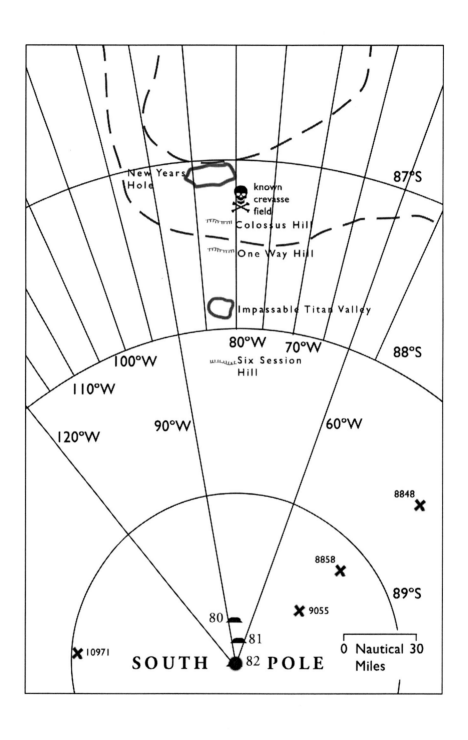

2 1

Days 80-82

Aftra SKIING NINE HOURS a day for 40 days straight, I was wrecked. Kelly suggested I sleep in an extra hour or two. If nothing else, lie there and let my body rest, even if I didn't sleep. I made every effort not to move a muscle, taking advantage of the two slack hours I gave myself. At 8 a.m., I felt refreshed and ready to tackle the final distance.

There were no weekends, holidays or any days off. Polar travel allows for little slack. Fatigue made the indistinct colored spots I had been seeing in the sastrugi become distinct and vibrant yesterday. Even with the ice obscuring the goggles, the raven I saw before now appeared all day. Hallucinations this strong told me my brain and body were running at the limit. I wondered what my brain would conjure up next, as I had never experienced this before. It felt as though I was in a laboratory experiment.

The wind had risen to a ripping 35 knots, making navigation slow and tedious. The roar was a welcome distraction, drowning out the mind junk threatening to fill my head. A ground blizzard made it impossible to see waypoints farther than 100 feet, necessitating constant compass checks. That was okay, though, because I couldn't see through the ice buildup in my goggles anyway. No matter what I wore, I was blind.

Using my counting technique, I still made headway, even though at a measly mile per hour. I had not dropped to this low a mileage since late November. But, in a way, I welcomed the terrible weather. I reached the point that I ignored the noise in my mind, even though it gave me countless excuses to stop. I forged on. Keeping track of two different counts in my mind made all the difference. If I let the aches, pains and discomforts bubble to the surface and distract me, I started to lose count. One of the rules of the game was if I lost count, I would have to start all over again. Although I never lost count, I had to take breaks. I stayed completely focused on moving forward. When I stumbled or the sleds snagged on unseen sastrugi, the harness shifted and sent bolts of pain to my brain, more than once making my eyes water.

Through the storm, a beautifully colored sunbow appeared. Although it was indistinct, the colors were vivid. I knew that it signaled snow. The weather was falling apart quickly, in time for the last two days of the journey. That was fine with me. If Antarctica was to remind me how difficult it was, I welcomed it.

Camp AC78
89°46.357'S 64°35.881'W
Distance: 5.8 nm, Time: 6 hours, Elevation: 9,161'
Distance to South Pole: 13.5 nm

Sunday, January 20, 2013 Day 81

During the night, my heel split open and hip pain made sleep all but impossible. For all the help the hard track should have given me, it ended up being a curse all the way to the end of this expedition. In fact, based on the throbbing and sharp pain I experienced in my hips and toes, I suspected these pains would be with me for some time after the expedition. Ultimately, it wasn't worth it.

Everything seemed to be in slow motion today. My skiing slowed. The wind howled. Cloud after cloud of snow blew into my face. My compass swayed back and forth in a trance-like motion. My gait and hand motion felt disconnected. Everything seemed surreal. Though I know it was a purely psychological effect, it seemed even my watch was not keeping the time.

I knew that I did not want to ski too long tomorrow, so I put in an extra half hour at the end of the day. I wanted to ski into camp standing rather than stumbling from fatigue. ALE had contacted the South Pole station about my arrival, so I wanted to have my act together as I arrived. With a whiteout most of the day, it was difficult to tell if I was even moving. The station was huge and yet I had seen no trace of it. As thoughts of failed navigation filled my head, apparitions momentarily materialized through the white haze.

Black forms appeared on the horizon. At first it seemed like a train of vehicles moving in the distance, like the Thiel's traverse rig. Stopping and squinting, I saw the mass was immobile. This was an exciting sign. But the blots were unclear. Taking a compass sighting of them, they were far off course of where I was supposed to be. Unfamiliar with how the station appeared at a distance, I imagined that these black blocks were some sort of outbuildings, far away from the Pole. For being this far out and them being fairly off course, I did not comprehend what they were. After seeing nothing but white and blue for so long, shapes meant little to me. My brain dreamt up outhouses and vehicles. These specters soon disappeared into the whiteout. I was left wondering if what I had seen was real, or was I hallucinating again?

As much as I wanted to rush through the evening routine, I stuck to the procedure I'd used for almost three months. There was no way I was going to wreck anything at the last moment. Hoping to make a wild run to the station, I knew I was still at least five hours out. I would rather arrive refreshed. It was impossible to sleep from the excitement. This was far worse than counting the minutes until Christmas morning as a child. I could not remember how long it had been since I was this excited about anything. I lay there, swaddled in my sleeping bag, listening to the wind beating the tent, knowing this was the last time I would be out here by myself, near nothing.

It was both sad and exciting.

Camp AC79
89°52.668'S 32°17.367'W
Distance: 8.4 nm, Time: 9.5 hours, Elevation: 9,100'
Distance to South Pole: 7 nm
Rations remaining: 5 days

M<small>ONDAY</small>, J<small>ANUARY</small> 21, 2013 D<small>AY</small> 82
(T<small>UESDAY</small>, J<small>ANUARY</small> 22, 2013 <small>AT THE</small> S<small>OUTH</small> P<small>OLE</small> <small>STATION ON</small> N<small>EW</small> Z<small>EALAND</small> T<small>IME</small>)

As excited as I was last night about the final approach today, I slept superbly. It was unexpected given all that had happened. A calm descended on me this morning as I shuffled through my gear. I now considered it differently than when I started. This little red tent had become my home in Antarctica for three months. I had some affection for it. Though it was no different than the other tents of the same design, this one had kept me alive through the worst weather and hardest times I had ever experienced. And now, today, it would all be over.

Desiring as much time at the pole as possible, I dressed, decamped, started skiing on time at 9 a.m. Using the compass, I made my way on the suggested GPS course of 172° for the first 75 minutes. All seemed perfect until I checked the GPS. Something was amiss. As the station was invisible, there was nothing to ski toward. Even though I had traveled 1.2 nm from my camp, I had only moved 0.6 nm closer to the VLF marker along my bearing.

What the…?

Something perplexing happens to the GPS display right at the Pole, roughly 30 miles out. The track on the screen curves dramatically to the right and far off the main screen. It was a peculiarity of mapping coordinate systems. Though the GPS displays orthogonal coordinates, the world is on spherical coordinates. Other than at the north and south poles, the orthogonal system works perfectly. The GPS does not show polar coordinates. Where all the longitude lines meet, orthogonal coordinates veer off the display. The second issue was that, right near the Pole, the GPS always shows a 180° bearing to reach the Pole, regardless of the longitude. This, combined with the magnetic pole lying off the Antarctic coast over 1,000 miles away, made navigating the last few miles to the geographic South Pole problematic. Even though I had been on course for 700 miles, my minor error of two miles east meant, had I continued on the compass bearing suggested by the GPS, I would have continued into oblivion on the eastern Antarctic plateau.

This was grievous.

Powering up the GPS, I watched it as I skied. The bearing needle on the screen showed I was 30° off course. My cheeks flushed with embarrassment. How could I make such a potentially tragic mistake this close. My GPS was set to True and not Magnetic North. No matter where I was when near the South Pole, the GPS indicated I should remain on a bearing of 180°. Recalling my briefing, ALE probably warned me to be careful about navigation near the Pole. As that was three months ago, the details were foggy. I resumed skiing, slowly shifting to the right until the travel arrow matched on the curved line toward the Pole. The compass showed my course as 157°, far from the GPS recommended bearing of 178°. Since there was nothing to navigate by, I stowed the compass and shimmied my way toward an invisible finish line. And then for the briefest of moments, the station appeared, along with an antenna tower. It was exactly on the bearing I needed to travel! Then, as quickly, the station disappeared. But the antenna was still barely visible on the horizon. Excited, I pocketed the GPS and picked up speed, barreling toward the still visible steel tower.

Soon, far in the distance, stubby black poles appeared. Though my hips and feet were absolutely killing me, I kept telling my body to shut up. Left. Right. Left. Again and again. And then, after hundreds of miles, the first sign of civilization appeared in the snow: a tattered piece of plastic garbage, half-stuck in the ice. Humans were near. After another full hour of skiing, tiny poles in the distance turned into a seemingly infinite line of flags stretching out to the antenna still invisible in the whiteout. Checking the GPS one more time, I shut it off and headed straight for the series of flags.

The first was two miles away from my camp.

With my feet screaming in pain, the station materialized out of the formless white and solidified. A sign welcoming me to the outer rim of the South Pole station made me quake with excitement. I phoned ALE and let them know I was on final approach to the Pole.

"Hello! It sounds like you made it to the Pole after quite a trip," said Celine, an ALE operator.

"Thank you," I replied. "If you can, please set up a tour with the South Pole station."

"We'll raise them on the phone and see what we can do," she said with joy in her voice.

Clicking the phone off, I yelled "Woooo!" into the light breeze.

Even after following the trail of flags, it took another hour to reach the NGO (non-governmental organization) camping area, labeled as the "World's Southernmost Resort." I was glad the operators at the pole had a sense of humor. I appreciated that after so long in the field. Setting up my tent, I made water and called ALE to find out what time my station tour was. They said if I could be there in one hour that would be great. Signing off, I immediately shut off the stove. Making water was no longer important. I could not be late for my appointment. Bundling up, as it was extremely cold and I would no longer be dragging a sled to stay warm, I set out for the Pole.

At 4:40 p.m., I touched the ceremonial pole. After savoring the moment for a few minutes, I skied over to the true geographic pole, exactly 90ºS, at 16:52 p.m. The points are separated by several hundred feet.

"Wooooo!" I yelled again and again. I was not worried about waking up the station crew. As the station was designed to keep out -100º temperatures, I was sure the insulation would repel my feeble yell.

After a little searching, I found the station entrance on the far side away from the markers. Opening a massive freezer door, Shannon warmly greeted me and allowed me to drop my coats in their storage room. As I was considered a tourist at a National Science Foundation research station, I had to be escorted at all times. She showed me a Project Ice Cube sensor, a neutrino detector designed to be buried two miles under the ice by the station. On display were previous geographic pole markers and flags. She entertained all of my questions with utmost patience, as I hoped to glean what I could from the massive effort to reach the Pole.

I also stamped my passport with the South Pole Station stamp on January 22, 2013. As the station ran on New Zealand time, I was transported over the dateline from my arrival on January 21 in mere seconds. I knew the gift shop only accepted cash, so I had brought plenty of it, as clothing items were not cheap here. After 20 minutes at a once in a lifetime visit to the South Pole for my sponsors and supporters, Shannon handed me off to Weeks Heist, the winter station manager. He in turn showed me the conference room. There, separated from me by a plate of glass, was Amundsen's original journal from his 1911–1912 expedition.

"I'm guessing that not a lot of people get to handle that book," I joked.

"Ha ha, not too many, that's for sure," was his reply.

"There are so many mementos of history in just this little room, it blows my mind."

"It's good you like it, that you appreciate it."

Surprisingly, Weeks was also an embedded software engineer. We shared thoughts on why we had both ended up at the South Pole. He, too, had seen the entirety of his life's story played out as he worked in his Manhattan cubicle.

"Although the work was a good challenge, I could see all the way to my death," he said.

"Like, the classic American story?" I asked.

"Yes, like moving to the New York suburbs, and having 2.5 children, two cars and such like everyone else."

"That sounds familiar."

"Just because I made a pile of money did not mean I was satisfied."

"No, I completely understand that. It's why I'm standing here, too."

Looking at him, I saw a mirror version of myself, minus the frostbite.

Weeks even allowed me to use the toilet on the station. I was relieved to be out of the weather. I was shocked at how I appeared, as I had not seen myself in a mirror for a full three months. With tape and glue all over my face, I thought I looked poor.

"Sorry to be a mess. I have not seen myself in a mirror in months," I told him.

"No, not at all. Some people actually come into the station with their cheeks completely frozen off. You look really good."

"Thanks."

"We're quite surprised how good you look considering how long you have been out."

"You're not the first person to mention being out this long," I laughed.

He told me about the 300 Club. To be a member, one had to hang out in the sauna for a half hour at 200 degrees, then they run to the ceremonial pole when it was -100 degrees outside. All done naked. They span a range of 300 degrees. I thought it would be fun to try, though I'd have to work here in the winter for the chance to do it. I wondered if they require witnesses for this activity. Another peculiarity about the South Pole was the elevation and the permanent low pressure system over the area, affecting the barometric pressure. Most of the time, the physiological atmosphere felt like an altitude of 12,000 feet rather than 9,000 feet. Walking up stairs was a real workout.

The facility had countless amenities. No one hurt for activities to do here. Crafts, computers, music rooms, a full basketball court, weight room, two reading rooms, a recreation room with a pool table, sauna and music room were all available for station personnel on their days off. As they work six days on for 9 hours a day, they're busy. The satellite link provides internet for 14 hours a day. It was crawlingly slow at best, but it was something. The hydroponics lab grows 35 pounds of vegetables per week. The humidity in the room induced a wild, hacking cough in my chest. I had experienced no humidity for 85 days. It was a shock to my system. The entertainment library still had VHS and Betamax tapes available.

"We're probably the only place on Earth that still has Beta tapes," he said.

For a place where crew are allocated two two-minute showers and one load of laundry per week, people looked happy. Was their sense of smell as crippled as mine? Or they had a strong tolerance and a generous supply of deodorant.

"Thank you so much for showing me around," I told Weeks.

"One more thing: Jeffrey Donenfeld would like to meet with you tomorrow morning, your time, to chat about your trip. That is, if you wouldn't mind."

"Sure, of course! I'd be happy to talk about it."

"Great, meet him at this freezer door at 8 a.m. and you guys can hang out and chat."

Once out of the station, I skied back to the geographic pole and circled it clockwise 35 times, turning back time and allowing me to relive my 39th birthday. It was the only place on the globe to do this reliably, since the North Pole is reported to be under water these days. On stepping out the door, I felt uncompressed. Though the station was fascinating, it felt claustrophobic as I had lived under the open sky for so long. Now 38 years old again, I skied back to my camp, a full kilometer from the station, and powered up the satellite phones to make the most important calls of the trip: those to my sponsors and supporters.

Kelly had a large crowd waiting in Jackson Hole to give me a stunning cheer when I came on the line. It was fun to hear such a group of people waiting on me. It was a risk to know when I would call exactly. It surprised me, as I did not expect such a crowd, thousands of miles away. My phone calls lasted far past midnight, as I had many to make. After disconnecting from the last call, I crawled into the sleeping bag and fell asleep instantly.

Camp AC80
89°59.420'S 17°14.451'W
South Pole
Rations remaining: 4 days

TUESDAY, JANUARY 22, 2013, DAY 83

I slept solidly, though it was a short night. I had stayed up way too late making my calls, but I was glad I took the time to make them. Jeffrey Donenfeld met me at the station deck in the morning before his shift. We had hoped to be able to talk in one of the quiet rooms, but per National Science Foundation and station rules, I was not allowed to stay inside. So, instead, we had to go out to the ceremonial pole to chat. We weren't even allowed to stand on the outside deck. The station has a small, 149-person community. As such, information spread faster than the flu. Once one visitor was allowed to stay inside, then everyone else would clamor to do the same. As I didn't want to stir up any trouble, I accepted it. I shared some of the highlights of the trip, and Jeffrey enjoyed all the stories about the cold experiences.

Once we were too cold to talk any more, I bid him adieu. Off to my camp I strode and contacted ALE about my pickup today.

"The weather is questionable at Thiel's Corner, so it's iffy if we'll be able to pick you up," said Celine.

"I understand. You don't want to come all this way just to have to return without cargo," I said.

"Please call us hourly with a weather report so we can update the flight."

"Okay, can do."

My job was to let them know how the pole landing strip looked. This data was key because ALE did not want the plane to fly all this way and then be unable to land. After learning from the South Pole staff that the flags I skied along were used to measure atmospheric distance visibility, I was able to accurately report the horizon, visibility and wind conditions. It was not until 4 p.m. that I was notified that the plane was cleared to land at 5:30 p.m., so I needed to be ready.

The plane touched down a few minutes after 5:30 p.m. That was impressive timing for Antarctica! The crew related that they had a sketchy time landing at Thiel's Corner for my cache drop, flying in blind due to the white out. I was glad they were skilled and able to safely land to refuel. I helped them run the pump to refill the aircraft and was soon ensconced on my private charter flight back to Union

Glacier. I was not the only cargo. There were four 55-gallon drums of jet fuel sitting right in front of me. As this seemed to be normal, I let go any nervousness about their proximity and instead focused on the landscape.

Three months of effort was undone by a neat six-hour flight. It was fun to refer to the GPS and recall what I was doing at these locations. I wasn't able to identify any specific sites, like *Impassable Titan Valley*, but I saw massive rivers of sastrugi snaking across the landscape. From our altitude of a few thousand feet, the hills, valleys and domes were invisible, though I knew they lurked under us.

The crew generously offered me a ham and cheese sandwich, apple and soda. That was the best, freshest and tastiest sandwich I had ever had in my life. I had tasted nothing fresh since leaving Union Glacier 83 days earlier. Before, I had looked at ham and cheese as the lowliest of sandwiches. Now, I appreciated the texture, flavor and moisture. The fresh meat certainly beat anything I brought with me.

We landed at midnight and I was escorted to the huge mess tent. Everything looked so different from when I had left. It was as though I was visiting for the first time. Inside was over half the ALE staff. They all cheered me when I entered. I was utterly stunned and, for once, was bereft of words. It was a rare moment. Thanking everyone for their support and tolerating my snail's pace, I was happy to see so many smiling faces up well past their bed time to receive me. The overflowing plate of pasta, meat and wine was better than any five-star dinner I'd had, anywhere in the world.

As the crowd congratulated me and trickled off to bed, I sat for a while and absorbed it. Inspecting the Antarctica pin map, I saw myself as a tag of paper, a tiny green triangle marching across the Antarctic wastelands. It didn't even seem real that I was back here, with the relative comforts of a huge tent, cot and pillow. The spaciousness of the tent felt strange, as though I was in a hotel suite. The space felt odd, as though there was too much of it. Once I lay down, I was unconscious in minutes, oblivious to the world.

JANUARY 23-24, 2013

The next two days were spent milling through Union Glacier camp. In between eating corpulent meals, I returned for snacks every hour. It was impossible to resist, considering the schedule I had maintained for the past three months. After eating, I would shuffle back to the tent and lay down. I rested but did not sleep. So many thoughts rolled through my mind, of the places I had been, what I had seen and what I experienced. The last climbing groups returned from Mt. Vinson, so they shared their stories of successes and near tragedies on that mountain.

The staff remarked that I was a scarecrow, as though I had bought my clothing two sizes too large. The doctors checked me over and declared me to be uninjured considering how long I had been out. There had been one case of frostbite this season and several injuries from slips and falls. One significant one was Jean-Gabriel Leynaud, a French filmmaker, who I had met when I returned to camp. He had flown out to the plateau to film and broke his leg in a fall. I was shocked to hear this, as he was fit and strong, not someone I would have expected that to happen to. ALE was coordinating a medical evacuation for him while disassembling the camp for the season. I felt bad for him, as he was congenial, high-spirited and strong.

The serious shock came at dinner on the 23rd. A Canadian Kenn Borek aircraft had gone down while flying through the Trans-Antarctic mountains. They were flying en route to an Italian research base in Terra Nova Bay when the aircraft's emergency locator beacon activated. The only reason that beacon triggers is if there was a hard surface strike. As the weather was poor in the area, no overflights or rescue were possible, though the flight crews at Union Glacier stood by to fly and help at a moment's notice. These administrative staff reminded everyone to be extra vigilant.

"It is the end of the season and, unfortunately, the injuries are almost inevitable," said Steve Jones to the staff during lunch. It seemed end-of-season injuries and problems were not uncommon. For all the modern technology in the world, being in Antarctica was still like being on an alien planet when problems arose.

The ice melter ALE brought down was used for hot shower water, a necessity for the staff. As they work seven days a week, I was sure the shower keeps everyone clean and healthy. I was allowed to use the shower to peel off my three-month old grime. To extend the single bucket of hot water, I filled it with ice chunks, creating a lukewarm mixture. Though the water was cooler, it allowed me to scrub myself down several times. The economy I learned during expedition turned out to be useful for an unexpected luxury experience.

Steve and I reviewed the Antarctic expedition statistics during the afternoon and I was stunned. I was the second only American and only the 29th person ever to solo to the South Pole in the 101 years of Antarctic trekking. And, I had made the second longest solo in the field. Aleksander Gamme was first, but he round-tripped. I was the 298th human to ever make the long distance trip ever, in all of humankind.

"Thousands have stood on Everest, as a point of comparison," said Steve.

He also asked me about how I felt about the snow tractor tracks being used as an aid or assistance.

"Although I thought I could ignore navigation, it ended up being a fallacy. I had no idea where that road went. Following it put me off-course more than once."

"Yes that was very true," he said.

"Also, the sleds never dragged in the tracks, so I ended up injured and slower."

"The sleds didn't track properly, then?"

"No, they always pulled to the side. Also, the tracks wander around, so following them actually added significant distance. In the end, I think it hurt and slowed me down. I wish I'd never found them."

Richard Parks was forced to request a pickup on January 24th. He still had 90 miles to cover in four days. It was impossible. Plus, ALE needed to be able to strike camp and fly out on the 29th. If they could not recover Richard due to weather, they would have to delay closing Union Glacier. Apparently, he was only the third person ever to need a bailout. As expected, the staff was harried racing around Union

Glacier as they tried to close camp on time.

ALE notified me that they were flying the Ilyushun-76 in on the afternoon of the 24th, so I needed to be ready to go. Although there was no wind at camp, I had to dress as though I was going into the worst conditions. The wind was strong at the mouth of the glacier compared to the camp, a few miles away. Many ALE staff members also acted as ground crew, assisting the aircraft with landing. When conditions were poor, they used smoke pots and mirrors to guide the jet, indicating where the runway was. This was a reminder of the remoteness and dangers of Antarctica. A huge, modern cargo plane still relied on ancient techniques to ensure a safe landing.

When we boarded, we were all treated to regular airline seats. They were luxurious compared to the carpet-covered plywood seats of last October. Cushions felt like cheating after never having anything comfortable to sit on for three months. The flight back was over a continuous bank of clouds. I never saw the vast expanse of the southern ocean through the viewport. It didn't matter, as I was so tired I slept most of the flight.

Punta Arenas, Chile

Stepping off the aircraft in Punta Arenas was a shock. Smells of grass, dirt, smog, asphalt and every other worldly odor assailed me. I had smelled nothing but my own odor and rotting food for three months. The sensation overwhelmed me. Normally, my sense of smell was passable, so this was a sensory overload. It was as though I had returned from an alien planet and experienced Earth for the first time. Nothing felt "right." Darkness, stars, darkness, headlights, cars, darkness, no ice and trees. All were foreign. Even the hotel room felt claustrophobic. The bed did not even feel right. I missed my sleeping pads and bag.

I ran into Vilborg at the Condor de Plata hotel when I arrived in the evening. She said she received calls from both the prime minister and president of Iceland. A popular blog published her story and she was soon on the front page of the national newspaper. She had made national news in Iceland and was overwhelmed by the response.

Unsure if she liked it, she did not let it go to her head. She said the conditions were so extreme this year that no one finished their goal.

"Look at this. Hannah had a client drop out. Roland was supposed to cross the continent but had to stop at the Pole," she said with a light Icelandic accent.

"That's pretty rough," I said.

"I had to be resupplied after trying to go solo. You couldn't make the round trip."

"Oh, you had to take a resupply in the end?"

"Yes. There was not any other choice," she acknowledged.

"I'm sorry that it didn't work out."

"That's okay. Eric Larsen had to bail on his bike attempt."

"And," I interjected, "Richard Parks had to be picked up."

"No kidding?"

"Yes, he was over 140 kilometers away, so he had no chance," I replied.

"I would have rather failed in the most difficult conditions than succeeded in relatively easy ones," she said.

"That was pretty amazing to meet you out there," I mentioned.

"I debated even approaching you, as others are very hard core and don't want to be disturbed."

"No, I loved it!" I assured her.

"That was good. I decided to take the risk and say hello. I could not figure out what the odd sastrugi was, so I had to go see. It ended up being your tent," she chuckled.

In the end, stopping by did not ruin her unsupported status, the conditions did. The pains near the end intensified for her, too. We discussed how other people felt, like this was a huge deal. Yet it seemed perfectly normal to either of us. Yes, it was difficult, but it seemed a logical consequence of what we were doing.

Vilborg also shared that she was forced to take a full sick day off, as she developed food poisoning from rotten salami. I told her about my not eating the meat I brought, as it looked like it had thawed. She responded by nodding her head. As she had been ahead of me by several days, she skied through deeper snow in the last two degrees.

By the time I arrived there, the wind had packed the surface down. Although I loathed the wind that assailed me in the last degree, it ultimately helped me out. Antarctica seemed to be the only place where bad weather and occasional strong winds were in fact helpful.

The next morning, I met with James Hayes from ALE for breakfast. We talked about our different perspectives from opposite sides of the satellite phone. He was stunned I stuck it out, too. I related the reasons I had left my engineering job and did the trek. He understood my reasoning as he had a similar experience. It seems many people who traveled to Antarctica desired a different experience, outside of the norm.

It did not take too long for Kelly to arrange my flights to bring me back home. The flight schedule allowed for two days in Punta Arenas. I did little sightseeing. As I hobbled from all the aches and pains, I was unable to walk far. I did enjoy a fancy dinner at La Marmita, a restaurant near the ALE office. It was the first fancy food I had eaten since October last year. The llama steak was savory and a welcome break from freeze-dried meals. Other than speaking with the hotel staff, I had few interactions with people. For as much as I yearned to talk with and learn about the people, my poor Spanish hindered me. Even though I looked like a madman with wild hair and beard, the Chileans treated me no differently, for which I was thankful.

All too soon, I and my gear were crammed into a puny taxi, heading to the airport. While jammed under the ski bag, I passively watched the landscape roll by. It seemed like a dream. The sights and sounds of southern Chile still seemed extraterrestrial. I suspected I would feel this way for some time after living in Antarctica.

(Left) *Roald Amundsen's original diary from his 1911-1912 expedition to the South Pole. It is encased behind glass in the South Pole Station's main conference room.*

(Main) *After 82 days on the ice, covering over 700 miles through brutal Antarctic conditions, I reached the South Pole. The pole does have a red and white candy stripe on it.*

(Main) *After three hours of skiing on an extremely cold day, my breath formed this four inch icicle stuck to my fleece face protector.*

2 2

SOMETHING MORE DIFFICULT

ON ARRIVING BACK to the United States, I was reintroduced to the western world. In Santiago and Punta Arenas, in relatively poor Chile, the luggage carts were free. I simply grabbed one and was free to use it. But in Los Angeles, each cart cost $5. It was a shock to think about the difference in perspectives between the two countries. As I had no cash on me, I hauled four heavy expedition bags from the international to the local terminal.

Soon, I was in San Diego. A mob of people shocked me at the commuter terminal, cheering me as I strode through the automatic doors. Kelly arranged to have family, friends and supporters drive out to greet me. They even brought along a television crew! The number one question everyone asked me was what was the first food I was going to eat. I had months to contemplate it.

"A carne-asada burrito from my favorite taco shop in south San Diego," was my immediate response. Although I had not had any particular food cravings while on the expedition, the hunger for a meaty meal was impossible to resist.

KUSI, one of the San Diego local television stations, was also at the airport to cover my return. They had featured my departure back in

October and were now producing a follow up. In a few days, I was in the studio and on television talking about the expedition. One funny comparison they made was with the recent cold in southern California. They had been through a cold snap, meaning 40–50°F. Reporters were dressed in heavy down jackets and alpine gloves. It was fun to watch, as I had worn less clothing in -30° temperatures in Antarctica, the biggest ice box on the planet. We all had a laugh at that.

It was so comforting to be back and visiting with my family, girl-friend and friends. We fairly rushed about, meeting up with people I had not seen since last year. Everyone asked similar questions, which I happily repeated answers to. The uniqueness of the experience made retelling it a joy every time. People responded with the same over-whelmed look.

"How in the world could you stay alone for so long, eating the same thing every day, seeing nothing, and not have gone nuts?" was the constant refrain.

"I did see things. There were colored spots. A raven was in the sky," I said.

While talking with Kelly about my expedition, she said she deleted the part about seeing the raven from my blog.

"I thought you were just making that up," she said.

"No, quite the contrary. It was as real as it could have been," I replied.

"Well, I thought you were just going a little crazy, so I removed the raven part."

"No, you're kidding! I swore I saw it so many times."

"I know, but I did not want people to think you had gone crazy."

"Thank you for watching out for my sanity," I said.

"I'm sorry, hopefully that was okay?" she asked.

"No worries. I had plenty of crazy already, so leaving the raven out changed nothing."

Steve Jones said it was common for trekkers to hear mice under their skis. I only heard my name called out on Christmas Eve, but heard nothing abnormal past that. The amount of butter I consumed was what astonished people the most. It was inconceivable to consume two sticks of butter a day and still lose 25 pounds.

Mom and dad said they slept far better once I returned to San Diego.

"We did not even realize we were sleeping poorly until you came back. As soon as you were here, we talked and realized we had both completely slept through the night. We were relieved you were home in one piece," mom said.

As a turnabout, I had a terrible time sleeping for the first month after returning. The beds were perfectly comfortable. The temperature was comfortable. City noises were nothing compared to the roar of my tent in gale force winds. It was just the opposite. Everything was too comfortable. I was enclosed in a box. There was nothing that, if I did not do it, would cost me my life. My inability to sleep was from what was going on in my head. Learning that the three man crew of the Kenn Borek Twin Otter had perished also weighed on my mind.

More than once, I woke up yelling, drenched in sweat. The ALE doctors warned me something like this could happen. They said that I should grab a couple of good books, then go somewhere and relax with them. During the second half of the expedition, I longed to be somewhere requiring only two decisions. This first was which beach to choose and the second was which drink to have in my hand. Kelly and I were off to Hawaii in February to fulfill that desire. It was a no-stress trip, something I hadn't done in a long time.

Antarctica was by far the most stressful place I have ever been. There was constant pressure to make mileage. Everything needed maintenance to prevent deterioration. If I did not take care of myself, I would disintegrate. My feet would develop serious blisters, fingers would split and start bleeding, and there were joint, muscle and connecting tissue injuries to avoid. There was nothing relaxing about Antarctica.

Although I've worked at places that were incredibly stressful at times, those stresses were left at work. I had solace when I was home. On the seventh continent, there was no real refuge. Even my tent, my only shelter, was under threat of being shredded or blown away. But, the only decisions were my own out there. No one demanded I do anything, made choices that took me away from my family and friends, nor was there the worry of being stepped on for political gain. Antarctica simply presented itself as it was. There was no hidden agenda. It never told me what an expert job I did only to stab me in the back later. There was none of that. After working for 16 years and dealing with those issues, the joy, pain and satisfaction of Antarctica was refreshing. I had only one goal. Though I did not complete the round trip, I had the record for the longest time ever to reach the South Pole. It was not the greatest accomplishment to hang on the wall, but there will likely be no one who will have more go wrong, nor take longer than I.

The question facing me now was what to do next. I had completed arguably the second most difficult trek in the world. After talking with Vilborg about her plans, a seed of an idea was germinated. She now planned to capitalize on her new-found fame and climb the Seven Summits. And, if she succeeds at that, she only has to trek to the North Pole to achieve the explorer's grand slam. As she had also crossed Greenland, she has two of the three classic polar crossings. After completing this trek, she was confident in her ability to conquer high peaks. With her stamina and performance, I was sure she would succeed. I had not thought about the grand slam until discussing it with Vilborg. Now, it was constantly on my mind.

After examining the maps, talking with people who have been there, and learning that no expedition was allowed to go in 2011 or 2012, the North Pole presents a formidable challenge. Thinking about it has kept me up many nights. Antarctica was supposed to be a luxury trip compared to crossing the Arctic ice. Open water, polar bears, salty ice, humidity and far colder conditions are some of the challenges in the Arctic. After returning from the most difficult expedition I have ever undertaken, traveling somewhere even tougher makes perfect sense. I realized my dream of going to Antarctica. I never gave up. Changes happened and I accepted them. Now, I have to develop and move forward with my dream of skiing to the North Pole. I expect people will say I'm crazy. Then again, they told me I was crazy for going to Antarctica, too.

(Main) *Walking on a solid, slick ice tarmac over to the Illyushin-76. Antarctica gave me a 35 knot wind at -5°F, for a windchill of -36°F, as a departing gift.*

(Below left) *The maintenance staff at the station has a polar sense of humor. I was required to camp over half a mile from the Pole at this resort.*

(Below right) *The manufacturer of the flag pole at the Scott-Amundsen station had a once in a lifetime opportunity to design a finial that can honestly be utilized in exactly one place in the world.*

Aaron Linsdau Speaking Engagements

Take your organization and event to the next level. Aaron Linsdau's message of setting goals, making changes, and never giving up resonates with audiences. He is unique in that he is one of only two American's to succeed in skiing from the edge of Antarctica to the South Pole alone.

This expedition is ten times more difficult than climbing Mount Everest, and that's with a team. Being alone increases the challenge to an even higher level. Aaron presents the psychological and emotional experience of how he managed obstacles, what it took, and examines the sacrifices he made to succeed. He shares how he coped with failure, achieving what only a handful of other people ever have.

Aaron collaborates with your organization to deliver the right message for your team. He relates his experience to your challenges, providing you with exactly what you need. Aaron tunes his talks for what you want to convey to your people. Contact Aaron today and start moving toward your goal.

"Never Give Up"

Contact Aaron Linsdau through **www.sastrugipress.com**
For additional information, visit **www.ncexped.com**

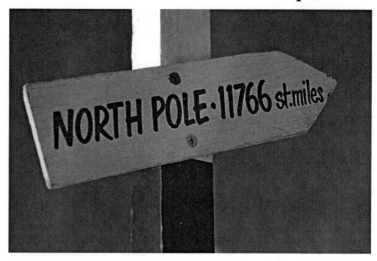

Enjoy other Sastrugi Press adventure titles

Journeys to the Edge by Randall Peeters, PhD

Ever wonder what it's like to climb Mount Everest? Or to even have the energy and motivation to do it? Well, the idea isn't as far-fetched as it may seem, even though very few people in the world have climbed Mount Everest. It requires dreaming big and creating a personal vision to climb the mountains in your life.

In Journeys to the Edge, Randall Peeters shares his successes and failures and gives you some directly applicable guidelines on how you can create a vision for your life. With this in hand, nothing is impossible, whether it be the mountains of career, social, domestic, financial, or spiritual success. Even climbing a big mountain to satisfy a lifelong dream is possible.

These Canyons Are Full of Ghosts by Emmett Harder

Driven to find his fortune in the most desolate and forbidding landscapes on earth, one prospector learns there is more to finding gold than just using a shovel and pickaxe. These riveting tales of modern Death Valley prospecting will give you insight into what drives a person to keep looking for the next big strike. During his explorations through the massive national park, Emmett Harder discovers a famous lost gold mine, loses another one, and crosses paths with Death Valley's most notorious resident: Charles Manson.

The Blind Man's Story by J.W. Linsdau

Imagine one's surprise to be hiking in the great Northwest and coming across someone who spends his summers living high on a bluff – and that someone is blind, with a fascinating story to tell.

That's what happened to journalist Beau Larson, while on vacation near a mountain town called Fools Gold. He returns to work, but his chance meeting leads to intrigue when his newspaper sends him back to Fools Gold to cover a dispute between local timber workers and environmentalists.

Beau finishes his report, but soon discovers one of the key environmentalists interviewed has been murdered. He again finds himself in Fools Gold only to learn there is more to "The Blind Man's Story" than he thought.

Visit Sastrugi Press on the web at **www.sastrugipress.com** to purchase the above books directly from the publisher. These titles are also available at your favorite bookstore or online retailer.

Other major Antarctic expeditions

2012-2013 season

Vilborg Arna Gissurardóttir

Vilborg Gissurardóttir was the first Icelandic person, either woman or man, to ski from the coast of Antarctica to the South Pole. She had originally planned to ski the 1130 km (701 mile) journey in 50 days. Her plan was not to be the fastest skier on the route. But rather she planned to do the entire expedition solo, which means without mechanical assistance or resupply. As she had planned to reach the South Pole in 50 days, she had brought supplies for exactly that many days, leaving little room for complications. This made her sled rig light, enabling her to travel quickly. This was her second expedition of 2012, as she had skied across Greenland in spring.

Roland Krueger

The industrial designer from Germany left the Ronne-Filchner Ice Shelf, better known as the Messner Start, headed for the South Pole on November 24, 2012. Once he reached the Pole, after covering 900km, he planned to continue on to the Axel Heiberg Glacier at the Ross Ice Shelf. To do this, he brought 64 days of supplies in a 130kg (286 lb) sled. In 2005, Roland Krueger became the first German to ski unsupported and unassisted from the Messner Start to the South Pole, with an international team of five, in a then record-setting time of 34 days. The conditions were fast, as the surface was hard and there was little snowfall or sastrugi to contend with.

Hannah McKeand

Hannah McKeand holds the Guinness World Record for skiing from the coast of Antarctica, from either the Messner or Hercules Inlet, to the South Pole a remarkable six times. Working with Antarctic

Logistics and Expeditions, Hannah McKeand works as a guide and camp manager. She holds a speed record for skiing from the coast to the South Pole as a soloist and is still the fastest woman to do so. Hannah also made an attempt to ski to the North Pole, too. In 2012, she guided clients from the Messner start to the South Pole. She reported experiencing conditions unlike anything she had seen in over 10 years trekking across Antarctica.

Eric Larsen

Eric Larsen, from Colorado, is an accomplished polar explorer. He has trekked to both the North and South Poles. As he has traveled to each pole more than once, he decided to try something new for the 2012-2013 Antarctic season. He flew down with a fat tire bike, designed to roll over hard snow and ice. With his bike and over 200 pounds of supplies, he hoped to be the first person ever to ride a bike to the South Pole. All that stood in his way was 700 miles of ice and sastrugi. When leaving the Hercules Inlet, he needed crampons to push the bike up to the plateau, a precursor to what he was to experience on his way.

Richard Parks

After skiing on a last degree trip to the South Pole in 2010, Richard Parks learned he did not have enough of Antarctica. After completing the Adventure Grand Slam in a single year, he returned to Antarctica, planning to undertake an unsupported and unaided expedition to the South Pole. As he was experienced, he planned to make a fast dash for the pole with limited supplies to keep the weight down. However, he had problems even before reaching Antarctica.

It was a privilege to share the adventure with all of them.

Where possible, all positions, elevations, distances, and measurements have been noted. As some information was not recorded in the expedition journal, it was omitted from this manuscript. If the original information recorded in the journal conflicted with surveyed information, the official record was substituted.

1 nm (nautical mile) is equivalent to 1.15 statute miles
1 L (liter) of fluid is equivalent to 1.057 quarts